P9-CQV-997

Changing
Lives
Through
Preaching
and Worship

LIBRARY OF CHRISTIAN Leadership

Changing Lives Through Preaching and Worship

30 Strategies for Powerful Communication

Marshall Shelley, General Editor

MOORINGS
Nashville, Tennessee
A Division of The Ballantine Publishing Group, Random House, Inc.

Library of Christian Leadership
CHANGING LIVES THROUGH PREACHING AND WORSHIP

Copyright © 1995 by *Leadership*/Christianity Today, Inc.

The material in this book was previously published in *Leadership*, by Christianity Today, Inc.

Scripture taken from:

The *Authorized King James* version (KJV) of the Bible.

The HOLY BIBLE, NEW INTERNATIONAL VERSION®. NIV®. Copyright © 1973, 1978, 1984 by International Bible Society. Used by permission of Zondervan Publishing House. All rights reserved.

The *New Revised Standard Version* (NRSV) of the Bible. Copyright © 1989 by the Division of Christian Education of the National Council of the Churches of Christ in the United States of America. Used by permission.

The *Living Bible* (TLB) © 1971 by Tyndale House Publishers, Wheaton, Illinois 60189. Used by permission. All rights reserved.

Library of Congress Cataloging-in-Publication Data

Changing lives through preaching and worship / Marshall Shelley.   general editor. — 1st ed.
     p.   cm. — (Library of Christian leadership ; 1)
    "Was previously published in *Leadership*, by Christianity Today, Inc."—T.p. verso.
    ISBN 0-345-39596-4 (hardcover).
    1. Preaching. 2. Public worship. 3. Pastoral theology. I. Shelley, Marshall. II. Leadership (Carol Stream, Ill.) III. Series.
BV4211.2.C44 1995
264—dc20
                                  95-9144
                                  CIP

First Edition: July 1995

10 9 8 7 6 5 4 3 2 1

Contents

good!

Foreword

It has become fashionable to bemoan today's lack of leadership —"Where are the leaders who can take us from where we are to where we ought to be?"

In both secular and religious circles, it's the cry of countless voices. The unspoken assumption seems to be that no real leaders were born after World War II. The years immediately after the war are seen as the heyday of leadership, when generals, prime ministers, evangelists, parachurch agency founders, and other giants walked the earth. Armies were strong, organizations vigorous, and the mood triumphant.

But during the 1960s, the mood changed. The folk song asked, "Where have all the flowers gone?" And people began asking the same about leaders. Authority became something to be questioned. Power something to be distrusted.

The effects of this attitude linger forty years later with the new millennium upon us.

Where are the leaders? we ask. Many consider the current crop of people filling positions of responsibility today not to be real leaders, but mere officeholders. We still feel ambiguous about granting anyone authority and power, even while lamenting the lack of leadership.

For more than a dozen years, I've served as an editor with a publication called *Leadership,* a practical journal for church leaders dedicated to strengthening those in ministry and helping them toward biblical faithfulness and pastoral effectiveness. Part of my job was to find living examples of Christian leadership. Was that possible? In an era of anti-authoritarianism, had genuine leadership become extinct?

I'm happy to report that reports of the death of Christian leadership were greatly exaggerated. Faithful and effective Christian leaders are indeed alive and well. The other editors at *Leadership* and I have enjoyed seeking out these men and women, interviewing them or encouraging them to write their reflections on various aspects of Christian leadership, and publishing them in our journal. Many times, their stories have moved us to laughter, tears, anger, amazement, and—often—awe at the way God chooses to use ordinary human beings in extraordinary ways.

This book and the others in The Library of Christian Leadership focus on the unique aspects of Christian leadership. This series is not just for pastors, but for anyone interested in moving people in a Godward direction.

We're delighted to offer these books, packed with insights that are biblically shaped and then fired in the kilns of day-to-day ministry. Our prayer is that the experiences and reflections of these Christian leaders will make you, in turn, a better Christian leader.

We hope future generations can look back and see not a lack of leadership but thousands of examples of Christians who model and articulate their faith, and who motivate others to do the same. That is, after all, what Christian leadership is all about.

—Marshall Shelley
Executive editor, *Leadership*

Introduction

Most of the moments when God has changed me deeply have come during worship.

—KEVIN A. MILLER

I propose we change the sign on most church sanctuaries.

As I visit churches around the country, quite often I see this sign on the sanctuary doors: *Enter to Worship.*

But what the sign really ought to declare is: *Enter at Your Own Risk.* You are venturing into the zone of preaching and worship, and there you are going to encounter the holy and awesome God. Beware.

Writer Annie Dillard asked, "Does anyone have the foggiest idea what sort of power we so blithely invoke? Or, as I suspect, does not one believe a word of it? . . . It is madness to wear ladies' straw hats and velvet hats to church; we should all be wearing crash helmets. Ushers should issue life preservers and signal flares; they should lash us to our pews."

This book is soberly dedicated to two dangerous and life-changing arts: preaching and leading worship. There is one true, holy, and living God. To bring people before his radiance and to speak his word—can there be a greater challenge, a weightier responsibility, a more noble task?

* * *

As I look back over my Christian life, one fact juts up like a mountain crag: most of the moments when God has changed me deeply have come during worship.

I remember hearing Stuart Briscoe preach a sermon almost

fifteen years ago. He expounded the apostle Paul's words, "Woe to me if I do not preach the gospel!" In Stuart's careful treatment, those words from 1 Corinthians 9:16 hit me with force. I saw—suddenly, startlingly—that I, too, was a person under orders, an enlisted man. God had conscripted me for his assignments, and I could not selfishly determine my life's work. I could not squander my energies. A profound shame and judgment would come to me if I did.

That holy realization born during a sermon, birthed in worship, has never left. It is why I devote myself to strengthening the leaders of God's church through *Leadership* and through books like this.

Since I have been irrevocably altered through preaching and worship, I love and believe in them and God's ability to work through them. In those final minutes before worship, I feel the rush of adrenaline, much as a linebacker pacing the sidelines minutes before kickoff. I want to preach well; I want to lead worship with integrity.

I also feel awe and fear. I live with the mind-clearing realization that I will be judged more strictly as a teacher. Every idle word I speak will have to be accounted for. As Calvin Miller playfully thought of it, on the great Day of Judgment, there will be a march of cassettes past the throne.

Thus this book. It begins a new series, The Library of Christian Leadership, that draws together some of today's finest Christian leaders to speak honestly and helpfully about our common challenges. This inaugural volume on preaching and worship answers questions—deep and theological ones, basic and practical ones—that leaders face. It helps us approach the twin tasks of preaching and leading worship in a more faithful and effective way.

Leadership's associate editor, David Goetz, has selected, arranged, and refined what I believe is an outstanding collection. I wish it had been available to me years ago.

—Kevin A. Miller
Editor, *Leadership*

Contributors

Paul Anderson has been pastor of Trinity Lutheran Church in San Pedro, California, since 1970. A pianist and organist, he has written a number of praise songs and hymns. He also authored *Building Christian Character* and coauthored *Mastering Pastoral Care.*

Garth Bolinder is pastor of Hillcrest Covenant Church in Prairie Village, Kansas. He has also pastored Modesto Covenant Church in Modesto, California, and Evangelical Covenant Church in Woodstock, Connecticut. He is coauthor of *What Every Pastor Needs to Know about Music, Youth, and Education.*

Stuart Briscoe has been pastor of Elmbrook Church in Waukesha, Wisconsin, for more than twenty years. Before entering the ministry, he was a banking official in England. He has also ministered with Capernwray Missionary Fellowship of Torchbearers. He has authored numerous books, including *Fresh Air in the Pulpit,* and coauthored *Mastering Contemporary Preaching* and *Measuring Up.*

Steve Brown is president of Key Life Network, Inc., and Bible teacher on the national radio program *Key Life.* He is also professor of communications and practical theology at Reformed Theological Seminary in Orlando. He formerly pastored Key Biscayne Presbyterian Church in Florida. He has authored books such as *When Being Good Isn't Good Enough* and *How to Talk So People Will Listen,* and coauthored *A Voice in the Wilderness.*

Fred Craddock is the Bandy Distinguished Professor of Preaching and New Testament Emeritus of Candler School of Theology at Emory University in Atlanta. He holds a Ph.D. in New Testament from Vanderbilt University and has served churches in Tennessee and Oklahoma. He has presented the Lyman Beecher Lectures at Yale and has authored *Preaching* and *The Gospels* and co-authored *Preaching Through the Christian Year.*

Jim Cymbala is pastor of the Brooklyn Tabernacle in Brooklyn, New York. The church is home to the Brooklyn Tabernacle Choir, which is directed by his wife, Carol. The Brooklyn Tabernacle has planted several churches in other parts of New York City and features a Tuesday night prayer service attended by more than one thousand people each week.

Leighton Ford is president of Leighton Ford Ministries in Charlotte, North Carolina, which seeks to raise up younger leaders to spread the message of Christ worldwide. He also served as associate evangelist and vice president of the Billy Graham Evangelistic Association. He is the author of *Transforming Leadership.*

Richard Foster is founder of *Renovaré* and is the Jack and Barbara Lee Distinguished Professor of Spiritual Formation at Azusa Pacific University in Azusa, California. He is the author of several books, including *Celebration of Discipline, Freedom of Simplicity,* and *Prayer: Finding the Heart's True Home.*

Jack Hayford is pastor of Church on the Way in Van Nuys, California. He is the author of many books, among them *Worship His Majesty* and *Rebuilding the Real You,* and has coauthored *Mastering Worship* and *Who's in Charge?*

R. Kent Hughes has been pastor of College Church in Wheaton, Illinois, since 1979. He is author of *Disciplines of a Godly Man, Disciplines of Grace,* and *Liberating Ministry from the Success Syndrome,* and coauthor of *Mastering the Pastoral Role.*

Bill Hybels is founding pastor of Willow Creek Community Church in South Barrington, Illinois. He is the author of, among others, *Descending into Greatness* and *Fit to Be Tied*, and coauthor of *Mastering Contemporary Preaching.*

Tim Keller is pastor of Redeemer Presbyterian Church in Manhattan, New York, which he planted in 1989. Tim has also taught communication and leadership at Westminster Seminary and chaired an outreach organization to the homosexual community in Philadelphia. He is the author of *Resources for Deacons* and *Ministries of Mercy.*

John Killinger is professor of religion and culture at Samford University in Birmingham, Alabama. He has pastored First Presbyterian Church in Lynchburg, Virginia, and First Congregational Church in Los Angeles, California. He is the author of nearly fifty books, including *Fundamentals of Preaching* and *Lost in Wonder, Love, and Praise.*

Craig Brian Larson is contributing editor of *Leadership* and a freelance writer living in Arlington Heights, Illinois. He is the author of *Running the Midnight Marathon* and coauthor of *Preaching That Connects.*

Barry Liesch is professor of music at Biola University in La Miriada, California, and the author of *People in the Presence of God.*

Gordon MacDonald is pastor of Grace Chapel in Lexington, Massachusetts. Prior to that he served Trinity Baptist Church in New York City and was president of InterVarsity Christian Fellowship. His many books include *Ordering Your Private World, Restoring Your Spiritual Passion,* and *Mastering Personal Growth.*

Calvin Miller is professor of communications and ministry studies, and writer-in-residence at Southwestern Baptist Theological Seminary in Fort Worth, Texas. Before that he served as pastor of Westside Church in Omaha, Nebraska, for more than twenty-five years. His many books include *The Singer, A Requiem for Love, Spirit, Word and Story,* and *Empowered Communicator.*

Ben Patterson is dean of the chapel at Hope College in Holland, Michigan. Before that he pastored Presbyterian congregations in New Jersey and California. He is contributing editor to *Christianity Today* and *Leadership,* author of *Waiting: Finding Hope When God Seems Silent,* and coauthor of *Mastering the Pastoral Role* and *Who's in Charge?*

Steve Pederson is drama director at Willow Creek Community Church in South Barrington, Illinois. Before that he taught theater for fourteen years at Northwestern College in Orange City, Iowa. He earned a Ph.D. at the University of Iowa. He is the editor of *Sunday Morning Live,* volume 16, and director of the companion videos for the same series.

Eugene H. Peterson is professor of spiritual theology at Regent College in Vancouver, British Columbia. He pastored Christ Our King Presbyterian Church in Bel Air, Maryland, for twenty-nine years. He is a contributing editor of *Leadership* and is the author of numerous books, including *Five Smooth Stones for Pastoral Work, The Contemplative Pastor, Under the Predictable Plant,* and *The Message.*

Calvin Ratz is pastor of Brightmoor Tabernacle in Southfield, Michigan. Prior to that he served churches in British Columbia, Alberta, and Quebec, and spent eleven years as a missionary in Hong Kong and Kenya, East Africa. He is coauthor of *Mastering Outreach and Evangelism.*

Haddon Robinson holds the Harold J. Ockenga chair of preaching at Gordon-Conwell Theological Seminary in South Hamilton, Massachusetts. Formerly he served as president of Denver Seminary in Colorado, and before that he was on the faculty of Dallas Theological Seminary in Texas. He is the author of *Biblical Preaching* and coauthor of *Mastering Contemporary Preaching* and *A Voice in the Wilderness.*

Howard Stevenson has been associate pastor of music, worship, and the creative arts at First Evangelical Free Church of Fullerton, California, for the past 15 years. He served as music chairman for the Southern California Billy Graham Crusade at

Anaheim Stadium in 1985 and has been involved in music evangelism throughout the world. He is co-author of *Mastering Worship*.

Chuck Swindoll is president of Dallas Theological Seminary and speaker of the radio broadcast *Insight for Living*. Before that he was pastor of First Evangelical Free Church in Fullerton, California, for twenty-two years. His many books include *Growing Strong in the Seasons of Life* and *Laugh Again*.

Gardner Taylor is pastor emeritus of The Concord Baptist Church of Christ in Brooklyn, New York, which he served from 1948 to 1990. He has lectured, among others, at Yale Divinity School, Harvard Divinity School, and Colgate-Rochester Divinity School. He is the author of *The Scarlet Thread* and *Chariots Aflame*.

David Veerman is vice-president of the Livingstone Corporation in Illinois. He was one of the senior editors of the *Life Application Bible* and the senior editor of the *Life Application Bible for Students*. He has authored, among others, *How to Apply the Bible* and *Parenting Passages*.

Warren Wiersbe is a writer and speaker living in Omaha, Nebraska. Before that he was a teacher for the *Back to the Bible* radio broadcast and pastored Moody Church in Chicago. He is the author of, among others, *Living with the Giants*, *Preaching and Teaching with Imagination*, and *Be Myself*.

William Willimon is dean of the chapel and professor of Christian ministry at Duke University in Durham, North Carolina. He has served United Methodist pastorates in Georgia and South Carolina. His numerous books include *Peculiar Speech: Preaching to the Baptized*, *The Intrusive Word: Preaching to the Unbaptized*, and *A Voice in the Wilderness*.

Section 1:
Changing Lives Through Preaching

Every sermon should have for its main business the head-on constructive meeting of some problem which was puzzling the minds, burdening consciences, distracting lives, and no sermon which so met a real human difficulty, with light to throw on it and help to win a victory over, could possibly be futile.

—HARRY EMERSON FOSDICK

PART 1

Personality

1

Your Preaching Is Unique

*The experiences we preachers go through are not accidents;
they are appointments.*

—WARREN W. WIERSBE

It doesn't make sense!" said my pastor friend.

We were lingering over lunch and discussing the Bible conference I was conducting in his church. I'd just commented that the church was having a strong influence on the students and staff of the nearby university.

"What doesn't make sense?" I asked.

"Where you and I are serving," he replied.

"You're going to have to explain."

"Look, I'm really a country preacher with a minimum of academic training, yet I'm ministering to a university crowd. You write commentaries, and you read more books in a month than I do in a year, yet your congregation is primarily blue-collar and nonprofessional. It doesn't make sense."

The subject then changed, but I have pondered his observation many times in the intervening years. I've concluded it's a good thing God didn't put me on his "Pastor Placement Committee" because I would have really messed things up. I never would have sent rustic Amos to the affluent court of the king; I'd have given him a quiet country church somewhere. And I'd never have commissioned Saul of Tarsus, that "Hebrew of the Hebrews," to be a missionary to the Gentiles; I'd have put him in charge of Jewish evangelism in Jerusalem.

Why is it, then, that so many preachers do not enjoy preaching? Why do some busy themselves in minor matters when they should be studying and meditating? Why do others creep out of the pulpit after delivering their sermon, overwhelmed with a sense of failure and guilt?

The difference a witness makes

Without pausing to take a poll, I think I can suggest an answer: they are preaching *in spite of themselves* instead of preaching *because of* themselves. They either leave themselves out of their preaching or fight themselves during their preparation and delivery; this leaves them without energy or enthusiasm for the task. Instead of thanking God for what they do have, they complain about what they don't have; and this leaves them in no condition to herald the Word of God.

A *Christianity Today*/Gallup Poll some years ago showed that ministers believe preaching is the number one priority of their ministries, but it's also the one thing they feel least capable of doing well. What causes this insecure attitude toward preaching?

For one thing, we've forgotten what preaching really is. Phillips Brooks said it best: Preaching is the communicating of divine truth through human personality. The divine truth never changes; the human personality constantly changes—and this is what makes the message new and unique.

No two preachers can preach the same message because no two preachers are the same. In fact, no *one* preacher can preach the same message twice if he is living and growing at all. The human personality is a vital part of the preaching ministry.

Recently I made an intensive study of all the Greek verbs used in the New Testament to describe the communicating of the Word of God. The three most important words are *euangelizomai*, "to tell the good news"; *kerusso*, "to proclaim like a herald"; and *martureo*, "to bear witness." All three are important in our pulpit ministry.

We're telling the good news with the authority of a royal herald, but the message is a part of our lives. Unlike the herald, who only shouted what was given to him, we're sharing what is personal and real to us. The messenger is a part of the message because the messenger is a witness.

God prepares the person who prepares the message. Martin Luther said that prayer, meditation, and temptation made a preacher. Prayer and meditation will give you a sermon, but only temptation—the daily experience of life—can transform that sermon into a message. It's the difference between the recipe and the meal.

I had an experience at a denominational conference that brought this truth home to me. During the session at which I was to speak, a very capable ladies' trio sang. It was an up-tempo number, the message of which did not quite fit my theme; but, of course, they had no way of knowing exactly what I would preach about. I was glad my message did not immediately follow their number because I didn't feel the congregation was prepared.

Just before I spoke, a pastor in a wheelchair rolled to the center of the platform and gave a brief testimony about his ministry. Then he sang, to very simple accompaniment, "No One Ever Cared for Me Like Jesus." The effect was overwhelming. The man was not singing a song; he was ministering a word from God. But he had paid a price to minister. In suffering, he became a part of the message.

The experiences we preachers go through are not accidents; they are appointments. They do not interrupt our studies; they are an essential part of our studies. Our personalities, our physical equipment, and even our handicaps are all part of the kind of ministry God wants us to have. He wants us to be witnesses as well as heralds.

The apostles knew this: "For we cannot help speaking about what we have seen and heard" (Acts 4:20 NIV). This was a part of Paul's commission: "You will be his witness to all men of what you have seen and heard" (Acts 22:15 NIV). Instead of minimizing or condemning what we are, we must use what we are to bear witness to Christ. It is this that makes the message *our* message and not the echo of another's.

The myth of "The Great Sermon"

It's easy to imitate these days. Not only do we have books of sermons, but we have radio and television ministries and cassettes by the thousands. One man models himself after Charles Spurgeon, another after A. W. Tozer; and both congregations suffer.

Alexander Whyte of Edinburgh had an assistant who took the second service for the aging pastor. Whyte was a surgical preacher who ruthlessly dealt with human sin and then faithfully proclaimed God's saving grace. But his assistant was a man of different temperament who tried to move the gospel message out of the operating room into the banqueting hall.

During one period of his ministry, however, the assistant tried Whyte's approach, without Whyte's success. The experiment stopped when Whyte said to him, "Preach your own message." That counsel is needed today.

I am alarmed when I hear seminary students and younger pastors say, "My calling is to preach, not to pastor." I am alarmed because I know it's difficult to preach to people whom you do not know.

As an itinerant Bible teacher, I know what it's like to "hit a place and quit a place," and I can assure you it is not easy. After thirty years of ministry, which included pastoring three churches, I've concluded it is much easier to preach to your own congregation week after week. You get to know them, and they get to know you. You're not a visiting Christian celebrity, but a part of the family. It is this identification with the people that gives power and relevance to your preaching.

Every profession has its occupational hazards, and in the ministry it is the passion to preach "great sermons." Fant and Pinson, in *20 Centuries of Great Preaching*, came to the startling conclusion that "great preaching is relevant preaching." By "relevant," they mean preaching that meets the needs of the people in their times, preaching that shows the preacher cares and wants to help.

If this be true, then there are thousands of "great sermons" preached each Lord's Day, preached by those whose names will never be printed in homiletics books, but are written in the loving hearts of their people. Listen again to Phillips Brooks:

> The notion of a great sermon, either constantly or occasionally haunting the preacher, is fatal. It hampers the freedom of utterance. Many a true and helpful word which your people need, and which you ought to say to them, will seem unworthy of the dignity of your great discourse. Never tolerate any idea of the dignity of a sermon which will keep you from saying anything in it which you ought to say, or which your people ought to hear.

Preaching Christ, not myself

Let me add another reason for insecure feelings about our preaching. In our desire to be humble servants of God, we have a tendency to suppress our personalities lest we should preach ourselves and not Christ.

While it is good to heed Paul's warning ("For we do not preach ourselves, but Jesus Christ as Lord, and ourselves as your servants for Jesus' sake"—2 Cor. 4:5 NIV), we must not misinterpret it and thereby attempt the impossible. Paul's personality and even some of his personal experiences are written into the warp and woof of his epistles; yet Jesus Christ is glorified from start to finish.

During the past twenty years, I have been immersed in studying the lives of famous preachers of the past. Most of these ministered during the Victorian era in Great Britain, a time when the pulpits were filled with superstars. If there's one thing I learned from these men, it is this: God has his own ways of training and preparing his servants, but he wants all of them to be themselves. God has put variety into the universe, and he has put variety into the church.

If your personality doesn't shine through your preaching, you're only a robot. You could be replaced by a cassette player and perhaps nobody would know the difference.

Do not confuse the art and the science of preaching. Homiletics is the science of preaching, and it has basic laws and principles that every preacher ought to study and practice. Once you've learned how to obey these principles, then you can adapt them, modify them, and tailor them to your own personality.

In my conference ministry, I often share the platform with gifted speakers whose preaching leaves me saying to myself, *What's the use? I'll never learn how to preach like that!*

Then the Lord has to remind me he never called me "to preach like that." He called me to preach the way I preach!

The science of preaching is one thing; the art of preaching— style, delivery, approach, and all those other almost indefinable ingredients that make up one's personality—is something else. One preacher uses humor and hits the target; another attempts it and shoots himself.

The essence of what I am saying is this: You must know yourself, accept yourself, be yourself, and develop yourself—your best self—if preaching is to be most effective.

Never imitate another preacher, but learn from him everything you can. Never complain about yourself or your circumstances, but find out why God made things that way and use what he has given you in a positive way. What you think are obstacles may turn out to be opportunities. Stay long enough in one church to discover who you are, what kind of ministry God has given you, and how he plans to train you for ministries yet to come. After all, he is always preparing us for what he already has prepared for us—if we let him.

Accepting what we're not

I learned very early in my ministry that I was not an evangelist. Although I've seen people come to Christ through my ministry, I've always felt I was a failure when it came to evangelism.

One of the few benefits of growing older is a better perspective. Now I'm learning that my teaching and writing ministries have enabled others to lead people to Christ, so my labors have not been in vain. But I've had my hours of discouragement and the feeling of failure.

God gives us the spiritual gifts he wants us to have; he puts us in the places he wants us to serve; and he gives the blessings he wants us to enjoy.

I am convinced of this, but this conviction is not an excuse for laziness or for barrenness of ministry. Knowing I am God's man in God's place of ministry has encouraged me to study harder and do my best work. When the harvests were lean, the assurance that God put me there helped to keep me going. When the battles raged and the storms blew, my secure refuge was "God put me here, and I will stay here until he tells me to go."

How often I've remembered V. Raymond Edman's counsel: "It is always too soon to quit!"

It has been my experience that the young preacher in his first church and the middle-aged preacher (in perhaps his third or fourth church) are the most susceptible to discouragement. This is not difficult to understand.

The young seminarian marches bravely into his first church with high ideals, only to face the steamroller of reality and the furnace of criticism. He waves his banners bravely for a year or so, then takes them down quietly and makes plans to move.

The middle-aged minister has seen his ideals attacked many times, but now he realizes that time is short and he might not attain to the top thirty of David's mighty men.

God help the preacher who abandons his ideals! But, at the same time, God pity the preacher who is so idealistic he fails to be realistic.

A realist is an idealist who has gone through the fire and been purified. A skeptic is an idealist who has gone through the fire and been burned. There is a difference.

Self-evaluation is a difficult and dangerous thing. Sometimes we're so close to our ministry we fail to see it. One of my students once asked me, "Why can't I see any spiritual growth in my life? Everybody else tells me they can see it!" I reminded him that at Pentecost no man could see the flame over his own head, but he could see what was burning over his brother's head.

A word from the Scottish preacher George Morrison has buoyed me up in many a storm: "Men who do their best always do more though they be haunted by the sense of failure. Be good and true; be patient; be undaunted. Leave your usefulness for God to estimate. He will see to it that you do not live in vain."

Be realistic as you assess your work. Avoid comparisons. I read enough religious publications and hear enough conversations to know that such comparisons are the chief indoor sport of preachers, but I try not to take them too seriously. "When they measure themselves by themselves and compare themselves with themselves, they are not wise" (2 Cor. 10:12 NIV).

Although we are in conflict against those who preach a false gospel, we are not in competition with any who preach the true gospel. We are only in competition with ourselves. By the grace of God, we ought to be better preachers and pastors today than we were a year ago.

If we are to be better pastors and preachers, we must be better persons; and this means discipline and hard work. The "giants" I've lived with these many years were all hard workers. Campbell Morgan was in his study at six o'clock in the morning. His successor, John Henry Jowett, was also up early and into the books. "Enter your study at an appointed hour," Jowett said in his lectures to the Yale divinity students in 1911–12, "and let that hour be as early as the earliest of your businessmen goes to his warehouse or his office." Spurgeon worked hard and had to take winter holidays to regain his strength.

Obviously, we gain nothing by imperiling our health, but we lose much by pampering ourselves, and that is the greater danger.

The gift is sufficient

If God has called you, then he has given you what you need to do the job. You may not have all that others have, or all you wish you had, but you have what God wants you to have. Accept it, be faithful to use it, and in due time God will give you more.

Give yourself time to discover and develop your gifts. Accept nothing as a handicap. Turn it over to God and let him make a useful tool out of it. After all, that's what he did with Paul's thorn in the flesh.

Often I receive letters and telephone calls from anxious chairmen of pulpit committees, all of whom want me to suggest a pastor for their churches. "What kind of pastor do you need right now?" I always ask.

"Oh, a man who is about forty years old, a good preacher, a love for people."

If I don't interrupt them, they usually go on to describe a combination of Billy Graham, Charles Spurgeon, Jonathan Edwards, Mother Teresa, and the Lone Ranger.

"Forgive me," I usually say when they take a breath, "but that's not what I had in mind. What kind of ministry does your church need just now—evangelism, missions, administration, teaching, or what? After all, very few people can do everything."

The long silence that follows tells me the chairman and the committee have not really studied their church to determine its present and future needs. How, then, can they ever hope to find the right pastor to meet those needs?

Preaching is not what we do; it's what we are. When God wants to make a preacher, he has to make the person, because the work we do cannot be isolated from the life we live. God prepares the person for the work and the work for the person, and if we permit him, he brings them together in his providence.

God knows us better than we know ourselves. He'd never put us into a ministry where he could not build us and use us.

2

Voice of Authority or Fellow Struggler?

If an apparently strong-willed pastor admits struggles from the pulpit, it becomes a powerful preaching moment.

—STEVE BROWN

Our church had just signed a contract for a $3 million building project. I panicked when those I banked on to help pay for it refused.

So I called up every elder and deacon and cajoled them to pledge toward the project. I recruited someone to paste a large picture of our church on a cardboard box and cut it up into bricks of $10,000 each. I also convinced the elders and deacons to stand in front of the church one Sunday and announce their 100 percent support for the project.

Then, as a climax to all my work, I preached a hard-sell message, a the-time-for-fun-and-games-is-over sermon.

We raised the money, all right, but I was criticized severely. I so deeply offended one person, he left the church.

As I look back, I realize how manipulative the sermon was. I practically said that if people didn't give, they would get the fever! At that moment, the church didn't need a blistering prophet who threatened but a gentle pastor who encouraged. In retrospect, I should have identified with people: "This is a huge goal, and even I'm afraid to make the sacrifices required to fulfill it. But if we depend on God, he can give us courage to do it together."

I've been wrong in the other direction as well, being sensitive in the pulpit when I should have kicked the congregation in the seat of the pants!

This is one of the toughest problems modern pastors face. People need and want to hear how a pastor shares their struggles and pain. Nonetheless, a part of them longs to hear an authoritative word to guide their lives.

Different preachers bring different gifts to the pulpit. Some are proclaimers, with an authoritative word. Others are more intimate: "Let me tell you what God has been doing in my life." Naturally, we should major in our strengths.

Still, for most preachers in most settings, we need to be both authoritative and vulnerable if we hope to offer God's Word in a way that affects people deeply. It has taken me years to learn to do both well, and I'm still learning. Here are some principles I keep in mind.

A strong foundation

When a weak pastor admits to struggling in the faith, the congregation hardly takes notice. That's pretty much what members expect, given how feebly he or she has been leading the church. But if an apparently strong-willed pastor admits struggles from the pulpit, it becomes a powerful preaching moment.

That's one reason I believe the preacher should, first and foremost, be a proclaimer of God's Word. That gives us authority when we preach with authority and also when we preach as a fellow struggler.

But another reason to proclaim God's Word authoritatively is more critical: preachers are under obligation. We are handlers of holy Scripture, which bestows upon us the authority to herald its teachings. There's no getting around the fact that we're in a situation different from that of the listener.

Consequently, no matter what style we emphasize, we need first to establish ourselves as strong, authoritative pastors. Years ago, a pastor friend of mine gave me an insight into pastoring:

"Steve, people look at us as representatives of God. I don't like this, and it's not biblical. But the way they treat us is the way they feel they can treat God. So if you allow people to walk over you, they think they can do that to God."

Maybe I understood what he said because I instinctively have operated that way.

When I arrived at one church, I was young and ambitious, and the church asked me to target the youth; the church was slowly graying. So I began developing relationships with the teenagers in the church neighborhood. The basketball hoop in the church parking lot turned out to be an effective means of getting next to them.

I had served the church for only six months when the chairman of the trustee board nonchalantly mentioned, as we were standing under the basketball hoop, that the board had decided to remove the hoop.

I exploded. "No, you're not! By taking down that basketball hoop, you're sending a strong message to those kids. You asked me to attract young people here, but you'll be running them off."

The chairman waved me off, pivoted, and walked away.

I was livid. "Jack, don't walk away from me!"

He kept walking, but I persisted. I followed him up two flights of stairs smack into the middle of a trustee meeting. I sat down.

"Don't worry," Jack said to the other trustees. "Pastor and I are just having a little disagreement."

Then he added, "By the way, I've invited the pastor to come to our meeting." (Pastors were normally excluded from the trustee meeting.)

"Could I say something, Jack?" I asked. I paused and then turned to face the entire board. "First, Jack didn't invite me to this meeting. I'm the pastor of this church and don't need an invitation to a trustee meeting. Second, I will be at these trustee meetings from now on."

The air was heavy with silence, and I went on to complain about the backboard decision. But I had gained their respect. I can't lay claim to knowing consciously what I was doing, but in effect I was building a base of strength, from which I could operate in the proclamation mode on Sunday morning.

Gaining authority

It is critical to establish authority, especially for young pastors or those in new church settings. If they are going to have any success in the pulpit, their authority must be established early and maintained regularly.

One way, though it must be handled as carefully as removing asbestos, is by tackling conflict head-on. Once I switched job responsibilities of several of the church staff. I relayed my plans to the session, expecting them to approve my actions, as they usually did.

I was wrong. First they said they wanted to think about it; then they became increasingly negative. The issue ballooned into an all-out power struggle.

I decided this was a "resignable issue," so I called a special meeting. I opened the meeting boldly: "I'm not going to take responsibility for what happens in this church without authority to make staff decisions. If the staff begins to think I don't have the authority to hire, fire, and organize the staff as I see fit, I can't do what you want me to do. We're going to decide right now what we're going to do about this!"

After some discussion, one of them (who had initially balked at my changes) said, "Steve, we don't care how you arrange the staff. But if you don't want our input, don't ask us what we think."

Out of that we worked out a new set of agreements on our roles in the church.

I hated that meeting. The thought of confronting the board ate away at me, and I thought I was going to lose control at the meeting. I tried to talk myself out of it: *I'm not going to make any waves over this.* But then I realized how much of my leadership would be sacrificed if I didn't make waves. Establishing your authority takes a lot out of you, but sometimes you have to do it. That incident buttressed my overall credibility and increased my authority in the pulpit.

A second key is to become sensitive to the symbols of authority. When I entered ministry, I *looked* young. I knew I would have trouble preaching authoritatively if people thought of me as baby-faced. So I grew a beard.

Some pastors don robes (if their tradition permits it); others install larger pulpits. In any case, we are wise to make use of such symbols.

Key qualification

Of course, power can be dangerously abused, and spouting off foolishly can wind up losing you all credibility. To earn the right to confront, or even to use the symbols of authority, sacrificial pastoral care is required.

One pastor I know is the very image of strength and authority. At staff meetings he bluntly holds staff members accountable for their duties:

"I asked you to contact six visitors this week. Did you do it?"

"And I asked you to get cards out to all seniors. Did you do it?"

"Now this week, this is what I expect from each of you . . ."

He's a no-nonsense leader. But I once found out why he gets away with it.

He asked me to speak at his church one Sunday. One of his members picked me up from the airport, and on the drive to the church, I asked the driver what he thought of his pastor.

"I don't like him."

"Really?" I said.

"Yeah," he replied. "But don't get me wrong. I'll follow him to the pit of hell."

I became curious and asked why.

"When my mother was dying," the man said, "he didn't leave her side for forty-eight hours."

This pastor had earned his authority. When we preach, the sacrificial pastoral care we've given grants us a unique authority.

When it's time to get intimate

I'm not a naturally warm person, and in some pastoral situations that has been a problem.

When I first arrived at Key Biscayne Presbyterian Church, I developed a friendship with a man who launched *Dolphin* magazine. Three months before he died, he made a decision to follow Christ. The night before he died, he said, "Steve, a lot of people don't know that I've found faith in Jesus Christ. So when you're standing over my casket, I want you to tell those attending my funeral what happened to me and how it can happen to them."

The church was packed the day of his funeral, and I preached an evangelistic message, keeping my promise to him. Afterward, everybody was hugging and consoling his widow. She walked over to me at one point and gave me a hug. I hugged her, but I must have winced because she said, "Are you angry?"

"Ginny, not at all," I said. "I love you a lot, but I'm just not comfortable with hugging yet."

Now, years later, no one would believe this of me. I come across to many as someone who could be anyone's best friend. But this is something I've learned.

I'm a teacher. I'm driven to help people understand what I'm saying. I long to make Jesus Christ real to people. And if I'm going to communicate with the modern world, I'm going to have to be as much fellow struggler as herald of God's Word.

I began learning this by default. Several years ago, I developed a terrible pain in my hip; for almost a year I was forced to walk with a cane. I couldn't even stand up to preach. Every time I'd lean in a certain direction, a searing pain would shoot through my body.

But I still had to preach—that was my livelihood. So I found a stool, and with microphone and Bible in hand, I preached sitting in front of the church. Right before the sermon, someone would move the pulpit aside and replace it with this stool.

The move from the pulpit to the chair, I discovered, increased my effectiveness. The symbol of the big pulpit served only to accentuate my natural tendencies as a proclaimer. When that was removed, many in my church remarked that I had become less preachy. Instead of communicating, "This is the way it is," my sermons subtly shifted to "Can we talk together this morning?" Just as symbols can communicate authority, they can also communicate intimacy.

Also, if you want to communicate intimacy, few things are more effective than simply telling the congregation you care about them.

A pastor friend told me, "I'm in trouble in my church, and I don't know what to do." After some conversation, I concluded that although Bill loved his congregation, he had yet to communicate it to them. He gives you the impression he wants to be left alone; he has a natural scowl on his face. But it belies his real feelings.

So I told him, "Bill, you need to say from the pulpit, 'Guys, I know I look like I'm mad at you all the time, and I know you don't think I like you. But I think you're the best thing since sliced bread. I feel so privileged to be your pastor. I love you.' If you'd say that one time, you wouldn't be in trouble any longer."

Another help is the counsel of friends. One of my pastor friends has always been a strong proclaimer, partly because he looks like a movie star, partly because he's naturally arrogant. He knows arrogance is a problem. So some time ago, he said to his elders, "I know I'm arrogant, and I struggle with it all the time. I don't like that about myself. I want you guys to help me with this."

He never said this from the pulpit—that would have been to throw his authority out the window—but it was a winsome thing to do. It not only convinced his board that he was a fellow struggler, it gave my friend some periodic feedback about what he was communicating from the pulpit.

Finally, I need to make sure I know who I am. I'm a sinner and I'm a sufferer. And when I suffer, I want to make sure I drink the full cup of it, so that I can learn what God is teaching me. Most of all, I want to make sure I experience grace.

Then, whatever I say from the pulpit comes out okay. I don't come across as insensitive to people's situations. Nor do I seem like a pitiful wimp who knows nothing of God's victory. I can communicate "I understand" while proclaiming God's truth.

Mistakes to avoid

In becoming more vulnerable from the pulpit, we become vulnerable to some homiletic mistakes. Here are three I try to avoid.

First, I don't want to lose all control. Though I want to show people I have emotions, I don't want to lose my ability to speak to the situation.

One church I stepped into was a war zone—father against son, husband against wife—before and after I arrived. Actual fistfights had broken out in the narthex, which were reported in several of the Boston newspapers. The most divisive issue was the placement of the Communion table in the new sanctuary. When I candidated there, the search committee asked me, "Where would you put a Communion table?"

I, not knowing the significance of the issue, naively replied, "You can hang it from the ceiling for all I care." My smart-aleck answer got me the job. I was hired and then baptized into an ugly church fight.

Thankfully, I had Walter, a father figure whose gentle wisdom and love guided me through a morass of hatred and division. Walter and I prayed together almost every day before he contracted cancer. The night he died, I visited him in the hospital. He begged me to stay with him a little longer, but I had another obligation. The doctors told me he would be fine, so I left, promising Walter I would see him in the morning.

I would never again see him alive, however; Walter slipped away in the night. I was devastated. I had just lost my one pillar in what seemed to be a house of cards.

Three days later, I presided over Walter's funeral. And during the service, I fell apart. I would start to cry, and the organ would begin playing softly. Then I'd sit down until I regained composure. I'd stand up again, only to lose it again. Walter's death opened up within me a floodgate of emotion.

When the service finally ended, several people commented, "It was obvious you loved Walter," and "Your tears showed the depth of your feelings." They identified with my loss; I had mourned alongside them.

But as pastor, I owed the family a service that would glorify

God and comfort them in their mourning. Certainly it's appropriate to tell people how you feel, and shedding a tear or two is okay. But I have to remember I'm the pastor called on to do more than simply share my feelings.

Second, I don't want to overtell. Once we've found a crisis in our lives, it's tempting to retell it whenever we can to help listeners see that we know about crises.

A recent crisis for my wife and me came our way from the ocean: Hurricane Andrew. We found ourselves huddled in a small closet as the winds blasted South Miami. We believed our deaths were imminent. In the end, we lost our home and many of our possessions but not each other.

This was too good a story not to tell. So I did, again and again as the opportunity presented itself. Three months later, I was speaking at a gathering of leaders in Colorado Springs when it suddenly struck me that for the last three months I had relayed our story at every place I had spoken. *Enough is enough,* I concluded.

Third, I don't want to get too specific about some sins. Though we want to communicate that we're sinners, it's not always appropriate to go into details. Otherwise we undermine people's confidence.

Some sins, like my anger, I'm free to describe in detail—just as I've told stories in this chapter. Other sins, though, I talk about only in a general way. When preaching about greed, for instance, I might say, "With this sin I've prayed, 'Forgive me my sins,' " or "I've got a problem with this sin, but if you think I'm going to be detailed about it, you're crazy!" So, in one statement I can let people know I'm human, without being inappropriate.

The intimate herald

Many years ago, I spoke at a Youth for Christ retreat. I did everything I could, short of standing on my head, to communicate to those teenagers, but the entire front row of boys slept through the entire weekend of services. So later, when asked to speak at a large convention of teenagers, I initially refused: once bitten, twice shy. Eventually, though, I reluctantly accepted the invitation.

That evening, after the band finished their set, I got up to speak to an auditorium full of teenagers. Someone had left a stool on stage, so I sat down, adjusted my half-glasses, and opened my big black Bible to the evening's text.

Suddenly the room fell silent. The students listened almost breathlessly, hanging on my every word. I was not a little surprised, to say the least, considering the reaction of my last teenage audience.

As I reflect upon the dynamics of that evening, part of the effect, I believe, was my gray hair, my deep voice, and my sitting down in front of them. All of that combined to have some sort of guru effect on the audience. I became the intimate herald, one who identified with them yet who spoke a word from the Lord.

I urge preachers not to violate their personalities. We are most effective at what makes each of us unique: our gifts and abilities. Some of us will naturally lean more toward proclamation, others at being a warm, charismatic witness of God's truth. Yet I'm convinced that each of us, when we're preaching at our best, can employ both to great effect.

3

Passion or Polish?

*If, indeed, every word is brought to God, one can imagine the last
great gathering of the sermons of all ages replying to one issue:
Which sermons really counted?*

—CALVIN MILLER

The book of Jonah is the tale of a reluctant preacher. Jonah's
message, as we have come to know it, is: "Yet forty days, and
Nineveh shall be overthrown" (Jonah 3:4 KJV).

A brief eight words. Surely there is more: some clever and
imaginative introduction lost in the oral manuscript. There must
have been iterations, poetry, and exegesis. But they are gone,
and those eight words are all we know.

Such a miniature message seems anticlimactic. Even the king
of Nineveh had more to say than Jonah (see vv. 7–9). But the
lost sermon was preached and bore a stern word of necessity.
Verse 10 states its effect: "And God saw their works, that they
turned from their evil way; and God repented of the evil, that he
had said that he would do unto them; and he did it not" (KJV).

The results of sermons in the Bible seem to be of great importance. This is true of either Testament. Acts 2:40–41 speaks of
the dramatic results of Peter's Pentecostal sermon, and a few
days later we are told, "Howbeit many of them which heard the
word believed; and the number of the men was about five thousand" (Acts 4:4 KJV). While Jonah omits the statistics of his sermon, Luke was careful to note Simon's.

Preaching in the New Testament seems to emulate the authoritative style of the Old Testament prophets. Ever cloaked in the
otherworldly authority, preaching became the vehicle the early

church rode into the arena of evangelizing the Roman Empire. As common people of Galilee once marveled at Christ's authority in the Sermon on the Mount (Matt. 7:28–29), so the authority of Scripture-based sermons became the defense—sometimes the sole defense—of the men and women who pressed the strong alternative of the gospel.

No time to waste

From John the Baptist to the end of the New Testament era, the sermon, like the church itself, flamed with apocalyptic zeal. The prophets had preached strong declarations of the direction of God in history. Following Pentecost, the sermon was possessed of a new spiritual union, where the preacher and the Holy Spirit were joined. The sermon, like Scripture, was dictated by the Spirit. Because of a direct alliance with the Trinity, the preacher had the right to speak with God's authority, demanding immediate action and visible decisions. This "right-now" ethic saw the sermon in terms of the demand of God. When God demanded decisions, they could be tabulated as soon as the sermon was finished. Sheep could immediately be divided from goats.

The specific message was delivered by those who possessed the call. The rules of primitive homiletics were not defined. The sermon was the man; the medium, the message. The product was instant and visible. Faith could be tabulated by those who cried in the streets that they believed, admitted to baptism, and showed up for the breaking of bread and prayers.

Following the first head counts in Jerusalem, the fire of evangelism spread, pushed on by the hot winds of Greek and Aramaic sermons. Congregations sprang up as sermons called them into being. Without institutional structure, programs, or buildings, the church celebrated the simple center of worship—the sermon and that which the sermon created: the company of the committed, the fellowship of believers.

The sermon was not celebrated as art, though doubtless, art may have been an aspect of delivery. Art was not so important in the panicky apocalypticism of Century One. Zeal raged in the bright light of Pentecost, not art. The sermon was the means of reaching the last, desperate age of humanity. One needed not to polish phrases or study word roots—the kingdom was at hand—there wasn't time to break ground for a seminary. Church administration went begging. On the eve of Armageddon, committees and bureaus were unimportant. There was only one point to be made. All human wisdom was one set of alternatives: repent or perish.

This was also Jonah's sermon: repent or perish. Like those of the New Testament era, his was not a notable document. The sermon was the workhorse of urgent evangelism.

Jonah's sermon was powerful simply because it was not ornate. He who cries "fire" in a theater need not be an orator. Indeed, he is allowed to interrupt the art of actors. It is not an offense to the years of disciplined training to be set aside for the urgent and unadorned word: "The theater is on fire!" The bearer rates his effectiveness on how fast the theater is cleared, not on the ovation of the customers. The alarmist is not out for encores but empty seats. His business is rescue.

The book of Jonah concerns such reluctant and apocalyptic preaching. The royal family sitting at last in the ashes of national repentance illustrates how effective his urgency was.

This zealous declaration is the Word of God as it is preached today in growing churches. Those who would speak an artistic word must do it in churches already built. Further, those who admire the Fosdicks and Maclarens—and they are to be admired—must see that their artistry would be passed by in the slums of London, where Booth's drums and horns sounded not a "trumpet voluntary" to call men and women to the queen's chapel but the "oom-pah-pah" of the Cross. "Are you washed in the blood of the Lamb?" was an urgent question that nauseated Anglicans even as it intrigued the poor and downtrodden of England with its zealous demands.

What did Booth say? Who knows? Who cares?

What did Whitefield say? What Billy Sunday? What Finney, what Wesley, what Mordecai Ham? To be sure, some of their sermons survive. But essentially they viewed their preaching not in the Chrysostom tradition but the tradition of the Baptizer of Christ: "O generation of vipers, who hath warned you to flee from the wrath to come? Bring forth therefore fruits worthy of repentance" (Luke 3:7–8 KJV), or Simon Peter, who cried, "Save yourselves from this untoward generation" (Acts 2:40 KJV).

The coming of art

Here and there were men like Jonathan Edwards who combined the best of literary tradition and apocalyptic zeal. But there was a real sense in which Edwards, the Mathers, and the other Puritans supplied a pre-soap-opera generation with a cultural center. The better their apocalypse, the higher the otherworld fever of their gospel contagion. Their fiery tirades began to resemble the spirit of a matador, and the amens were the enthusiastic oles, where the champion was not Jehovah but the preacher. Kate Caffrey writes in *The Mayflower*:

> A strong style was favored—in 1642 John Cotton recommended preaching after the manner of Christ, who, he said, "let fly poynt blanck"—and the hearers judged each performance like professional drama critics. Two sermons on Sunday and a lecture-sermon or weeknight meeting, usually on Thursday, were the custom, with fines of up to five shillings for absence from church. Only those who wished need go to the weeknight sermon, which was accompanied by no prayers or other teaching. Yet they were so popular in the sixteen-thirties that the General Court of Massachusetts tried to make every community hold them on the same day, to cut down all the running about from one town to the next. The preachers protested that it was in order to hear sermons that people had come to New England, so the court contented itself with the mild recommendation that listeners should at least be able to get home before dark.

> Even condemned criminals joined in the vogue for sermons. On March 11, 1686, when James Morgan was executed in Boston, three sermons were preached to him by Cotton and Increase Mather and Joshua Moody (so many came to hear Moody that their combined weight cracked the church gallery), and the pris-

oner delivered from the scaffold a stern warning to all present to take heed from his dread example.

Sermons were so important that it is impossible to overestimate them. Hourglasses, set up by the minister, showed the sermons' length: a bare hour was not good enough. People brought paper and inkhorns to take copious notes in a specially invented shorthand; many thick notebooks filled with closely written sermon summaries have been preserved. The meeting house rustled with the turning of pages and scratching of pens. Sermons were as pervasive then as political news today; they were read and discussed more eagerly than newspapers are now.

These intellectualized, zealous Massachusetts Bay sermons were celebrated by sermon lovers throughout New England. In these meetinghouses the sermon grew in performance value. And yet the zeal and urgency were viewed as part of the performance.

The tendency remains. Now the zealot is a performer and the sermon a monologue celebrated for its emotional and statistical success. The burden is urgent but also entertaining. The preacher feels the burden of his word as the fire-crier feels the pain of his office. But he feels also the pleasure of its success, which is his reputation.

Ego being the force it is, the urgency of the cry often becomes a secondary theme. Artistry eclipses zeal.

In *Moby Dick*, Herman Melville tells us of Father Mapple's sermon on the book of Jonah. Listen to Mapple's artistic treatment:

Then God spake unto the fish; and from the shuddering cold and blackness of the sea, the whale came breeching up towards the warm and pleasant sun, and all the delights of air and earth; and "vomited out Jonah upon the dry land"; when the word of the Lord came a second time; and Jonah, bruised and beaten—his ears, like two sea-shells, still multitudinously murmuring of the ocean—Jonah did the Almighty's bidding. And what was that, shipmates? To preach the truth to the face of Falsehood! That was it!

This, shipmates, this is that other lesson; and woe to that pilot of the living God who slights it. Woe to him whom this world charms from Gospel duty! Woe to him who seeks to pour oil upon the waters when God has brewed them into a gale! Woe to him who seeks to please rather than to appal! Woe to him whose good name is more to him than goodness! Woe to him who, in this world, courts not dishonour! Yea, woe to him who, as the great Pilot Paul has it, while preaching to others is himself a castaway!

But perhaps Father Mapple's art can afford to be more obvious than his zeal: he is preaching in a church already there and is not delivering urgency but a *sermon on urgency!*

How shall we then preach?

For years I have felt myself trapped in this quandary. Growing a church causes me to speak of redemption, frequently and earnestly. My sermons often sound to me too Falwellian or Criswellian or Pattersonian, my sermons more zealous than artistic. It is their intent to draw persons to Christ, in which pursuit my church is engaged.

But you may object, "Is it only sermon that creates your church? Do you not use the manuals and conventional machinery of the church and parachurch?" Yes. There have been mailing programs, and such radio and newspaper ads as we could manage. In fact, has not the sermon become second place in the church? Evangelical Free Church denominational executive Bill Hull once said in a denominational symposium:

Let us candidly confront this chilling claim that the pulpit is no longer the prow of the church, much less of civilization, as Herman Melville visualized it in *Moby Dick*. Ask any pulpit committee after months of intensive investigation and travel: How many pastors in the Southern Baptist Convention are even trying to build their careers on the centrality of preaching? . . . Subtle but excruciating pressures are brought to bear on the minister today to spend all of the week feverishly engineering some spectacular scheme designed to draw attention to his church, then on Saturday night to dust off somebody else's clever sermon outline (semantic gimmickry) for use the next morning.

Is this not so? To some degree, I think it is.

But there are some of us who don't want it to be. We feel called to do the work of an evangelist and believe urgency can have some class, and be done with some artistry and/or enlightenment. For years I have listened to the sermons of Richard Jackson, pastor at North Phoenix Baptist Church, with great debt to his example. After he finished a long section in the Passion passage of Saint John, I had seen the Cross in a new light. During more than a year of sermons from that Gospel, more than six hundred were added to his church by baptism. Perhaps Pastor Jackson has taken the burden of urgency to the Greek New Testament and the credible commentators and has emerged to say, "Here is enlightened urgency."

Perhaps Swindoll has done it with certainty. Perhaps Draper did it with Hebrews in his commentary. The sermon by each of these, I believe, is a declaration of urgency that at the same time takes giant strides toward homiletic finesse.

A secular parallel commends itself, again noticed by Bill Hull:

With disaster staring him in the face, Churchill took up the weapon of his adversary and began to do battle with words. From a concrete bomb shelter deep underground, he spoke to the people of Britain not of superiority but of sacrifice, not of conquest but of courage, not of revenge but of renewal. Slowly but surely, Winston Churchill talked England back to life. To beleaguered old men waiting on their rooftops with the buckets of water for the fire bombs to land, to frightened women and children huddled behind sandbags with sirens screaming overhead, to exhausted pilots dodging tracer bullets in the midnight sky, his words not only announced a new dawn but also conveyed the strength to bring it to pass.

No wonder Ruskin described a sermon as "thirty minutes to raise the dead." That is our awesome assignment: to put into words, in such a way that our hearers will put into deeds, the new day that is ours in Jesus Christ our Lord.

I am not talking about dogmatism. Dogmatism is authority-sclerosis. It is an incessant filibuster—never mute, always deaf! Talking is easier and much louder than thinking. The growing church too often cannot celebrate new truth, for it is too long screaming the old ones. The familiar is the creed; the unfamiliar is liberalism and dangerous revisionism. The thinking person off the street may want to ask questions and enter into dialogue, but he finds that trying to ask a question is like shouting into the gale or trying to quote the flag salute at a rock concert. His need for reasons seems buried in the noise.

I have always applauded Huck Finn for deciding to go with Tom Sawyer to hell than with the fundamentalist Miss Watson to heaven:

> Then she told me all about the bad place, and I said I wished I was there. She got mad, then, but I didn't mean no harm. All I wanted was to go somewhere; all I wanted was a change, I wasn't particular. She said it was wicked to say what I said; said she wouldn't say it for the whole world; she was going to live so as to go to the good place. Well, I couldn't see no advantage in going where she was going, so I made up my mind I wouldn't try for it. But I never said so, because it would only make trouble and wouldn't do no good.
>
> Now she had got a start, and she went on and told me all about the good place. She said all a body would have to do there was to go around all day long with a harp and sing, forever and ever. So I didn't think much of it. But I never said so. I asked her if she reckoned Tom Sawyer would go there, and, she said, not by a considerable sight. I was glad about that, because I wanted him and me to be together.

The logic of the streets is doubly plagued by such images. Why would a robust, open-minded Christ so love an overcorseted, dyspeptic, neurotic Scripture quoter as Miss Watson? Hell, for all its fiery disadvantages, seems a quieter and kinder place than her heaven.

It is not that saying "Thus saith the Lord" is wrong, and yet we are all drawn by the counsel of a friend who says, "Let us look together at what the Lord saith!" When we become more authoritarian in dialogues, we need to be sure we are really speaking the mind of God and not merely strong-arming our own agenda in another's more mighty name.

What matters most

Still, as crass as it sounds, unless the preached word encounters and changes its hearers in some way, artistry and enchantment cannot be said to have mattered much. The sermon must not at last be cute, but life-changing. As Somerset Maugham said of certain writers, "Their flashy effects distract the mind. They destroy their persuasiveness; you would not believe a man was very intent on ploughing a furrow if he carried a hoop with him and jumped through it at every other step."

When the sermon has reasoned, exhorted, pled, and pontificated; when it has glittered with art and oozed with intrigue; when it has entered into human hearts and broken secular thralldom—when all of this has been done, the sermon must enter into judgment at a high tribunal. Like the speaker who uttered it, the sermon must hear the judgment of the last great auditor. If, indeed, every word is brought to God, one can imagine the last great gathering of the sermons of all ages—the *march of the cassettes past the throne.* Every word tried . . . a thousand, thousand sermons—indeed, a great multitude that no man could number: Peter Marshall, Peter the Hermit, Peter the apostle, Peter Piper, Peter Paul, popes, Carl McIntire, Oral Roberts, Robert Bellarmine, John R. Rice, John Newton, John Hus, Prince John—a thousand, thousand words from David Brainerd to Origen, Tertullian to Swaggart, Jack Van Impe to Arius, all at once replying to one issue: Which sermons really counted?

The God who is the ancient lover of sinners will cry to those sermons at his left hand, "Why did you not serve me? Why did not you love men and women enough to change them? You took their hearts, commanded their attention, but did nothing to change them. Be gone, ye cursed sermons, to Gehenna— be burned to ashes and scattered over chaos—for better sermons would have called chaos to unfold itself in strong creation."

PART 2

Practices

4

Listening to the Listeners

Preachers need an organized program of feedback to determine whether they have hit their target.

—Haddon Robinson

What do you think of sermons?" the Institute for Advanced Pastoral Studies asked churchgoers—and got an earful. Sample responses:

"Too much analysis and too little answer."

"Too impersonal, too propositional—they relate nothing to life."

"Most sermons resemble hovercrafts skimming over the water on blasts of hot air, never landing anyplace!"

No wonder sermons are occasionally mocked as "the fine art of talking in someone else's sleep." Communication experts dismiss them as "religious monologues." Communication flows best on two-way streets, they argue, while preaching moves in only one direction. And because congregations can't talk back to register doubts, disagreements, or opinions, many sermons hit dead ends.

But that's not the only hit sermons take.

Content overload

A second rap is that most ministers overcommunicate. They load new concepts and duties on their congregations before previous ideas can be digested and absorbed. Content keeps coming, but when frustrated listeners can't stop the conveyor belt, they stop listening.

Yet monologues afflict the clergy like a genetic disease. Experiments with dialogue sermons, in vogue a few years ago, have gone the way of the CB radio. What is more, those trained in theological seminaries, where content is king, succumb to the empty-jug fallacy. Getting ideas into someone else's head is akin to filling a jug with water. Preachers invest large segments of time gathering water from books, commentaries, and old class notes but seldom consider time spent with people a valuable resource. While they often possess the gift, knowledge, and fiery enthusiasm, their sermons sound like "manualese"—textbook exegesis. The empty-jug fallacy is summed up in a bit of doggerel:

> Cram it in, jam it in;
> People's heads are hollow.
> Take it in, pour it in;
> There is more to follow.

Heads are neither open nor hollow. Heads have lids, screwed on tightly, and no amount of pouring can force ideas inside. Minds open only when their owners sense a need to open them. Even then, ideas must still filter through layers of experience, habit, prejudice, fear, and suspicion. If ideas make it through at all, it's because feedback operates between speaker and listener.

The preaching efficiency gauge

In recent years, automakers have begun outfitting some models with fuel efficiency gauges to let drivers know how their habits affect consumption. Whenever you stomp on the accelerator, the needle plummets; whenever you drive gently, the indicator rises. Very quickly this feedback helps pinpoint wasteful actions.

Preaching seems to be a zero-feedback situation, a monologue with no return. It does not have to be so. The pull toward monologue can be broken. In fact, significant preaching has always involved dialogue. The most astute preachers allow their eyes and ears to program their mouths. As they stand in the pulpit, they respond to cues from the audience telling them how they are doing. As they prepare, they study not only content but also people, hearing the spoken and unspoken questions. After speaking, they listen intently to find out how they have done.

Most people do not realize that important feedback takes place during the act of preaching. Listening seems passive—a typical Sunday spectator sport. Yet able communicators listen with their eyes. They know that audiences show by their expressions and posture when they understand, approve, question, or are confused. People nod agreement, smile, check their watches, or slump in their seats. Great preachers do not build strong churches nearly as often as great churches through their feedback make strong preachers. These congregations give their preachers the home court advantage by actively listening to what they have to say.

Pre-sermon feedback

Feedback, however, begins as the sermon is still brewing. Here pastors hold an advantage over other speakers, since they interact daily with members of the audience. Yet this advantage is not automatic. To benefit, preachers must listen: to questions people ask, and for answers they seek. They must observe: needs (expressed or unexpressed, admitted or denied), relationships (personal, family, community), experiences, attitudes, and interests. Jotting down what they observe each day will help take note of the passing parade. This in turn colors and shapes the handling of biblical material and the approach to the message. Let a preacher take a truth from Scripture and force himself to find twenty-five illustrations of that truth in daily life, and he will discover how much the world and its citizens have to tell him.

This dialogue with the congregation and the wider community can be more focused. In order to develop a sensitivity to current questions, John Stott, the internationally known English minister, joined a reading group that met monthly. They explored the ideas and implications of significant books, usually secular, from a Christian perspective. At times they attended films or plays together and then returned to the church to discuss what they had seen.

When Stott preached on contemporary issues, he formed an ad hoc group of specialists to help him learn the personal dimensions of the problem. At some of these gatherings, Stott actively participated, while at others he merely sat and eavesdropped on discussions between different points of thought. As an outgrowth of the challenging dialogue, Stott's sermons, while solidly biblical, were as up-to-date as next week's newsmagazine.

Prepping the congregation

Pastors in smaller churches legitimately object that groups such as the one Stott created develop more easily in large urban or suburban congregations. Yet even in rural and inner-city communities, men and women wrestle with substantive issues, and many would welcome the opportunity to discuss contemporary life and thought with a minister.

Churches, large or small, can organize systems of feedback. A church in Iowa turns monologue to dialogue by basing its midweek Bible study on the passage for the *following* Sunday's sermon. The pastor provides notes explaining the text, and then the people divide into small groups to explore further meanings and implications for themselves. Out of this encounter, the pastor zeroes in on terms, ideas, and issues he must address and, as an added benefit, often finds illustrations and applications for his sermon. Surprisingly, everyone agrees studying the passage beforehand heightens rather than diminishes interest in the sermon. They are made aware of the biblical material, and they become curious about how the preacher will handle it.

A pastor of a small church in Oregon goes over his sermon with members of his board every Thursday at breakfast. Everyone reads the passage beforehand, and the minister takes a few moments to sketch the broad outline of his message. During the discussion that follows, each shares what the passage says and what it might mean to the congregation. While the minister prepares the sermon, he does not do so in solitary confinement; instead he benefits from the insights and experiences of others in the body of Christ.

Rehearsing the sermon aloud also offers opportunity for feedback. John Wesley read some of his sermons to an uneducated servant girl with the instruction, "If I use a word or phrase you do not understand, you are to stop me." By this exercise, the learned Methodist developed the language of the mines and marketplace. Many preachers have taken a lead from Wesley. Some have risked their marriages by practicing on their spouses. Since preachers' spouses marry "for better or for worse," they can cut their downside risks by offering constructive criticism. Some seminaries offer courses to equip spouses in making their mates' sermons better. Less courageous ministers—or those with weaker marriages—might run through their sermons with a shut-in or a friend willing to contribute an ear.

The lifeblood of communication

As people file out of the sanctuary on Sunday, they mumble appropriate cliches: "You preached a good sermon today" or "I enjoyed what you had to say." While these responses are nice, they are often little more than code words to get past the minister as he guards the door. Preachers need an *organized* program of feedback following the sermon to determine whether they have hit their target.

Oak Cliff Bible Fellowship in Dallas, Texas, devotes the last fifteen minutes of the service to questions and answers. Some sermons raise more questions than others, of course. When questions are few, members tell what the sermon could mean in their lives. Both questions and testimony not only benefit the people but provide immediate information to the pastor.

According to Reuel Howe, feedback sessions are more productive if the minister is not present. In his book *Partners in Preaching,* Howe suggests inviting six or more laypeople, including a couple of teenagers, to take part in a reaction group following the church service. The pastor does not attend, but the conversation is recorded. When the tape runs out, the session ends. The pastor listens to the recorded comments later in the week. Several questions structure interaction.

1. What did the sermon say to you?

2. What difference, if any, do you think the sermon will make in your life?

3. How did the preacher's method, language, illustrations, and delivery help or hinder your hearing of the message?

4. Do you disagree with any of it? What would you have said about the subject?

Laypeople find these opportunities stimulating. In fact, through them, many learn to listen to sermons more perceptively and develop a keener appreciation for good preaching. If the minister listens carefully, he will discover how his congregation responded, what they heard and did not hear, what they understood and did not understand.

However it comes about, feedback is the lifeblood of communication. Without it, preaching seldom touches life.

When the church was young, Christians gathered at a common meal for Communion and communication. As a teacher explained the Scriptures, listeners broke in with questions and comments. So lively was the feedback that New Testament writers like Paul wrote ground rules to keep this interchange under control. Later, as Christianity fell under the influence of Greek and Roman rhetoric, oratory replaced conversation, and dialogues became monologues.

The infant church possessed what the modern church must rediscover. Only as we talk with people—not at them—will preaching remain a vital and effective carrier of God's truth.

5

The Art of Positive and Negative Preaching

*As journalists know—and radio hosts like Rush Limbaugh
make a fortune on—the negative gets more attention
and interest than the positive.*

—Craig Brian Larson

I was coaching gymnasts at a local club for a few hours a week. As I took beginners from basic skills like hip circles on the high bar to more difficult tricks like giants, I repeatedly faced a decision intrinsic to the art of coaching: when to say what the gymnast was doing right and when to say what he was doing wrong.

Both were necessary. I couldn't help a beginner on the high bar by ignoring that he was about to swing forward with his hands in an undergrip position—he would peel in the front and fall on his head. "Don't ever do that!" I warned. "You'll break your neck."

But my ultimate goal was not just to avoid injury; I wanted these boys to become excellent gymnasts someday. So I encouraged them as they developed the fundamentals: "Good stretch. That's the way to hollow your chest. Nice scoop in the front."

Preachers face the same decision weekly. One of our most important decisions when crafting a sermon is whether to frame it positively (what to do, what's right, our hope in God, the promises) or negatively (what not to do, what's wrong, the sinful human condition). The choice between positive or negative in the subject, outline, illustrations, and application powerfully affects the tone of a sermon. It changes the response of listeners.

Surprisingly, it took a friend editing a piece of my writing to make me sensitive to the issue of positive and negative preaching. I found he had written a new conclusion. "I didn't think this ended well on a negative note," he explained, "so I've converted this to a positive conclusion."

I liked my original version, but as I considered the revised version, I had to admit the positive conclusion was more effective. It left a hopeful feeling, and that was appropriate.

Thereafter in my preaching, I became intentional about selecting positive or negative elements. And I have seen the difference it makes.

Same text, different sermons

Recently I preached from Malachi 1:6–14 and had to choose between positive and negative approaches.

Malachi 1 scathingly indicts the priests and Israelites for what they were doing wrong. The people were sacrificing to God their blind and lame animals. The priests were sniffing at the altar, complaining that it smelled and that the sacrifices were a burden. God angrily rebuked them because by such "worship" they were showing him contempt rather than honor.

This Old Testament passage forcefully portrays a failing that Christians can have—we may dishonor God by giving him our worst instead of our best.

In writing the sermon, I had several decisions to make. First, the subject could have been framed negatively: how people show contempt for God. I had to develop that theme to be true to the text, of course, yet I decided to do so under the umbrella of a positive subject: how to honor God.

If I had selected the negative approach, my main points would have been: We show contempt for God when we (1) respect a father or employer above God, (2) offer God what we don't value, (3) worship God as if he is trivial.

In the positive approach, I wrote this outline: We *honor* God when we (1) respect God above a father or employer, (2) give God what we value, (3) worship God in a way that reflects his greatness. I developed the points with contrast, explaining what the Israelites were doing wrong and then illustrating positively how we can do what is right.

That one decision early on drastically changed the application and emotional impact of the entire sermon.

My goal is not a simple fifty-fifty split between positive and negative messages. Rather, I want to know which approach I am using and *why*. The right balance of positive and negative preaching leads to healthy Christians and churches, and to sermons that people want to hear.

When to be negative

Both positive and negative elements are especially effective at accomplishing certain objectives. First let's look at four legitimate reasons to use a negative approach.

To show our need. Negative preaching takes sin seriously and leads to repentance, thus indirectly bringing the positive results of joy, peace, and life. It is in keeping with the model of Jesus, who clearly honored God's hatred of sin by telling people what not to do.

In his sermon "God Is an Important Person," John Piper used a negative approach to help listeners see their need to honor God:

> I've been to church-growth seminars where God is not once mentioned. I've been to lectures and talks on pastoral issues where he is not so much as alluded to. I have read strategies for every kind of recovery under the sun where God is not there. I have talked to students in seminaries who tell me of manifold courses where God is peripheral at best. I have recently read mission statements of major evangelical organizations where God is not even mentioned.
>
> I admit freely that I'm on a crusade, and I have one message: God is an important person, and he does not like being taken for granted.

In this case, the string of negative examples builds forcefully to show listeners their need.

To seize interest. As journalists know—and radio hosts like
Rush Limbaugh make a fortune on—the negative gets more attention and interest than the positive.

In his sermon "Power," Howard Hendricks immediately gains
a roomful of listeners with an introduction that reminds us our
culture is a mess:

> Humpty Dumpty sat on a wall.
> Humpty Dumpty had a great fall.
> All the king's horses and all the king's men
> Couldn't put Humpty Dumpty together again.

> What a perceptive parable of our generation. We live in a society
> in which everything nailed down is coming loose. Things that
> people said could not happen are happening. Thoughtful though
> unregenerate people are asking,

> "Where is the glue to reassemble the disintegration and disar-
> ray?" . . .

> Then we usually seek someone to blame. I saw an intriguing
> piece of graffiti in the city of Philadelphia some time ago.
> Scratched across the wall were these words: *Humpty Dumpty
> was pushed.*

After getting listeners' attention with negative news, Hendricks goes on to show that only Christ has the power to
straighten out our culture.

To accentuate the positive. The positive feels even more so
after it has been contrasted with the negative.

I appreciated this approach in Leith Anderson's sermon "Can
Jesus Trust Us?" Leith develops one point negatively to help us
grasp the positive.

> Jesus . . . trusted John with his love. It is a most extraordinary
> thing to be described as "the one whom Jesus loved," to be Jesus'
> best friend. It smacks of something inappropriate, but the fact is,
> that's what their relationship was.

I wonder what it would be like if such a thing were done today. . . . What would happen if in 1994 someone were identified from all of Christendom as Jesus' best friend? Editors would be lined up for an interview. That person would be on the cover of every magazine. What do you think it would do to that person's life? Do you think that person would write a book or cut a CD or go on the road on a Best-Friend-of-Jesus seminar? Wouldn't it have the high potential of ruining that person's entire life? Wouldn't there be a temptation to arrogance? Wouldn't there be the possibility of treating others in an inappropriate and disparaging way?

And yet, didn't Jesus have as much right to a best friend as any of us? If so, wasn't it critically important that he choose someone whom he could trust to be his best friend, with the confidence that person would never misuse their relationship?

By showing the negative way most people would handle such a relationship with Jesus, Leith makes the apostle John's response seem even more positive.

To warn of danger. If my son reaches toward a hot pan on the stove, it's no time for me to tell him what great potential he has. "Don't touch that pan!" is negative—and necessary. In a dangerous world, much of a responsible pastor's counsel is negative by necessity.

In his sermon "Take Your Best Shot," based on the crucifixion account, Gordon MacDonald uses a negative approach to warn of evils we must avoid.

Here are two major forms of evil erupting out of the human experience. One is the crowd's irrational, angry, brutal resistance against God, his purposes and his people. The other is Pilate's saying, "I don't want to be identified with it." In silence and complicity, he backs off, washes his hands, and decides it would be better to do nothing.

What bothers me most is my strong suspicion that I could have been in that crowd. . . . I can see the possibility of being so defiant against God that I would have joined the crowd saying, "Crucify him!" self-righteously justifying myself. I can also see myself as Pontius Pilate saying, "I don't want anything to do with this," and letting it happen.

It's not positive, but it is powerful, and it warns listeners of a danger to avoid.

When to be positive

At the core, however, New Testament preachers proclaim good news, a message that brings hope, help, strength, and joy. Jesus sums up the negative commands—don't kill, steal, lie, covet—in positive terms: Love the Lord and love your neighbor.

This positive approach works best when you have the following objectives:

To show the goodness of Christ. The negative often focuses on what people and Satan do. The positive focuses on God's answer, God's glory, God's nature, God's salvation. Christ-centered preaching requires the positive.

In his Easter sermon, "Victory for Us," Earl Palmer shows by an analogy from the Winter Olympics that Christ won a victory not only for himself, but also for us:

The high point of the Olympics from a sentimental standpoint is those award ceremonies. When the victors stand on those three pedestals, that's where everybody is crying. The three flags are raised, and the national anthem of the gold medalist is played.

Something else is signified there: not only did [the various skaters] win, but their countries won, too. Not only their countries but their parents. Notice how the cameras try to find parents in the audience and the skaters' trainers and sometimes a whole town in Wisconsin—they all share in that victory. That's what makes it great. They not only won for themselves, they won for us, too.

In the Easter narratives of the New Testament, two great affirmations are made. One affirmation is that Christ has won the victory, and it's his alone. But the second theme, perhaps more subtly portrayed but also present in all the Gospel narratives, is that we too win a victory on Easter day. Our Lord's victory is his vindication, but it's also our vindication.

The positive approach fits the theme of resurrection and life. ***To bring encouragement and hope.*** God wants people to experience hope, peace, acceptance, courage. Bad news makes people feel bad. So while the negative is useful, it is rarely helpful to leave that as the last word.

In his sermon "Listening to the Dark," Eugene Lowry comforts listeners from the story of God speaking in a still, small voice to the despairing Elijah:

> In the midst of the darkness of the cave finally came this voice. The voice came up close to the ear and whispered. And the voice said, "What are you doing here?"
>
> That's one of the most remarkable passages in all of Scripture. What do you mean, "What are you doing *here*?" Do you notice what the voice did not say? It did not say, "What are you doing *there*?"—as though God were distant and aloof, looking on to the scene of the cave saying, "What are you doing there, Elijah? Why are you there?" We're not talking *there,* we're talking *here*.
>
> God is in the dark. In fact, God is bigger than the dark. That's the promise. It is God's dark. God is the Creator of the dark. And the promise is that God will be present. . . . And so with the confidence of children of the Most High God, revealed in Christ, we may dare to endure the dark.

To build godliness. People need not only to stop sinning, but also to start doing God's will. Preaching is both destructive and constructive, tearing down what's wrong and building what's right. Preaching positively encourages people to do what's right.

In his sermon "No Ordinary People," Wayne Brouwer affirms the right things the people in his congregation are doing:

> One of the great privileges we have as pastors is to hear the things that people say to us when they first join us for worship and for

fellowship. Seven times this past week alone, I've heard things like this:

"I didn't know what Christianity was about until I came to First Church."

"You people at First Church made me feel welcome even when I didn't know what I needed in my own soul."

"You know," said one person, "I dropped out of church for many years. I didn't think I needed it. And then my friend brought me to First Church one day. Now I know what I've been missing. I'd like to become a member."

"People at First Church really live their faith, don't they?"

That's what they're saying about us. They're not really saying it about us. They're saying it about Christ in us.

This positive approach surely made Brouwer's congregation want to continue to accept newcomers.

To bring resolution. Sermons often have greater emotional impact when we begin with the negative, show the need, and then bring resolution by showing what God can do.

In his sermon "The Love That Compels," Stuart Briscoe shows the classic negative-to-positive form of Christian preaching: the sin of humanity and the salvation of Christ.

Human beings are not unlike volcanoes. Inside a volcano, the pressure builds until the top blows with a dramatic eruption of lava. At other times, cracks slowly and insidiously appear on the side of the volcano, and the lava flows out in a different manner. . . .

Inside each of us, there's a thing called *sin*. No matter what way our volcano was formed, whether we blow the top or leak streams of lava, it's the lava inside that's the problem. The ultimate disease is the problem, and there's nothing human beings can do about it.

God demonstrated his incredible love toward us when he took the initiative and determined to do something about the sin problem. He invited Christ to take our sins on himself and die our deaths.

God would no longer count our sins against us. He would reckon the sin to Christ and reckon to us the righteousness of Christ. That's love.

Notice that the negative opening doesn't find resolution until the positive conclusion.

How to change direction

As we ponder the purpose of our sermon, we may sense that we need to flip an element from positive to negative, or vice versa. Instead of saying what not to do, we want to focus on what to do. Or instead of illustrating what someone did right, we want to illustrate what someone did wrong. Here's how to make the switch.

Switching from negative to positive. In a sermon on James 1:24, I wanted to encourage listeners to persevere because it makes them mature in character. I suspected, though, that many of my listeners weren't overly concerned about growing in character. But I also assumed they don't want to crash and burn morally. So I began by using a negative example, trying to motivate them by showing them what to avoid:

No one wants to crash and burn.

On September 8, 1992, United States Air Force master pilot Don Snelgrove was flying over Turkey in an F-16 fighter. He was on a four-hour mission to patrol the no-flight zone established over northern Iraq to protect the Kurds.

Nature calls even for master pilots. He pulled out a plastic container, set his F-16 on autopilot, and undid his lap belt. As he adjusted his seat upward, the buckle on that lap belt wedged between the seat and the control stick, pushing the stick to the right and sending the plane into a spin.

As he struggled to regain control, the plane plunged 33,000 feet. Finally at 2,000 feet altitude, he ejected from the plane. Moments later the F-16 struck a barren hillside and burst into flames. Neither the pilot nor anyone on the ground was injured. But I'll tell you what: there was one very embarrassed master pilot. That F-16 burning on a hillside in Turkey cost U.S. taxpayers 18 million dollars.

Even inadvertent mistakes are terribly embarrassing. How much worse are the mistakes and failures that result from our weaknesses, flaws, and sins. But we don't have to crash and burn morally. We can develop godly character, and James 1:24 shows us how.

My goal was to use negative examples to motivate.

But I could have begun the sermon positively. Perhaps the congregation already desired character and needed only encouragement. In that case, I could have begun the sermon with a positive example of someone who inspires us with his or her noble character:

Inside each of us there is the desire to be a better person. Many of us would love to be more like Dr. Elizabeth Holland, a pediatrician from Memphis, Tennessee, who has served as a volunteer doctor for World Vision.

Once she treated patients in the middle of an African civil war, says writer Robert Kerr. In 1985 she performed one appendectomy in which "the 'operating room' was a mud hut deep in the jungle of Zaire. The anesthetic was an animal tranquilizer, which ran out in the middle of the operation. Outside, MiG jets were dropping bombs." Every time a bomb hit, dirt from the mud hut fell down on them. She performed a virtual miracle considering the circumstances, and her patient lived.

During the Angolan civil war, Holland routinely saw 400 to 500 patients a day. " 'I frequently wrapped broken bones in magazines and used banana leaves for slings,' she said."

Since food was in short supply, Holland ate a paste made from ground cassava-plant roots. "It tasted like glue," said Dr. Holland. "The first few days, I thought I would die. But then I got to where it tasted pretty good. Sometimes when it rained we could get a few leaves from the trees to cook in with it for variety."

Across the Angolan border was a minefield that often killed or injured civilians; Holland would retrieve them.

"She said, 'I learned if I got my nose down at ground level and crawled along on my stomach, I could see the mines. So I would make my way across, then throw the injured person over my shoulder and carry them out the same way I had come over.' "

Maybe we will never be forced to persevere as Elizabeth Holland has, but each of us can grow in character, and James 1:24 tells us how.

Notice that this example leaves a positive feeling in listeners; it assumes they want the best and can develop. The negative approach focuses on what to avoid; a positive approach focuses on what to attempt.

Switching from positive to negative. Familiar Bible passages can be presented in a positive or negative approach, depending upon the situation. Take, for example, the story of Peter trying to walk on water.

In his sermon "A Mind-Expanding Faith," John Ortberg drew from the text a positive main idea:

All of us are "would-be water walkers." And God did not intend for human beings, his children created in his divine image, to go through life in a desperate attempt to avoid failure.

The boat is safe, and the boat is secure, and the boat is comfortable. The water is high, the waves are rough, the wind is strong, and the night is dark. A storm is out there, and if you get out of your boat, you may sink.

But if you don't get out of your boat, you will never walk because if you want to walk on the water, you have to get out of the boat. There is something, Someone, inside us that tells us our lives are about something more than sitting in the boat, something that wants to walk on the water, something that calls us to leave the routine of comfortable existence and abandon ourselves in this adventure of following Christ.

But the same passage could be used in a negative approach: to point out Peter's mistakes to avoid. It might sound like this:

Peter was able to walk on water for a few steps. But in the middle of that walk toward Christ, something changed in his heart, and it caused him to sink.

Peter isn't the only one who has taken bold steps of faith to follow Christ. Many in this congregation are doing the same. In spite of great fear, you have begun to teach a Bible class or host a cell group or volunteer at the local hospital. Now that you've begun, you are beginning to see how challenging this really is, and you're wavering. You feel like you're going to sink. Let's see if we can learn from this account how to avoid what caused Peter to sink.

To change from positive to negative, look for what a text shows not to do.

The fine art of discipling

My two oldest sons competed on their high school gymnastics team last year. As the postseason meets began, Aaron, who was a senior, had the goal of qualifying for state. Ben, a sophomore, wanted to make it to sectionals.

In regionals both Aaron and Ben had poor meets, missing several routines. When they got in the car afterward, they were down in the dumps—even though they had both (barely) made the cut for sectionals. Probably they were a little embarrassed, not knowing how I would react (I competed in gymnastics in high school and college).

Although after some meets, I have pointed out flaws in their technique, this time I spent the next thirty minutes in the car telling them the bright spots, the specific things they had done well: "Aaron, that was the best double you've ever done off high bar. You were above the bar." "Ben, your plunge on parallel bars was unbelievable. You must have held it for five seconds!"

By the time we got home, they were smiling and talking about how much better they would do in the next meet. Their confidence had returned. One week later, Ben hit his routines as well as he had all year, and Aaron reached the goal that he had hoped for all year: he qualified for state.

We coach—and disciple—not only the body but the heart. The choice between positive and negative in our sermons is a critical part of training Christians who have the hearts of champions.

6

Illustrating with Simplicity and Power

The longer I study Jesus' method of communicating, the more convinced I am that his genius rested in his ability to simplify and clarify issues others had complicated.

—CHARLES SWINDOLL

The scene was thick. The clouds were heavy and dark gray. The mood was tense. It was no time to take a walk in the park or stroll down Pennsylvania Avenue. The smell of death was in the air. A decision was essential. With paper and pen in hand, the long, lank frame of a lonely man sat quietly at his desk. The dispatch he wrote was sent immediately. It shaped the destiny of a nation at war with itself.

It was a simple message—a style altogether his. No ribbons of rhetoric were woven through the note. No satin frills, no enigmatic eloquence. It was plain, direct, brief, to the point. A bearded Army officer soon read it and frowned. It said:

April 7, 1865, 11 a.m.
Lieut. Gen. Grant,
Gen. Sheridan says, "If the thing is pressed, I think that Lee will surrender." Let the thing be pressed.

A. Lincoln

Grant nodded in agreement. He did as he was ordered. Exactly two days later at Appomattox Court House, General Robert E. Lee surrendered. "The thing was pressed," and the war was ended.

Simplicity. Profound, exacting, rare simplicity. Lincoln was a master of it. His words live on because of it. When he was assaulted by merciless critics, many expected a lengthy, complex defense of his actions. It never occurred. When questioned about his feelings, he answered, "I'm used to it." When asked if the end of the war or some governmental rehabilitation program might be the answer to America's needs, he admitted quite simply, "Human nature will not change." In response to a letter demanding the dismissal of the postmaster general, he wrote, "Truth is generally the best vindication against slander." When encouraged to alter his convictions and push through a piece of defeated legislation by giving it another title, he reacted with typical simplicity, "If you call a tail a leg, how many legs has a dog? Five? No, calling a tail a leg doesn't *make* it a leg!"

Simplicity. The difference between something being elegant or elaborate. The difference between class and common. Between just enough and too much. Between concentrated and diluted. Between communication and confusion. Between:

"Hence from my sight—nor let me thus pollute mine eyes with looking on a wretch like thee, thou cause of my ills; I sicken at thy loathsome presence." and *"Scram!"*

Simplicity. *Economy* of words mixed with *quality* of thought held together by *subtlety* of expression. Practicing a hard-to-define restraint so that some things are left for the listener or reader to conclude on his own. Clear and precise—yet not overdrawn. Charles Jehlinger, a former director of the American Academy of Dramatic Arts, used to instruct all apprentice actors with five wise words of advice: *"Mean more than you say."*

It has been my observation that we preachers say much too much. Instead of stopping with a concise statement of the forest explicit and clear—we feel compelled to analyze, philosophize, scrutinize, and moralize over each individual tree—leaving the listener weary, unchallenged, confused, and (worst of all!) *bored.* Zealous to be ultra-accurate, we unload so much trivia the other person loses the thread of thought, not to mention his patience. Bewildered, he wades through the jungle of needless details, having lost his way as well as his interest. Instead of being excited over the challenge to explore things on his own, lured by the anticipation of discovery, he gulps for air in the undertow of our endless waves of verbiage, cliches, and in-house mumbo jumbo.

One dear old lady said of the Welsh preacher John Owen that he was so long spreading the table, she lost her appetite for the meal. I particularly like the way William Sangster put it: "When you're through the pumpin', let go the handle."

The longer I study Jesus' method of communicating, the more convinced I am that his genius rested in his ability to simplify and clarify issues others had complicated. He used words anyone could understand, not just the initiated. He said just enough to inspire and motivate others to think on their own, to be inquisitive, to search further. And he punctuated his teaching with familiar, earthy, even humorous illustrations that riveted mental handles to abstract truths. Best of all, he didn't try to impress. Such a captivating style led others to seek his counsel and thrive on his instruction.

As a fellow struggler earning the right to be heard Sunday after Sunday, let me offer this summary:

- Make it clear.
- Keep it simple.
- Emphasize the essentials.
- Forget about impressing.
- Leave some things unsaid.

Luther made it even more simple:

- Start fresh.
- Speak out.
- Stop short.

We've got the greatest message on earth to declare. Either most people have never heard it, or they've been confused because someone has garbled the issues. Jesus implies, "If the thing is simplified, they will surrender."

Let the thing be simplified.

7

Making Applications Personal

True Bible application involves discovering what the Bible is saying to me and then doing what it says.

—David Veerman

Terry gathers his family and quickly herds them into the station wagon. He has to get to church early to photocopy some handouts for the Sunday school class he teaches. Then there's choir, and after church several conversations about the committee he serves on. With seemingly boundless energy and enthusiasm, Terry is immersed in church activities. In his quiet moments, however, Terry worries. At home, his briefcase holds a doctor's report telling of a shadow in the X-rays of his lungs.

* * *

Ruth is known for her contagious smile and warm encouragement. As hospitality chairperson, she seems to know everyone in church. *How can she always be so up?* people wonder. While Ruth is succeeding at church, she believes she is an absolute failure at home. There is constant bickering with a teenage daughter, and she feels a growing sense of distance from her husband.

* * *

An honor student and a varsity volleyball player, Janet is the picture of the all-American girl. She's also actively involved with the church youth group and takes her faith seriously. But she wants to know how to bring what she believes into her everyday life, especially with her boyfriend, who lately has been pressuring her sexually. Janet sits in the back of the church and wonders.

*   *   *

Recognize any of those people? You've never met them, but you probably know many just like them. They fill our churches: men and women and young people, some desperate, looking for answers.

Steve Brown, president of Key Life Network and former pastor of Key Biscayne Presbyterian Church in Florida, says that when he preaches, he safely assumes seven out of ten people in the congregation have broken hearts. They especially need a life-changing word from God, something they can *act on* as well as know.

As a communicator, I recognize the value of applications, and the difficulty of making appropriate ones. In fact, in many sermons I hear (and some I've preached), the application simply is left out. Yet, as Jay Kesler, president of Taylor University, puts it, preaching a sermon strong on information but weak on application is like shouting to a drowning person, "Swim! Swim!" The message is true, but it's not helpful.

A friend once said of his former pastor, "The closest he came to application was occasionally to end his sermon with, 'And you?'" I'm sure he wanted to drive home his sermon, but although the spirit was willing, the application was weak.

Why the difficulty?

If applications are desirable, why are they so often lacking? As I've talked about this with pastors, and especially as I wrestled with applications as senior editor of the *Life Application Bible*, I've identified several reasons.

Hard work. This is, perhaps, the main cause of application deficiency. They're tough. They demand time and effort.

When our team began working on the *Life Application Bible*, we wanted (1) to help our readers ask the right questions, and (2) to motivate them to action. That twofold response was our definition of *application*.

I anticipated little difficulty writing application notes. After all, I'd spent two decades in youth ministry challenging young people to follow Christ and teaching them how to grow in the faith. But my assumption was wrong; finding applications was tough work. I found it enjoyable to research and explain textual questions, cultural influences, and theological intricacies, but I couldn't easily make the bridge to real life. Even now, after years of writing application notes, I find it doesn't come easily.

Wrong assumptions. I used to assume the audience would make a connection between the lesson and their lives, a common mistake. None of us wants to insult the intelligence of our listeners, and so we lay out the Bible story, the theological insights, or the timeless truths, and leave the rest to them. But most people, I found to my dismay, can't make the mental jump. Our congregations don't want to be spoon-fed, but they do need to be led.

Fear. We may fear being "too simplistic." We may think we have to speak deep, complex truths or broad, general principles to proclaim properly the Word of God. There have been times when I've subconsciously tried to show off my education. How easy it is to preach to ourselves, splitting the finer points of theology, extrapolating the etymology, or considering the cultural context, while the congregation waits for a life-changing challenge!

I've worked hours crafting sermons I then delivered with confidence, only to have people stare back with a collective ho-hum. It's not that I wasn't prepared or "pre-prayered," or that I stumbled or stuttered. In fact, the congregation probably learned something, and I heard quite a few post-sermon comments such as "That was interesting" and "Good job."

But nothing was said about changed lives. For fear of oversimplifying, I simply had been nonspecific. I had failed to move to application.

No training. I've spoken to many preachers who bemoan their lack of training in applying Scripture. While grateful for the intensive work in other areas of homiletics and theology, they express need for a dose of reality. "I wish I'd been taught how to relate the Word to the needs of real people," said one.

A misunderstanding of what application is can weaken

preaching. If I'm unsure of my goal, I'll definitely have trouble hitting it. So what is effective application?

What application is not

Let's begin by listing what *isn't* application.

First, application is not additional information—simply giving more facts. Whether in detective work or in Bible study, gathering facts begins the process, but it doesn't complete it. The facts need to be used.

For instance, it's good to know that Matthew was a tax collector and that tax collectors conspired with Rome to become rich, exploiting their countrymen. Such information puts Matthew in context and helps us understand the Bible. But to become useful, the information needs to become wedded to action a listener might take.

Second, application is not mere understanding. Understanding God's truth, the step that must follow fact collecting, is vital. We need to know what the Bible means, not just what it says. Again, however, a sermon left here is incomplete. Many people understand biblical truths, but the truths make no impact on their lives. I may understand that Jesus quoted Scripture to counter Satan's attacks in the wilderness and that the Word of God is powerful. But so what? How would *I* ever do that?

Third, applying the text is not merely being relevant. Relevance explains how what happened in Bible times can happen today. For example, we can describe Corinth as similar to many cities today—wild, filled with idols, violence, and sexual immorality. Relevant description can make us more open to application. But this step still falls short since it doesn't tell us what we can do about the situation we recognize.

Finally, illustration—explaining how someone else handled a similar situation—doesn't qualify as application. Illustrations shed light on a passage and show us how someone else applied truth to his or her life. But it remains removed from the individual—from us.

If each of these four aspects of Bible exposition isn't application, what is? What steps can we take to apply the Bible to life?

Applications at their best

Simply stated, application is answering two questions: *So what?* and *Now what?* The first question asks, "Why is this passage important to *me?*" The second asks, "What should I do about it today?"

Application focuses the truth of God's Word on specific, life-related situations. It helps people understand what to do or how to use what they have learned. Application persuades people to act.

For example, Luke 5:12–15 reports Jesus' touching and healing a leper. Beyond describing the horrors of leprosy in the first century (information) and pointing out the similarities to people with AIDS today (relevance), application asks the congregation to think about who they may consider untouchable and challenges them to touch those people for Christ. It asks, "Whom do you know who need God's touch of love? What can you do today or this week to reach out to them?"

Or take the story of Samson and Delilah in Judges 16. Much more than an interesting piece of Jewish history, it shows how desire can deceive a person into believing a lie. When we explain this story to young people, we can apply it through a direct challenge. First, they must decide what kind of people they will love *before* passion takes over. Second, they must understand that unless a person's faith, personality, and temperament are as gratifying as his or her kisses, the result is pain and self-destruction. An application here is to exercise patience in their relationships.

Application moves beyond explaining the text and stating the timeless truths. It makes the message personal and challenges people to act. For this to happen, four steps are necessary:

1. The listener must receive the message: *Do I understand what was said?*

2. The person should find reason to reflect on his or her own life: *What does the message mean for me?*

3. The individual needs to identify necessary behavior changes: *What should I do about it?*

4. The person should lay out a plan or steps to make a change: *What should I do first?*

Keeping these steps in mind during sermon preparation can help us preach a sermon that moves people from receiving the message to taking action. But how do we determine an appropriate application in the first place?

Preparing for application

I use what I call the Dynamic Analogy Grid to discover possible applications in a Scripture passage (see illustration on page 65). Whether my text is a verse, a paragraph, or a chapter, this tool helps me move from the words and their meanings to God's Word and his message for the people in the pews. Here's how I work through the grid, using my other Bible study tools and my knowledge of people.

I work across each horizontal row of three boxes, starting with boxes 1 through 3. These three boxes deal with the information in the text. I decide what the passage says about humankind's need/problem, God's action/solution, and humankind's necessary response/obedience. That helps me put the passage in its cultural-historical context and determine the biblical principle or timeless truth.

If, for example, the passage chastises the people of Israel for idol worship (let's use 1 Samuel 7:3–4), I'd want to know what gods were idolized, how they were worshiped, and what problems ensued for the Jews. That would fill box 1. Then I'd want to determine God's action or solution for this problem (box 2), and how he wanted the people of that day to respond (box 3).

Next, I'd move to boxes 4 through 6, which put the text into a contemporary context. When filled in, these boxes make the text relevant.

DYNAMIC ANALOGY GRID

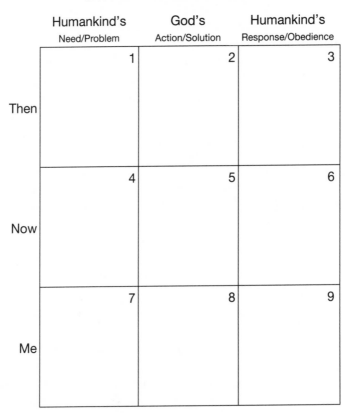

	Humankind's Need/Problem	God's Action/Solution	Humankind's Response/Obedience
Then	1	2	3
Now	4	5	6
Me	7	8	9

For box 4: What are the idols today? Of course there are differences, but which of our problems, pressures, and temptations are similar to those of the people of Israel back then?

For box 5: How does God's solution for the Jews then parallel his actions for Christians today?

For box 6: What response does God want now? What does God want people to do? This answers the question *So what?*

The final step is to fill in boxes 7 through 9. This applies the passage personally as I think of specific needs in my community and congregation. This leads us to answer the question *Now what?*

For box 7: What is one example of a similar problem I'm

facing now? Or what are we facing as a church that's similar to idols?

For box 8: What is God telling me as an individual, or us as a church, to do about it?

For box 9: Then what, specifically, does he want me or us to do first? What are some steps we should take today to rid ourselves of idols or to reorder our priorities?

Preaching for application

Here's how one pastor used the grid. Hebrews 1:4 introduces the theme of the preeminence of Christ, saying that Christ is greater than the angels. The problem at that time (box 1) was that Hebrew Christians were in danger of falling back into Judaism, and many were fascinated with angels. Simply stated, God's solution (box 2) was to use the author of Hebrews to emphasize the superiority of Christ, that he alone is sufficient for salvation. First-century believers were challenged (box 3) to understand Christ's true identity, to worship only him and not to ignore salvation (2:3).

For the "Now" row, this pastor decided that most people today don't have old religions to fall back into, but several new ones entice us, such as the New Age movement and cults, which permeate all areas of our society (box 4). People easily follow theological tangents. People today need to understand the superiority of Christ over all religions (box 5). Christ is better—the only way. And we need to challenge believers to keep their eyes on Christ and to trust only him (box 6).

After filling the first two rows, this pastor understood the context, the biblical principles, and the relevance of those principles. He could answer *So what?* The final step was to consider the people of his congregation and what possible actions they should take. He applied the message to both unbelievers and believers wavering in their faith.

For unbelievers, confused by the supernatural talk in society and unfamiliar with Christ (box 7), he emphasized the "great salvation" described in Hebrews 2:3 (box 8) and challenged them to trust Christ (box 9). The Christians sidetracked by theological gurus or fascinated by faddish ideas and theologies (box 7 again) need to reject heresies that diminish Christ, to center their lives on Christ, their only authority and hope of salvation (box 8). One possible way they might do that (box 9) would be to learn more about orthodoxy, perhaps by reading a Josh McDowell book or joining an adult study on the topic at the church.

"Christ is greater than the angels" became more than a truth to affirm. It came alive as a message that challenged people to act.

I usually prepare by working from left to right, as I've illustrated above, but when I speak, I sometimes move down the boxes vertically, one column at a time. That moves from people's problem then, to society's problem now, to my (or our) particular problem; from God's solution then, to God's solution now, to God's solution for me (or us); and from humankind's expected response then, to humankind's expected response now, to my (or our) specific and personal response. That adds variety.

Here's another suggestion: Lloyd Perry, homiletics professor emeritus of Trinity Evangelical Divinity School, recommends a subpoint of application for every main point in the sermon. In other words, he recommends not leaving all the applications until the end, when people are least likely to be listening because they're tired or thinking about lunch. If we're running late, we're tempted to generalize or skip the challenge to action if it's lumped at the conclusion. Perry suggests we sprinkle applications throughout.

Mining for applications

If I want to prepare applications that hit home, I find it best to think through the needs of the people to whom I'm speaking. Needs may be categorized many ways. For example, I generally think in terms of felt needs, hidden needs, and spiritual needs.

As the adjective suggests, *felt* needs relate to what people are feeling. Felt needs include physical and social pressures at the front of their awareness. Hunger is a felt need, as is loneliness or conflict or guilt.

Hidden needs are those things people need but aren't aware of at the moment. An engaged couple needs to know about conflict resolution, for example, but might not recognize it before the wedding. Other hidden needs a congregation might have include the needs to tithe, to have patience, and to be good stewards of time.

Obviously, such needs could fit under the heading of *spiritual* needs. But what I'm calling spiritual needs are God's special demands on life and the implications of what it means to call Christ Lord. Being involved in church, sharing the faith with others, studying the Bible regularly, and praying consistently are some of the spiritual needs that come to mind.

Another way to expose a congregation's needs might be to think through the following eight areas of personal application:

1. Relationships (for example, with family, friends, neighbors, coworkers, fellow believers).

2. Conflicts (in marriage, with children, at work).

3. Personal burdens (sickness, family pressures, death, loss).

4. Difficult situations (stress, debt, hindrances).

5. Character weaknesses (dishonesty, lack of integrity, anger).

6. Lack of resources (in time, energy, money, materials, information).

7. Responsibilities (work demands, church programs, volunteer efforts, home projects).

8. Opportunities (learning, working, serving, witnessing, etc.).

When I read this list while thinking of my audience, the Holy Spirit often shows me a need to address. I keep this list nearby as I study a text on which I'll speak.

Mike Marcey, my pastor at Naperville Presbyterian Church in Illinois, prepares applications by thinking through the types of people in the church—not specific individuals, but categories of people. He considers visitors, who are new in town or who've come out of curiosity. He also thinks of the more mature Christians in the congregation, who want to grow in their faith. And there are people in personal crises. The list goes on. Reminding himself of the various types of people present keeps Mike tuned in to the various needs for application.

Another way to locate appropriate applications is to look for them as we relate with people and observe the world. Needs may surface during pastoral calling, hospital visitation, conversation after services, counseling appointments, youth work, board meetings, newspaper reading, and so forth. It's not hard to find areas to apply the Bible to life.

The other day I was rushing down the highway. I pulled behind the line of cars awaiting the left-turn arrow at the stoplight. Finally the light changed, but the man in front of me didn't budge. I figured he hadn't seen the light change, and so I gave a tap on my horn. No movement.

"What's wrong with this guy?" I muttered, and I hit the horn again and again. Finally he put his arm out the window and pointed to the left. Coming down the highway was a fire truck with lights blinking and siren wailing.

In short, I needed both patience and perspective—a need many people have, and one I can address in an application some time.

Some people study, study, study, and do very little about it. They act like a football player who loves the game and knows the plays by heart, but who seldom practices or plays.

Others do, do, do, and spend little time in study. They act like the athlete who runs, throws, and catches footballs by the hour, but who spends no time understanding the rules of the game or learning the playbook.

True Bible application involves both studying and doing. It is discovering what the Bible is saying to me and then doing what it says.

We've been given the awesome responsibility of presenting and explaining the Word of God. We must be sure to tell our listeners everything they need to know about the text and context—history, culture, archaeology, theology, and etymology. But we can't neglect application.

"Keep putting into practice all you learned from me and saw

me doing," Paul writes, "and the God of peace will be with you" (Phil. 4:9 TLB). Our job: to explain what God wants people to know and do about his eternal commands, promises, and truths, and then to offer them ways to *do* it.

8

Offering an Honest Invitation

The only proper reason to give an invitation is that
God calls people to decision.

—LEIGHTON FORD

Not a few of us have been turned off by public invitations that offended our theology, our integrity, our sensitivities.

Some "altar calls" I wish I hadn't heard, and I doubt they altered anyone. I recall a healing evangelist during my younger days who cajoled and threatened his audience until the number of people God had "revealed" to him came forward that night. But I also recall another man with the gift of healing who laid his hands gently but with authority on those who came to kneel at the altar of an Anglican church.

I remember an evangelist in the Wheaton College chapel whose finger swept the audience like an avenging angel; his invitation was so broad we felt we should come forward if we hadn't written our grandmother in the last week! He squeezed and pleaded as if Jesus were some kind of spiritual beggar rather than the royal Lord. But I have seen Billy Graham stand silently, arms folded, eyes closed, a spectator, as a multiracial throng of Africans, Europeans, and Asians surged forward in South Africa to stand together at the cross.

How *do* we give an honest invitation?

The real inviter

First, we must be *honest before God.* The only right we have to ask people to commit their lives for time and eternity is that God is calling them. The gospel message is both an announcement and a command: it tells what God has done and calls people to respond. "God was reconciling the world to himself in Christ, not counting men's sins against them. And he has committed to us the message of reconciliation. We are therefore Christ's ambassadors, as though God were making his appeal through us. We implore you on Christ's behalf: Be reconciled to God" (2 Cor. 5:19–20 NIV). *God is making his appeal through us.*

I am to present his message faithfully and give his call, trusting him with the response and giving him the glory. My part is to be faithful; his part is to produce fruit.

During a series of meetings conducted by R. A. Torrey years ago, there was no response the first several nights. Homer Hammontree, the songleader, came to Torrey in distress.

"Ham," the evangelist replied, " 'it is required in stewards, that a man be found faithful.' Good night; I am going to bed."

Then came a service with tremendous outpouring of the Spirit and a huge response. Hammontree was exultant. Again Torrey said quietly, "Ham, 'it is required in stewards, that a man be found faithful.' Good night; I am going to bed."

I find it hard to be as cool as that, but I do admire Torrey's sense of honest faithfulness to God.

Why am I doing this?

But then I must also be *honest with myself.* Why do I give an invitation? Because it's expected in my church or tradition? Because *I* need the affirmation of seeing people respond visibly?

Or, on the other hand, do I *not* give an invitation because I fear embarrassment if people don't respond? Or criticism because it's *not* part of my group's tradition?

The only proper reason to give an invitation is that God calls people to decision. From Moses ("Who is on the Lord's side?") through Elijah ("How long will you waver between two opinions?") to Peter ("Repent and be baptized, every one of you") and Paul ("I preached that they should repent and turn to God and prove their repentance by their deeds")—the scriptural tradition is *crisis preaching* that calls for a decision. It has been noted that almost everyone Jesus called, he called publicly. Picture him directing James and John to leave their boats, Zacchaeus to climb down from the tree, the lame man to rise and walk.

None of us has completely pure motives. We are a mixed people. That is why I must continually pray, "Lord, let me not give this invitation because I need to see results. Let me not shun it because I am afraid or because someone might criticize. I must give it solely because you love these people, you want them to know you, and you have told me to tell them that."

Up-front and open

Then I must be *honest with the audience*. Many people would like to know God, but no one has ever asked them clearly.

Tony Campolo, a Philadelphia sociologist, was seated at a state prayer breakfast next to the governor and found that he was sympathetic but had never committed himself to follow Christ.

"Why not?" asked Campolo.

The governor honestly replied, "No one ever asked me."

"Well, I'm asking you."

To his surprise, the governor responded, "Okay, I will."

The Scriptures use many metaphors to describe the step of faith: coming, following, kneeling, opening, receiving, turning. An invitation is a symbolic expression of that spiritual reality. It is nothing more, nothing less—and we need to explain that.

When I ask people to come forward at the end of an evangelistic meeting, I try to make it clear what I am asking them to do. At the beginning of the sermon I may say something like this: "Tonight at the end of my talk I am going to ask you to do something about it, to express your decision. I am going to ask you to get up and come and stand here at the front. This is an outward expression of an inward decision.

"Just as you make a promise to someone, mean to keep it, and shake hands on it—just as a young couple come to love each other, want to give themselves to each other, and then openly express that covenant in a wedding—so I am asking you to express your commitment. There is nothing magical in coming forward. Walking down here doesn't make you a Christian. You could come down here a thousand times with your feet, and it would make no difference at all if that's all it was. But as you come here with your feet, you are saying with your heart, 'God, I am coming to you and leaving behind those things that are wrong and sinful. I am trusting Christ as my Savior, and I am coming to follow him in his church from tonight on.' "

People need to know what responding to your invitation means and what it doesn't mean. They need to know that they must be open Christians, not private believers, and that this is a *way* of expressing that. It is also important that they know it is not the only way. While confession is required (Rom. 10:9), nowhere does Scripture demand that people raise a hand, come forward, or sign a card to confess Christ.

In my evangelistic invitations, I usually say so. "You don't have to come forward to be a Christian, but you do have to confess Christ and follow him openly." Some people are almost too shy even to come to church or be part of a crowd, let alone ever to come forward. Some overscrupulous souls live all their lives with a scar because they didn't come forward at some particular invitation. They need to know they can come to God in the quiet sanctuary of their own hearts and then express it in the faithfulness of their living. But they also need to know there is something about the open expression that seals that inner faith.

Others need to be told honestly that they must not put off God's call. "Not to decide is to decide" may be a common saying, but it is true. To hear the Shepherd's voice and shut ourselves to the sound is spiritually dangerous. An honest invitation will say with tenderness but seriousness, "Now is the day of salvation."

Some need to hear that Jesus is an alternative, not an additive to the good life. Through the Cross he offers free grace, but not a cheap grace that has no Cross for us. Our Lord is not the Great Need Meeter in the Sky. Our invitation is not "You have tried

everything else. Now put a little Jesus in your life." Mickey Co-
hen, the Los Angeles racketeer, wanted to know why, if there
were Christian politicians and Christian singers, he couldn't be a
"Christian gangster"! It was news to Mickey that Jesus didn't
come to ratify his sins but to save him from them.

More than one method

How then to give the invitation? It should be prepared as
carefully as the rest of the message and the worship.

Should an invitation be given at every service? Each pastor
and evangelist will need to settle that according to circumstances. I think an invitation should regularly be given in
churches of a size and situation where numbers of visitors and
non-Christians are likely. Almost every Sunday morning at Hol-
lywood Presbyterian Church, Lloyd Ogilvie would say, "I know
that in a congregation of this size, there are those whom God is
calling."

Other preachers may need to sense the leading of the Spirit
and extend the invitation at the times and seasons when pastoral
work and visitation seem to indicate people are ready. Some
churches, particularly in England and Australia, schedule
monthly guest services, perhaps the first or last Sunday morning
of the month, when members bring friends to whom they have
been witnessing. They know an evangelistic presentation and
appeal will be made.

Every invitation should be surrounded with specific prayer
that the Holy Spirit will direct people to Christ. But the preacher
and praying people in the seats should cultivate a spirit of prayer
throughout the entire service. Evangelism is a spiritual battle,
and I am convinced that unbelief and indifference can create a
field of resistance. Faith and prayer, on the other hand, can
contribute to an atmosphere of expectancy and response.

An honest invitation, in my judgment, should begin at the
outset of the message. People should know what is going to
happen rather than having something sprung on them. Billy
Graham begins giving the invitation with his opening prayer. I

have already explained my approach. Then the invitation is repeated throughout the message as the truth is applied. I do not mean people are told over and over to take some action, but repeatedly they are asked, "Is this you? Has God been speaking to you about this and this? Are you sensing that God is calling you?"

Many good methods have been used. The simple, straightforward appeal to walk to the front and stand or kneel during the singing of a hymn is often effective. Following the example of some English evangelists, I sometimes use an "after-meeting," in which the congregation is dismissed and requested to leave while all interested people are invited to remain for a ten-minute explanation of how to make a Christian commitment. In some Lutheran churches, people are invited to come kneel at the altar or to take the pastor's hand as they leave and quietly say, "I will," if they are responding to the gospel appeal.

I have seen Vance Havner ask people to stand one at a time and openly say, "Jesus is my Lord," particularly in an invitation for rededication. At some evangelistic luncheons or dinners, blank three-by-five cards are on the tables, and everyone is asked to write a comment at the same time. Those who have invited Christ into their lives during a prayer are asked to include their names and addresses as an indication of their decision. It may be helpful to have those persons bring their cards to the speaker or leader, which could then open up personal conversation and counseling.

At First Presbyterian Church in Winston-Salem, North Carolina, worshipers who desire prayer for healing or problems are invited to come at the close of the service and kneel at the altar rail for prayer. It would be easy to add an invitation to those who wish to become Christians to join them.

There is no one way to extend the invitation, but in every situation there is surely some way. The essential elements are opportunities for (1) directed prayer and (2) simple biblical counseling. In a large evangelistic meeting, those who come forward may be led in a group prayer, but that is not enough. They need to express their faith to God individually before leaving.

In my crusades, counselors are instructed to come forward at the beginning of the invitation. Why? Not to prime the pump, but to assist people, for it can be scary to walk forward publicly and particularly to stand alone. So there is no misunderstanding, I explain openly that these are counselors who are coming to lead the way. Lloyd Ogilvie often has selected elders stand at the front during the closing hymn to welcome those who respond. In any case, counselors should be trained ahead of time and provided with simple literature on the basics of Christian faith and walk. Their interaction with people deciding to follow Christ can happen at the front of the church or in a quiet room nearby. Quick and dependable follow-up in the next forty-eight hours both by telephone and by a visit in person must also take place.

Do's and don'ts

In giving the invitation, *do* pick up the feelings of those in the throes of decision. Empathize with their fear of embarrassment, of not being able to follow through, of what others will say. Hear the inner voice that tells them this is too hard, or they can wait—it's not important. *Don't* berate or threaten. *Do* explain very simply what it is you are asking people to do. If you want them to get up, walk forward, stand at the front, face you, and wait until you have had a prayer, tell them exactly what will happen.

Don't "bait and switch"—asking them *only* to raise their hand, and then *only* to stand, and then *only* to come forward. This is not to say we should never give an invitation in two steps, but it does mean we must not trick people or make them feel used.

Do make the meaning of the invitation clear. I don't think it's wrong to give an invitation with several prongs: salvation, rededication, renewal. I do think it's wrong to make it so vague that it's meaningless. *Don't*, on the other hand, overexplain so you confuse.

Do wait patiently, giving people time to think and pray, knowing the inner conflicts they may be facing. Sometimes those moments seem agonizingly slow for you, but be patient. *Don't*, however, extend and prolong when there is no response, saying "Just one more verse" twenty times, until the audience groans inwardly for someone to come forward so you'll stop. *Do* encourage and urge people gently, repeating your invitation once or perhaps twice. But don't preach your sermon again.

Do give the invitation with conviction, with courage, with urgency, with expectancy. But *don't* try to take the place of the Holy Spirit.

To find balance in these matters is not easy. I find it helps if I ask God to speak *to* me as well as *through* me.

What if no one responds? Do you feel embarrassed? Have you fallen flat on your face? You may. I have felt that any number of times. But the embarrassment passes, and what remains is the conviction that you have given an honest invitation to the glory of God, and even if no one responded, they faced the decision to follow Christ. Who knows when what they have seen and heard will be used to bring them to faith?

And if people do respond? You can rejoice and pray that they will follow Jesus in the fellowship of his church and the tasks of their daily lives.

PART 3

Pressures

9

A Tough Audience: The Jaded

One reason the modern world ignores our preaching is because it rarely hears anything from us it cannot hear from Dear Abby or Leo Buscaglia.

—William Willimon

A Christian fraternity and sorority group wanted me to talk on being a Christian on Duke's campus.

"For starters," I said, "I expect that by this weekend some of you will be in bed with somebody you're not married to, maybe with somebody in this group. What could I say to you tonight to give you the resources to refuse to do that?"

They got mad. Some of them said, "Wait. We're a *Christian* group. How dare you say something like that!"

"You look normal to me," I replied, "and I know the statistics, that few college students remain virgins any longer. I'm not doing this to attack you; I'm a preacher, and I'm supposed to be giving you what you need to live a Christian life."

After the group calmed down, one student said, "But why do preachers always act like sex is the biggest sin in the world?"

"That's a good question," I said. "Sounds like you know your Bible, because sex isn't the biggest problem according to the Bible. Still, we assume that if we can just get you to say no to this, a relatively little thing, there's no telling where we could go from here."

We live and minister in a culture that scoffs, gets riled, or worse, patronizes with polite interest the truths we preach. An important role of today's pastor is preaching truth to a disinclined world, to unbelievers who don't take us seriously, to nominal Christians who don't want to "overdo religion." How do we convince such people that there is something better, deeper, more significant they can give their lives to?

It's in the fine print

Let me begin with a caution: let's not start feeling sorry for ourselves, as if our current, increasingly pagan situation is all that new.

It would be fun, I think, to ask the writer of Acts, "What do you think about the modern disinterest in the gospel?"

Luke probably would say, "Has anybody physically beat you for preaching the gospel? That's the response we got."

Luke, of course, has amazing confidence in the power of the Word, despite the hardships; his story is one of the Word leaping over boundaries. Some, in fact, have accused Luke of homiletical triumphalism: "Preaching makes things happen! Look at Peter—he preached, and a couple thousand people showed up for baptism."

But triumphalism? Stephen preaches a few verses later, and they beat the stuffing out of him. Christian communicators can hope for baptisms, but we have to recognize the "beatings" that also may come our way. Our modern dilemma is not new: preachers throughout Christian history have struggled with delivering the good news to an indifferent and sometimes hostile world. It's always been listed in the fine print of the Christian preacher's job description.

It's been a long time, though, since I've had the tar beaten out of me for the gospel (or since I've had two thousand seek baptism!). More typically I've gotten the gentile response in Acts: scoffing or patronizing disinterest. It's like Agrippa and Felix, who say things like, "My, we haven't heard anything this interesting in a long time. We ought to get together and talk about this again. Of course, everything is relative, and we don't believe one way or the other."

I think Luke might say to us, "What you're reading as modern disinterest is just the good old pagan response to the gospel. Resistance is nothing new."

The response we get, however, isn't the issue. The issue is to bear apostolic witness, regardless of how hard it is.

My friend Stanley Hauerwas and I were speaking at a gathering of Methodist ministers. During the following question-and-answer time, one of them stood up and said, "I preached on racial justice in my church, and things went from bad to worse. My children were mocked at school. And the congregation called the bishop and complained about my sermons. Then my wife was fired from her job. As a result we had to move; I was assigned to a church in another city."

My heart went out to this poor brother, but not Hauerwas's.

"God is a nasty employer," said Hauerwas, with a shrug of his shoulders. "He's a big God, not a fake. And that's what it's like to work for a real God. Does anybody else have anything to say?" No one whined after that.

When we signed on to work for God, we signed on for the baptisms as well as the beatings. We should expect nothing less than the reaction the apostles got: opposition or just plain befuddlement.

From the bottom up

Let's admit it: one reason the modern world ignores our preaching is because it rarely hears anything from us it cannot hear from Dear Abby or Leo Buscaglia. I've met people who've given up on us because we're so bland. I rarely hear that people leave our churches because we're too involved in social activism, too liberal, or too conservative. I do, though, hear a lot of people confess, "I'm bored. I never hear anything interesting. The sermon is so drearily predictable."

Many are indifferent to our message because we've often softened it, tried to make it palatable to modern ears. People don't want that; instead, living as they do in a relativistic, lost culture, they desperately yearn for a moral compass.

One day I was in a sociology class to talk on marriage. Divorce came up, and I was saying, "Well, here are the words of Jesus, and there's been a debate within the church over their interpretation." I was trying to leave room for the many nuances.

Suddenly a student broke in and said, "This is just the kind of mealy-mouthed junk the clergy is saying these days: 'Divorce is not right, but on the other hand it may be okay.'"

Other students pitched in, "Yeah, yeah. You tell him!"

After class I pulled the student aside and asked about his response. I was surprised when he said, "Well, my old man left us for his secretary when I was sixteen." We spent the next two hours talking about that.

The cultural flotsam of the sixties looks different when you're looking at it from the bottom up. Divorce isn't seen as "an exciting new option for personal freedom" but as abandonment by one of the parents.

For many people, the teachings of the Bible are radically novel ideas. I was talking to a young woman on Duke's campus who'd been working with Habitat for Humanity in Americus, Georgia. She mentioned her astonishment at their discipline: "One thing about that group—you can't have sex down there with other people."

"Oh, really?"

"Yeah, they kick people out for that. They said they've found that sex among group members destroys community. They have too many important things that need to be done for people to be messing up everything by sleeping together."

It was a new insight for her. She was intrigued that people thought something more important than sex.

Even many who've grown up in church have been utterly unscathed by Christian morality.

I once asked a Duke student if he intends to have sex before marriage, and he said, "Yeah. Why not?"

"You grew up in a church, and you don't think anything is wrong with that?" I asked.

"I never heard that anything was wrong with it," he said. "What do you mean?" He was utterly naive, though he had grown up in a Christian church.

People are ripe for a voice that gives them something worth living and dying for.

Entertaining truths

At the same time, we mustn't ever kid ourselves about people's motives for showing up in worship.

I asked one student who'd been ushering several Sundays, "How do you like chapel?"

"I like it," he said.

"What do you think about the preaching?"

"Well, I like that, too."

"What do you like about it?"

"I just, ah, like it."

I kept pressing him for specifics. Finally he said, "Look, Dr. Willimon, I'll be honest with you. I come to chapel to meet women."

"Thank you," I said. "This has done me good. In case I should ever become presumptuous, I will remember this conversation."

I've had to come to terms with the fact that people come to church for a host of reasons—most of them bad, theologically. Though ultimately they are searching for meaning in their lives, we shouldn't naively assume people are hanging on our every word. If we're going to try to reach the disinclined, we're going to have to preach in a way that engages their attention.

In the book Stanley Hauerwas and I wrote together, *Preaching to Strangers*, Hauerwas remarks that one of my sermons was marvelously entertaining. I took that as a great compliment; boredom is not a virtue. I don't mind entertaining, as long as I'm faithful to the text.

When I was in high school, my sister gave me a book entitled *Public Speaking as Your Listeners Like It*, which impacts my preaching to this day. Its main point was the ho-hum rule: assume your listeners are never interested in what you're interested in. The book recommended picturing the listener as a guy who's been dragged there by his wife and doesn't like the looks of you. He thinks he knows more than you do and is incessantly looking at his watch.

Your job: to convince him your subject is the most important thing he will hear the rest of his life.

The ho-hum rule doesn't mean I eschew less palatable subjects. Just because my listeners could care less about the Jebusites doesn't mean I don't preach on the Jebusites. My task as a preacher is to convince them that they really do care about the Jebusites. To do this requires us to use an array of communication techniques to get them to care.

One way I do this is by being controversial. I intentionally assault the congregation with the gospel so they'll huddle together for protection.

One Sunday before Christmas, a guest preacher didn't show up because of icy weather, so I preached a spur-of-the-moment sermon on John the Baptist. In the sermon I said, "Imagine putting John the Baptist on a Christmas card and saying, 'Our thoughts for you at this special time of year are best expressed by the one who said, "You brood of vipers! Who told you to flee from the wrath to come?" Merry Christmas.'"

People kept telling me afterward what a great sermon I'd preached. I thought the sermon was a little harsh as I looked back at it. So I spent the rest of that week asking people, "Why was that a good sermon?"

They said, "You were right, and we're ready for some honesty about our condition."

Another way to engage people is to speak frankly and strongly about issues people face.

In one sermon on discipleship, I said:

Look, our capitalistic economy would love to keep you having sex all the time. They'd love to sell you blue jeans and perfume; this is the way they anesthetize you. They want to convince you there's nothing more significant in life than orgasm.

They want to convince you that this is what adults do, that this is the most important part of your humanity. It makes a whole lot of difference in the way you look, how you dress, and the kind of glances you give. They want you to believe that. And you have been converted into that beautifully.

"But it's a lie," I said. "I hate to break the news to you: sex is not all that great. It's all right. I know what you're thinking: you think I'm saying this because I'm forty. But I've been doing it a lot longer than any of you have—and I say it's not that big a deal. You're about as good at it now as you'll ever get. And you can't get saved doing it.

"Isn't it funny how the Bible hardly ever mentions sex?" I concluded. "Jesus didn't want to talk about sex; he wanted to talk about discipleship. Jesus is only interested in sex as it relates to discipleship. If it keeps you from being a faithful disciple, it's a big deal. Otherwise, have a good time."

A student once said to me, "This morning's message was a typical Willimon sermon. You went in, you hit them in the gut, and you left." I have a dual purpose in being controversial and frank: the message of the Bible is controversial and frank, and such preaching engages people.

The serious role of humor

Another way I engage the listener is through humor. Listeners are vulnerable to humor. One of my more delightful vocations in life is demonstrating how wonderfully funny and ironic the gospel is.

Jesus tells an ironic parable in which he compares a banquet to the kingdom of God. In Luke's account, a man throws a party and sends invitations to those lucky enough to receive them. Nobody shows up, however. The man gets ticked off and then invites the local riffraff, who have nowhere to go on a Saturday night.

Then he essentially says, "Oh heck, we've cooked all this food. Go on out and bring in anybody. Bring in the good and the bad. You brought in these nice crippled people. Go bring in anybody."

Jesus' point: the kingdom of God is a party we wouldn't be

caught dead attending. It's a ridiculous, humorous parable that sets up the listener for its punch line: we spend our whole lives avoiding certain people only to wake up and find that, in the kingdom, they're the people we have to eat next to for eternity. I find that story wonderfully entertaining and funny but also biting. Its humor sets up the listener for the hard truth.

Martin Luther King, Jr., once preached a sermon in which he recalled being stabbed by a deranged woman. He mentioned that, after the stabbing, the newspapers reported that a doctor had said, "If Dr. King had sneezed he would have died." A little white girl from Connecticut, he said, later wrote him a letter saying, "Dear Dr. King, I'm real glad you didn't sneeze."

So King said, "If I'd sneezed, I wouldn't have been down in Birmingham." Then, "Well, if I had sneezed, I wouldn't have been able to go to Stockholm to get the Nobel Prize." He went on and on, listing the places he wouldn't have been if he had sneezed. His wry humor invigorated the sermon so that the congregation responded, shouting *Amen*s and laughing with him.

Vitality set loose

Ultimately the only thing keeping me at delivering God's outrageous truths to the disinclined is that I'm convinced this Christian stuff is true. What ought to cause me to lie awake at night is not that somebody found me boring or my message outdated but whether I've been faithful to my appointed calling to preach the Word.

And one reason I continue to think this stuff is true is what happens as a result of preaching it. At Duke, it's like I'm in a laboratory, and all the ministerial variables are stripped away until only preaching is being tested. I've seen time and again that preaching can take the unbeliever into belief, and the nonchalant believer into deeper commitment.

Several years ago Jim Wallis, editor of *Sojourners* magazine, preached at Duke Chapel. He gave his radical *Sojourners* pitch, and two days later a Duke freshman told me, "Dr. Willimon, I want to thank you for bringing that man down here. I went back to my dorm, and I called my parents and told them I wanted my name removed from the rolls of the church I grew up in."

"Oh, no!" I said. "Why would you do something like that? I don't want angry calls from your mother."

"I grew up in that church—a Christian all that time," he replied, "and nobody ever spoke about Jesus and the poor. I did what Wallis said: I looked through my Bible, and it's unbelievable how much it says about the poor and the rich, and about God's love."

This kid was bubbling about how he was going to spend his Christmas break working for Habitat for Humanity.

It's beautiful to see that kind of vitality let loose. Sometimes even the disinclined are radically transformed by the power of the gospel's truth. Scary, isn't it?

10

A Tough Topic: Godly Sex

It would be much easier to dodge preaching about sex. But there'd be no rescuing people from the devastation of misused sexuality and no leading them to the joy of God's intentions for this gift.

—BILL HYBELS

I once had a professor who asked, "How often do you entertain thoughts about prophecy?"

One student answered what most of us thought: "About twice a year—once around Christmas, and again some time around Good Friday when I hear Isaiah 53."

"Okay," the prof replied. "Now, how many times in a given *day* do you have sexual thoughts?" Silence. The professor had accomplished his purpose. How many times do you hear biblically relevant preaching on human sexuality—something people are thinking about all the time?

That question stuck with me, and when I began ministering with youth, I put his advice to work. After all, what's on the minds of teenagers?

But as I got older, it occurred to me that *I* was still interested in sexuality, even though I was married and pastoring a church and years removed from the hormone battles of puberty. And I know I'm not alone, because every time I preach on a sexual matter, the church grows quiet in a hurry.

Sex is on our minds.

Anything that occupies that much of our thought life and powers that much of our personality ought to be addressed from the pulpit, because some of those thoughts are misguided and in need of God's correction. To not preach about sex would be to desert my post at one of the most active battle fronts in our culture.

Why rush in where angels tiptoe?

I realize preaching about sexual matters is fraught with possible problems. I could offend people. I might embarrass somebody, including myself. I might even distract the thinking of those listening.

Yet I can't ignore the topic.

Marriages are struggling because of misleading information about this subject. Young people are making mistakes because they're getting their behavioral cues from all the wrong sources. Singles are wrestling with sexual dilemmas. Sex is a subject begging for a clear Christian word.

For example, if we were to ask the married couples sitting in church on Sunday morning, "How many of you at this point in life are having a great physical relationship with your spouse?" my educated guess would be that 30 percent or fewer would say they have a vital relationship. If that's true, and my study and experience would say it is, 70 percent of deacons and Sunday school teachers and trustees and churchgoers and *pastors* are experiencing a measurable amount of sexual frustration.

People can tell themselves, *I'm not going to let my sexual frustration affect me.* But some way, somehow, some time, it will seek an outlet. What I'm trying to do through my preaching and our other ministries at Willow Creek is to spark dialogue, because talking can be an acceptable outlet. I say, "Let's *talk* about it. Let's not let frustration build until someone runs off with a willing partner, because that's a terrible way to solve the problem." We're committed to talking about sex responsibly, as opposed to ignoring it until eventually it causes unnecessary damage.

Recently I preached a sermon series titled "Telling the Truth to Each Other," and one sermon illustration told of a husband talking openly with his wife about the sexual frustration he was

feeling in the relationship. That illustration telegraphed the message that it's legitimate in marriage to talk about sex in that way.
Frustrations don't need to be pushed underground until they
emerge in the wrong place. Yes, telling the truth can get messy
and complicated, but we at least need to try. The response I read
in the congregation was agreement. Talking about it from the
pulpit, daring to bring sex into the open, gave them the sense
that such communication could happen in their marriages as
well.

My hope is that such frank talk on Sunday morning can lead
to more open expressions throughout the week, so people can
get the help they need. At a retreat, one man from our church
stood among his friends and said, "I need your help. My wife
was sexually abused as a child, and she repressed those memories so thoroughly that she wasn't aware of them until about two
years ago when everything snapped. Although she's now receiving counseling, this has thrown our marriage up for grabs. I'm
trying to juggle my church work and my kids while struggling to
keep our marriage together. I'm in real pain."

The group got up from their seats, sat him on a chair in the
middle, and huddled around to pray for him. There were tears
and embraces for this man who now didn't have to bear his
burden alone. He felt able to disclose his difficulty because we've
made it known in our church that you can talk about sexual
things. The group he chose was appropriate, a small fellowship
where his revelation would be heard with love and would not be
misused or spread.

Besides making sex a permissible subject of conversation, my
overarching concern is that people understand human sexuality
as one of God's good gifts, part of his grand design for us. I
preach each week to non-Christians who are seeking Christ in
our fellowship. Many have stereotyped Christians as rather Victorian—joyless, repressed people who think of sexuality as dirty
and vulgar. I want them to know that sexual impulses—even
strong ones—are not necessarily evil.

When I talk openly and without embarrassment about God's
wonderful design for human sexuality, speaking positively and
in a God-glorifying way, that's big news for many. It breaks open

their stereotypes of dreary Christianity and accusatory preachers.

Of course, I go on to explain how sexuality is a highly charged, God-designed drive that we need to understand and submit to the lordship of Jesus Christ because it can be used for great good or enormous destruction.

Direct and indirect preaching

I preach about sex in two ways: directly and indirectly. If I'm going to do justice to the many aspects of human sexuality, I need to take a direct approach. I dive into the subject, develop it, explain it. That's why occasionally I'll devote a whole series of sermons to the subject.

For example, I have tackled such topics as sexual fulfillment in marriage, romance, unfaithfulness, homosexuality, sexual abuse, pornography, unwanted pregnancies, and sex and the single person. However, although sex is not a taboo subject at Willow Creek, I do limit the subjects I cover.

Because I have many young ears present in worship services, I have never approached topics such as masturbation or sexual experimentation by married partners or sexual aberrations. These are doubly volatile since perhaps 90 percent of parents have never talked with their children about such topics. I don't want to be the first to bring them up with children present. That would violate the parents' rights. Instead, I encourage people to read suggested books on the topics or to stay after the services and talk with me or one of our counselors. And in private settings like that, I've found people will be very candid.

The second method I use in preaching about sexual topics is more indirect, what I call *maintenance statements*. These I sprinkle throughout the rest of my preaching to remind people of the full-blown lessons they've received in previous sermons. Even though I recently may have preached a whole sermon on marital fidelity, in the midst of a sermon on, say, the woman at the well, I'll throw in a maintenance statement: "The woman was floundering; she had lost the meaning of faithfulness to her spouse, just as she had never known faithfulness to her Lord."

This double-pronged approach keeps me from thinking, *I handled human sexuality in that sermon on David and Bathsheba.* I'm able to cover topics substantially through direct sermons and then reinforce my points continually through asides in the context of other messages.

Even with ample reason to preach about sex and a clear method for doing it, however, I still approach the pulpit with fear and trembling, because I know how difficult it is. But I've found help from five principles I've learned over the years.

Putting sex in perspective

Whenever I speak about sex, there is one impression I definitely do not want to leave: that misappropriated sex is the *one* sin the church and God cannot tolerate. I don't want to give it that kind of press, because I'm not sure Scripture does.

When I preach about illicit sex, I do call it a sin, as I would any other sin. I say it's wrong to break God's sexual code. But my main emphasis is on the downside of disobedience: Not "God will never forgive you for that!" but "If you don't obey the Lord in this area of life, eventually you'll find yourself in deep weeds." I deemphasize obeying rules for rules' sake alone and emphasize instead the dire consequences of breaking God's rules.

Alcoholism provides an analogy. I prefer to foster healthy attitudes toward alcohol by approaching it this way: "Do you people have any understanding of what physiological addiction is? Do you know how many thousands of times in the laboratory a monkey will push a lever to get another fix for its addiction?" That catches people's attention. Then I say, "Do you have any idea what chemicals do to brain cells? Do you know that a great many fatal traffic accidents are caused by driving under the influence of alcohol?" Then I can say, "Now you can understand why God says, 'Don't mess with alcohol in a way that could lead to addiction.' This stuff will enslave you, but God wants to set you free. Isn't God wonderful for saying, 'Stay free of this stuff'?"

People leave that kind of sermon thinking, *Thank you, Lord, for sparing me from something that could get its claws on me.*

How different that is from the sermon that declares, "God says you can't drink anymore!" People leave that kind of sermon with the thought, *Well, drinking can't be the worst sin in the world, so I'm going to do it no matter what God or anybody else says!*

I approach the topic of sex similarly: "God gave us the rules for our protection. You break them at your own risk. In fact in these days, you can die from promiscuity." I paint as vivid a picture as I can of sexuality run amok, and I never have a problem with attentiveness at this point. People have stumbled enough to know I'm not exaggerating. It's not uncommon for people to cry during such sermons. They know.

But then I always hit the positive side: "If you keep those benevolent rules and experience sex within God's well-defined boundaries, it can be a wonderful gift of intimacy and ecstasy."

Unfortunately, preaching this way isn't easy. It's relatively simple to preach *against* some sin, but I have to work overtime to develop *positive* and edifying messages on sexuality. For instance, preaching on "Thou shalt not commit adultery" is a lot easier than giving a message on the positive side: "How to Affair-Proof Your Marriage."

If I'm short of sermon-preparation time and really scrambling some week, my temptation is to develop a "thou shalt not" message. But if I'm a better disciplinarian of my schedule, and if I'm truly thinking and praying about my people and how they will receive the sermon, I'll put in the extra work to show the rewards of the righteous, inspiring people to obedience rather than castigating them for wrongdoing.

Being sensitive to pain

People are sensitive about their sexuality. For instance, try questioning my masculinity and watch what I do! I'll throw up emotional walls, if not my fists. We're like that when our sexuality is impugned. So I try to be tender when I talk about these matters of the heart. Since people's understanding of their sexuality—and their practice of it over the years—touches so close to their personal core, they are particularly aware of their shortcomings and sin.

In the area of sexuality, the guilt is unbelievable. I simply cannot talk about "sins against your bodies" or spout "thou shalt not's" without being sensitive to the depth of pain most people already feel concerning sex. If I cannot include a word of grace, I may do irreparable damage.

In addition, if the women in my church are typical, and I have no reason to believe they aren't, as many as half of them have had a destructive or unwanted sexual experience forced on them. Several studies bear this out. That means whenever I speak about sex, as many as half the women must deal with the pain, guilt, and unresolved feelings brought by these episodes. Therefore, I dare not treat the subject lightly.

Early in my ministry, I was naive about this reality and rather oblivious to the heightened sensitivities. I would speak on how wonderful human sexuality is. I'd go on about what a pleasurable experience it is and why God designed us as sexual creatures.

Finally a few women were thoughtful enough to pull me aside and say, "Bill, that's great for most people to hear, but the truth of the matter is, some of us have been scarred by this 'wonderful gift of God.' Frankly, we think sex was a rotten idea."

That was hard to hear. Such attitudes were foreign to me. In the sheltered Dutch enclave where I was raised, the men would have hanged anyone who laid a finger on a girl! But today we run across the ugly scars of misappropriated sex all the time.

I had to learn that whenever I talk about the beauty of human sexuality, I have to qualify my words: "But some of you have seen the other side of this good gift; you've been victimized by those displaying their depravity by the abuse of sex." And I must speak many words of comfort and understanding.

Providing a means of grace

Reassurances that God's grace covers sexual sin are fine, as are other expressions of comfort. But I have another responsibility when I preach about sex: I need to offer tangible ways for people broken by adverse sexual experiences to find healing.

A while back I studied the problem of pornography prior to preaching on it. As I neared the end of a protracted preparation period, I realized how many people are addicted to porn. I had to look in the mirror and say, *Am I going to handle this subject with integrity, or am I going to pontificate about it and leave a bunch of trapped and wounded people feeling even worse about what they're doing?*

Giving them the word of grace—telling of God's forgiveness—was one thing, but actually dropping them a rope to pull them out of the pit was something else.

I decided to ask a Christian counselor to put together an Alcoholics Anonymous–like support group for those who were ready to deal with their pornographic addiction. Such a group would need to function under close supervision because of the nature of the problem. The week after I preached on pornography and announced the forming of the group "to hold one another accountable in breaking free of that harmful addiction," more than fifty gathered. The group has continued and has had an effective ministry.

Unless I give people something to grasp as they let go of sexual problems, they have only their disoriented equilibrium to keep them from returning to their problems. Marriage-enrichment groups, group-counseling programs, mutual-accountability groups, discipleship programs with mature leaders—these offer people a way to begin to remedy their denatured sexuality.

Injecting humor

I work hard at humor; it's one of the toughest parts of sermon preparation. As long as it's used appropriately, its importance when preaching can hardly be overemphasized. Some people come to church not expecting to find themselves enjoying the experience. If I can get them laughing, they relax and become more open to what I'm about to say.

Particularly in preaching about sex, humor is the perfect counterbalance to the weightiness of the topic. With all that pain and guilt and sin-talk floating in the air, with people feeling nervous or perhaps expecting to be offended, anything I can say that disarms them for a moment is precious.

In one sermon I wanted to communicate the idea that sometimes even the best-laid plans in marriage go awry. I told the story of one anniversary night when I took my wife, Lynn, to the honeymoon suite of a luxury hotel. I told how I bought her flowers, took her out to dinner, had a special treat brought up to the room—the works. Of course, I was looking forward to the romantic agenda I had in mind. When we finally turned off the light, Lynn noticed a crack in the curtains letting in light from the parking lot. She got up in the dark, crossed the room, closed the curtain, and returned across the even-darker room. But just as she got to the bed, she stumbled into the bedpost and gashed her forehead. The cut was so bad I had to take her to the emergency room for stitches, which effectively took the twinkle out of my eye that night.

Our people laughed, and I was able to reach into *their* lives at that time because I had touched a universal point of connection: humor.

Yet humor must be appropriate. Once in an attempt to communicate with nonchurched males in the congregation, I let slip a flippant remark. I was referring to an ostensibly successful man, who doesn't think he needs Christ because "he's got a big home, a high-paying job, a condominium in Florida, a nice wife and two kids, and *a little thing going on the side.*" I said it matter-of-factly and went on from there to make my point.

What I had neglected, and what I was reminded of by a number of women in our church, is that being the victim of an extramarital affair is a devastating experience. Many never get over it. My offhand remark about "a little thing going on the side" showed how drastically I had underestimated the impact of the words. We can't wink and make light of something that painful. I would rather not use humor than use it at someone's expense.

Being transparent

One surefire way to ruin my effectiveness when preaching about sex is to speak as if I'm not subject to sin or sexual temptation: "I've got this sexuality thing all figured out. It's not much of a problem for me, and I'm going to straighten out you people in the next twenty minutes so you can get your passions under control as I have." That's pontificating, not communicating.

In the years before I started Willow Creek, I don't recall once hearing a pastor make reference to his own sexuality. Does that mean pastors aren't sexual beings? Is that an area of our lives we don't want others to emulate? The longer we're silent, the larger those question marks become.

When I preach about sex, generally I want to be able to say, "Friends, here's who I am. I love you people more than I value your impressions of me, and we've got to talk about some important things here." I include myself in the conversation, because as a pastor, I'm called not just to feed the flock, but also to model as best I can the kind of life Christ would have me lead. Since part of that life is my sexuality, I'll occasionally make reference to personal subjects, like the fact that Lynn and I have had a physical relationship that sometimes is satisfying and sometimes is not so satisfying. Then I point out the universal factors behind a satisfying relationship.

People tell me such candor is appreciated. It says we don't always have to have wonderful sexual experiences even if we'd like to brag that we do. I like to give people the sense that we can be men and women together who have cut the pretense and stopped pretending.

There remain, however, seasons in my marriage when, because of pressures and difficulties in our relationship, it would be destructive to me personally to try to address the subject of sex. When *I* am in turmoil about it, I don't need the added pressure of speaking about it as if all were well.

That's not to say I dare speak only out of my strength, because there are times when I speak out of my weaknesses, too. But I need to be fairly healthy before I preach, or I find I begin to launch into thunderous "thou shalt not's" only out of my own frustrations. I'll be more pastoral and effective if I wait until I have cooled down a little and can be more balanced.

Perhaps one other caution is appropriate: Personal transparency is for a purpose—identification with the congregation—not for mere verbal exhibitionism. Before I use personal references, I obtain Lynn's permission, because I would never share an illustration that would violate the intimacy and integrity of our marriage. I also pass questionable illustrations by our elders and ask them how they feel about them. They veto any personal anecdotes that are inappropriate.

But they encourage me to be open. They, along with me, want my messages to say authentically: "I need to hear this message as much as I need to give it, because I live where you live. I'm listening to myself as I preach."

The payoff

Preaching on the subject of sex is one of the hardest things I do, so it would be much easier to dodge it. Then I'd have no personal soul-searching, no controversy, no possibility of offending people.

On the other hand, there'd also be no rescuing people from the devastation of misused sexuality and no leading them to the joy of God's intentions for this gift.

I've discovered when I preach on sex, invariably I go home encouraged. The last time I spoke about marriage, I talked afterward with numerous couples who echoed what one said: "We're not going to settle anymore for less than a satisfactory sexual relationship. We're going to work on this, with a counselor if necessary, until we flourish in our physical relationship. We don't want to frustrate each other to the point that we break out of this marriage and have an affair we may never get over."

When I preach about sexual purity, I often hear from people

who have been convicted by the Holy Spirit and have determined to put impurity away. Just recently I spoke with a new Christian from our fellowship who had been living with a woman for three years. I told him that as painful as it would be, he really had no other choice but to separate. I listened to him and prayed with him and promised to help him walk through the experience.

As he left, he said, "I can't thank you enough for forcing the issue, because there's one side of me that's screaming, *I don't want to cut this off!* and the other side of me says, *But I have to.* I just needed someone to put the pressure on me. Thanks for doing that."

That's what happens when we preach—humbly, prayerfully, and lovingly—the truth about sex.

11

A Tough Time: Crisis Moments

Strong leaders are known for their landmark sermons.

—JACK HAYFORD

Whatever a pastor's position on wine drinking, it's not hard to marshal proof texts. I believe a case can be made either way. Although it's a controversial subject, several years ago I needed to deal directly with the subject with our Servants Council, a group of several hundred key people in our congregation.

As I wrestled with the issue in my study, I felt the internal pressure of being responsible for these leaders and their influence on our whole congregation. They needed a shepherdlike spirit instilled in them for rightly guiding all whom they taught and touched. This had to be explained in a loving way, rather than legalistically. My heart whispered, *You better help them see this clearly. Most of our people are going to decide what's right and wrong based on what you say and how you act.*

I also was concerned with external pressure, about the larger Christian community, that others might pass judgment on me. I could hear some saying, "Hayford is soft on drinking" (for not out-of-hand declaring a teetotaling stance) or "Hayford is a legalist" (because I concerned myself with the issue).

Strong leaders are known for their landmark sermons (and sometimes lynched for them). Landmark sermons are the defining moments of a church and a pastor. Without them there are no boundaries, no rallying points, no banners in the sand; there is nothing to communicate vision and goals, policies and practices, beliefs and standards.

Like Joshua's landmark recitation of the law with its blessings and curses at Mount Ebal, landmark sermons are memorable, weighty, conclusive, directive, never inconspicuous. After hearing them, the congregation feels that a line has been drawn in the sand—or in stone.

Some will regard your landmark sermon as a familiar "oak tree" on the church landscape, guiding them in the way they should go; others, deeming the sermon a garish neon sign, will wish it didn't mark the land. But no one can ignore such sermons or their consequences.

What classifies as a landmark sermon? How can we make them more effective? When should they be given?

The purposes of landmark sermons

Landmark sermons are highly visible for good reason. They tower above the normal weekly sermon because they accomplish at least one of six purposes.

To address questions that weigh on people's consciences. Ethical and theological questions bear heavily on many people.

Dozens of women who have had an abortion have committed their lives to Christ in our church, for instance. Sooner or later most accept God's forgiveness, but they wonder, *If that really was a person who was aborted, where is he or she now?* Their guilt and concern can be unbearable. Those who have suffered a miscarriage can raise the same question.

After counseling several women, I decided to preach a sermon on what happens to the soul of an aborted child. In a message titled "Short-Circuited into Eternity," I took a clear sanctity-of-life stance but was not condemning. I made it clear that the child had not reached an age of accountability and thus was innocent in God's sight.

Many Christians worry in silence about other troubling issues: Have I committed the unforgivable sin? Will God forgive my divorce and remarriage? Can a "backslider" be forgiven? What if my job requires me to work on Sunday? Preaching on such subjects can clearly guide people through their confusion.

To prepare the congregation for a church project. Several years ago we purchased an $11 million church complex as a second facility. Before I proposed this move, I preached for ten weeks in the book of Joshua on the subject "Possess Your Tomorrows." The main idea of this series—God promises us many things, but we have to move in and "possess" them—became part of the spiritual rationale for buying the property. Of course, it also encouraged individuals to "possess" what God had ordained for them.

Whether it's building a church, beginning more children's ministries, or launching small groups, people in the congregation need the motivation, insight, and challenge that can come only from their pastor's sermons.

To put landmark moments in biblical perspective. When the big earthquake hit San Francisco in 1989, I heard some say God was judging the homosexual community of that city. Landmark moments beg for landmark sermons, whether the issue is God's judgment, end-times prophecy, or the morality of war.

The week after the San Francisco earthquake, I chose as my text Christ's comment on two tragedies: the collapsing tower that killed eighteen and Pilate's mixing some of his victims' blood with their sacrifices. The consensus was that these victims were more sinful than others. But Jesus refuted the conventional wisdom.

My sermon's main point was "If God is judging San Francisco, we'd all better dive under our chairs right now." I acknowledged that while such a catastrophe *could* be an expression of God's judgment, it is a mistake to conclude it happened because some people are more deserving of judgment than others.

Although I had expressed many of that sermon's ideas in bits and pieces before, the landmark moment made it a landmark message.

To change policies. Over time, a church may shift or evolve in regard to membership policies, leadership qualifications, whom to marry or bury or baptize, to whom to serve the sacraments, lifestyle, and nonessential doctrinal matters. Such controversial topics beckon for a landmark sermon or series of sermons.

In the early 1970s, the predominant stance in my tradition had been that all divorced persons were unmarriageable on biblical grounds. Wrestling with the whole truth of the Scriptures, being driven there by tough questions that were raised in my soul as I talked with broken people, I came to a different conclusion: that persons divorced prior to their decision to follow Christ were eligible for marriage on the grounds that their past was forgiven and forgotten by God.

I preached a sermon on the subject on a Sunday night and concluded the message by performing the wedding of a couple who had each been divorced under those conditions. (Our policy, though, is not simplistic or arbitrary: there are specific stipulations governing how each situation is handled.)

To confront cultural trends. A year after the PTL scandal and five weeks after Jimmy Swaggart's problems came to light, I decided to preach a sermon on restoring fallen leaders. I had heard so many advocate that because God forgives a fallen leader, his sins should not disallow him from continuing in ministry; that if he repented, he could continue in leadership without a period of probation. I challenged that.

In my sermon I made what I feel is a biblical distinction: God forgives us instantly, but being forgiven isn't the only qualification for Christian leadership. Being forgiven isn't the same thing as rectifying character. Scripture says that potential leaders must be tested and proven over time to see whether certain essential qualities are present in their lives. I concluded that a leader who violates the qualifications of leadership must again be proven and tested over time before being restored to a position in the church.

To bring healing at times of human failure. When key members fall short of biblical morality, it shakes the church. Several years ago the daughter of one of our elders gave birth to a child out of wedlock. Later, when the issue of her immorality had been resolved, she asked for the child to be dedicated in church. We did so on a Sunday night. I preached a sermon on justice and mercy, asserting that we are obligated to stand on the side of mercy even when we run the risk of appearing to have sacrificed righteousness.

I concluded that sermon by calling the girl and her child forward, and the congregation joined me in dedicating this child to the Lord. No one felt standards had been sacrificed, and everyone recognized God's mercy was being manifest.

I also called to the platform the baby's grandfather, our elder. "John [not his real name] has submitted to the board his resignation as an elder," I announced. "We did not ask for his resignation, but he knew that at this time his family required his special attention, and so he did the right thing in submitting it."

There wasn't a dry eye in the place.

Mistakes to avoid

Landmark sermons have their own special temptations. Here are some mistakes I try to avoid.

Sensationalism or exploitation. When the news first broke about Magic Johnson testing positive for HIV, I considered preaching on sexual morality. The more I thought about it, though, the less I liked the idea.

It was a judgment call; many ministers did preach on it, of course, and I may have missed a landmark moment. But since I serve in the Los Angeles area, I felt I would be sensationalizing the subject or capitalizing on someone else's tragedy.

To test whether I'm tempted to sensationalize a theme, I ask myself these questions:

1. Am I concerned with this theme mainly to draw a crowd or to truly edify the flock?

2. Am I dealing with it substantively and biblically, or merely "grabbing a topic" and then glossing over the problem and only giving a superficial "lick and a promise" with a quick verse or two?

3. Is the issue crucial to the moment? Can I wait—should I wait—until a more profitable moment?

Giving the message to the wrong group. Some messages are suited for smaller circles within the church because of the differences between followers and leaders, males and females, children and adults, new Christians and mature Christians, the young and the old, the committed and the peripheral. What will be a landmark for a small group in the church may be irrelevant or confusing to some of the Sunday-morning-only attenders.

I did, in fact, deliver a message at the time of the Magic Johnson incident but only to our men's group. I felt the message was more appropriate there.

Imbalance. When I spoke to our leaders on the subject of wine drinking, I showed them the Scriptures that support both sides of the issue, but then I took my position: "I can't make a biblical case against wine drinking, but I feel this is one of those rare times when the Bible has a double standard for leaders and followers. That is why, personally, I have made a commitment never to drink alcoholic beverages of any kind."

I'm always concerned about touching all the bases and have found that people respond to that. Several of the elders in our church are attorneys, and some have specifically commented, "Pastor, I appreciate the way you cover all sides of these controversial issues. I feel we can make valid decisions because the whole case is presented." A balanced message shows respect for people's intelligence and confidence in their spiritual decision-making abilities. This doesn't mean I don't draw a conclusive point, but I do speak with respect toward positions I oppose.

Keys to effectiveness

I have a strong sense of anointing as I prepare and deliver landmark sermons. I sense that these messages are more than simply teachings or exhortations; they're prophetic. I'm presenting the counsel of God conclusively and categorically on a critical issue.

Still, I recognize the human dimension. Many factors can make people more or less receptive to what I'm going to say. Here are some of the things I do to make my landmark sermons more effective.

Maintain the tensions. Our tendency is to try to resolve the dynamic tension of truth, to oversimplify or go to extremes, but I have found that the truth is found in tension.

Ten years ago one member of our singles group worship team had a recurring problem with severe depression. He took medication to counteract it, but at times he would neglect his prescription and the chemical imbalance would bring terrible suffering. At one such time he took his life—jumping off a building near downtown.

Although only a fraction of the congregation knew him, he was a significant leader to enough singles that I felt I had to address the subject of suicide.

In my sermon, I emphasized the comforting grounds of our salvation—the grace of God and the death of Christ—but I also stressed our moral responsibility as stewards of God's gift of life. Such tensions may make landmark sermons controversial—but they also become inescapably confrontational and memorable.

Point to the overarching principles of Scripture. Universal principles are crucial to every decision, question, or problem that landmark sermons address. My job is to find the big picture in a particular situation, for overarching principles provide the deepest insights and broadest perspectives.

In 1990 and 1991, as the Persian Gulf crisis dominated the headlines, I preached on such issues as, "Does God Desire War?" "How Patriotic Should I Be When My Country Is at War?" "What Is My Christian Responsibility During a War?" I can't answer big questions about war without touching on great themes: how God views the nations, especially Israel, and how God views secular authority. Landmarks are built with huge stones and deep foundations.

Take adequate time. There are no landmark sermonettes. My landmark sermons take an hour to an hour and fifteen minutes to deliver (I usually give them on Sunday night). When I'm preaching a definitive word, I can't be sloppy or shallow, and I can't be brief, superficial, or simplistic. I take pains to exegete Scripture, select and define terms, frame the big questions, and focus the issue. I distinguish carefully between what I do—and don't—mean.

While preaching through a five-installment overview of the

book of Ezekiel on Sunday nights, I decided to spend an entire sermon on chapter 18 (fathers and children should be punished for their own sins, not for the sins of the other). I had become increasingly concerned about the trend to rationalize our failings by blaming our family of origin or assigning blame for one's sin or immaturity to abusive people in the past. I frequently saw people using these ideas as an escape, instead of vigorously pursuing a transformed life in Christ.

I didn't want to appear to oppose twelve-step programs or support groups (I don't). Nor did I want to seem impatient with spiritual "turtles," God's slow-grow children. But I did develop a fourteen-point contrast between the world's system of healing and God's system of healing (for example, "Justify or forgive yourself" versus "God has justified and will forgive you" and "Break codependence and liberate yourself" versus "Submit to repentance and God's deliverance"). When I gave the message, we distributed a chart summarizing the points.

Such thoroughness is also necessary when discussing awkward subjects. I once did a sermon about masturbation. Although I normally go to the pulpit with only an outline, for that sermon I wrote out nearly a full manuscript. The possibilities for unintentional double entendres or awkward moments were so great, I spent the extra hours to ensure that I had not only the right ideas but the right words. Some sermons require that type of precision.

Although this is hard work for me—and the congregation—I have found that people will listen to a more didactic message patiently and with interest if they care deeply about the subject.

After my Ezekiel message, as I was preparing to dismiss the service, I leaned on the pulpit and said, "I need to tell you, at times like this I feel a real heaviness. I don't apologize for anything I said, but I'm sorry for keeping you so long tonight."

The message took more than ninety minutes, and virtually no one moved. After the service and over the following week, I received a flood of comments from people who appreciated my taking the time to do the subject justice.

Consider a series. Sometimes I just can't say all I need to in one sermon. So I occasionally preach a landmark series.

Some especially nettlesome subjects are best approached in stages, that is, with months or years between sermons. I may need to nudge the congregation into the truth, to let them process the Scriptures one step at a time.

That's the way it turned out with my divorce and remarriage sermons. The first sermon addressed the subject of Christians divorced before their conversion; the second sermon, three years later, addressed rare instances when Christians divorced after their conversion may remarry. I didn't calculate this development, but time and understanding helped people digest the teachings.

When appropriate, I branch off into related issues and applications. Since so much groundwork has been laid, it's a perfect time to show how this subject relates to other doctrines and practices.

In the message from Ezekiel that addressed the family-of-origin "escape clause," I applied the truths about Christ's power to transform us to how and why we do "altar calls" and "altar services." We have found these times, when we call people to come to the front of the church, to make or renew their commitment or for the laying on of hands, to be one of the most life-transforming steps a Christian can make. I was able to develop the subject more meaningfully than if I had preached "The Purpose of Altar Calls" as a stand-alone message.

Relieve the tension. Landmark sermons address serious, sensitive, sometimes awkward subjects. The tension can be exhausting both for me and for the congregation. Relieving that tension two or three times in a long message can make the waters much easier to navigate, and that increases the congregation's ability to receive.

Discreet and timely humor not only breaks the tension but also keeps me human and personable. On the occasion I dealt with a particularly delicate sexual topic, I preceded it with a reading that illustrated the confusion of a camp director: A Victorian prude inquired too obliquely regarding rest room facilities at the camp. The woman's undue caution in not risking suggestive speech set the scene for a hilarious exchange of letters; absence of directness brought no answer whatsoever. It set the atmosphere for me to be direct and also created a sense of "humanness" in the room as we approached a very human subject.

When humor would be inappropriate, I ask people to turn to their neighbor and repeat some positive affirmation. I began the suicide message by announcing to the congregation the title of my sermon and explaining about the death of the individual. I knew everyone was feeling heavy. So I said, "Although we're going to talk about the sin of suicide, I want to remind you that we serve a mighty and merciful God. I'd like for you to turn to the person next to you and gently say, 'We serve a mighty and merciful God.' "

As they said those words, all across the auditorium you could see faces relax somewhat and people shift into more comfortable positions. Everyone was emotionally better able to face what we had to talk about after that.

Sometimes we'll pause for fifteen seconds of praise and thanksgiving for some encouraging truth: "Let's take a moment and praise God for the hope of eternal life with Jesus."

Relate personal experience. Sometimes divulging personal experiences that triggered my message helps make the sermon more personal, authentic, and powerful.

When I discussed wine drinking with our leaders, I told them why: I was raised in a teetotaling environment. Years ago, however, I realized how moderate amounts of wine with foods such as pasta or red meat benefited my digestion. I occasionally drank a glass of wine for this reason.

One Saturday morning, about three years after I began this practice, two events changed my habits. First, early in the morning as I was in prayer, the Lord "spoke" clearly to me: I was no longer to drink wine. Nothing I knew of had prompted this "word" to me. It was pointed, and my response was absolutely unhesitant. But, a few hours later the same day, I went to a counseling session not knowing why the wife of a young leader in our congregation had scheduled the appointment. She related how a Christian leader whom we both knew had gone to a restaurant with her husband, drank too much wine, and convinced her husband to think nothing of it. She was understandably troubled.

I didn't say anything to her about how the Lord had dealt with me just hours earlier, but the coincidence of those two events happening on the same morning was not lost on me. I felt God was unmistakably saying, "I'm dealing with you first."

When I recounted this to our leaders, I didn't mandate they act on the basis of my experience; I presented the Scriptures. But my story illustrated the heart of my message and showed how the Lord was teaching about the "cost" of leadership.

Symbolize the message when possible. A few years ago I spoke at an urban conference in Washington, D.C., on the subject of reconciliation. About a thousand pastors and leaders attended, 75 percent of whom were black.

In my message I admitted that during the civil-rights movement I had unknowingly, but in reality, violated our unity in Christ. What to the black community was a revival of God's grace in establishing justice, I had viewed as a social inconvenience. Although I agreed that blacks had suffered injustice, when I saw leaders of the Caucasian Christian community marching in demonstrations, I regarded them as liberals straying from the important issues of the gospel. But, too late, I came to realize how many like me had "missed a moment" to appeal in God's name for sacred justice. I said to the group: "You had a revival that was a great blessing to you, and I didn't see it. I didn't rejoice with you. I didn't help you. I was not a brother."

At the end of my message I asked one of the black pastors to come forward as a representative. I got down on my knees before him and asked his forgiveness. (I had asked his permission in advance to invite him forward.)

After the service, an aged black elder embraced me and said, "Pastor Hayford, I never thought I'd see the day when a white man would say and do what you did today." The symbolic action riveted the point.

Choose the opportune moment. Since a landmark sermon is a prophetic moment, I can't pencil it on the calendar as I would any other message. Several factors signal when the time is ripe.

Sermons of mine that have proven to be landmarks have been delivered with a strong feeling for God's heart. Often we sacrifice God's love on the altar of his truth. But I have sought to bring both passion for God's holy truth (reflecting his righteous nature) and his endless compassion (which reflects his merciful and loving nature). If either is lacking, the message falls short.

As I prepare a landmark message, I also have a growing sense of anointing best described as a sense of mission and authority. Even before I come into the pulpit, I feel clothed with a mantle of grace to declare a vital word. The message, fully gestated, is ready for birth.

However, events may demand immediate response. When that worship leader in our singles group committed suicide, I felt I had to bring that message within two weeks. World or local events also call for a landmark word on short notice. When responding to the headlines, I must hammer while the iron glows red.

Landmark messages are extraordinarily demanding. They strain my emotions and study time. They force me to wrestle with great issues. They draw criticism. And I know I will have to face some repercussion for people following incorrectly what I say (usually people who didn't listen to all I said).

Despite these pressures, however, as I prepare and deliver landmark sermons, I commonly have as deep a sense of God's presence as at any time in ministry. As a result, I view landmark sermons as one of the highlights of my pastoral ministry. And shouldering pressure is a small price to pay for a sermon that serves as a can't-miss-it, unshakable oak tree in our church for years to come.

PART 4

Perspective

12

The Sweet Torture
of Sunday Morning

The question every preacher has to ask himself is, "Is this the best I can give?" If the answer is yes, that is all we can do.

—Gardner C. Taylor

As a young man, I recoiled from the idea of being a preacher. I wanted to go to law school and become a criminal lawyer. My boyhood friends in Louisiana tried to discourage me from that idea; at that time no black person had ever been admitted to the Louisiana bar, and my well-meaning friends asked me where I was going to practice law—in the middle of the Mississippi River?

In my senior year of college, I was admitted to the University of Michigan Law School. But before I left, I had a fearful automobile accident; it touched me at the very center of my being, and through that experience I heard the Lord's call to the ministry. I felt both an enormous relief and a great embarrassment—for several years.

So I did not start off with any great confidence or sense of appreciation and awe about being a preacher. I wasn't sure it was a worthwhile thing for a young, healthy, thoughtful man to do. Even when I came to Concord Baptist at thirty years old, I still had some of that in me.

While I'm a better preacher than I was thirty years ago, I'm not as good a preacher as I want to be. After many sermons I still think, *I didn't get at it the way I should have.* Now and then I get a wonderful sense of having been delivered fully through a sermon, but it doesn't last long, and by Tuesday or Wednesday that sermon begins to look awfully wooden and stale.

Still, I know I'm a better preacher than I was when I started. I have a sense that I'm preaching closer to the heart of the gospel. But that doesn't mean Sunday mornings come any easier. Here is my weekly journey of moving from idea to Sunday morning.

Beginning the journey

I think of a sermon as a journey, a trip I want to make. I want to know where I'm starting, how to get there, and where I'll end up. Getting an idea is the beginning of that journey.

I rarely know what I'm going to preach about on the Monday or Tuesday before a Sunday preaching date. But by Tuesday night —and this is a mystery to me—some idea will come. An idea may spark by looking through some of the things I've read, or by what Alexander Maclaren called "sitting silent before God." I also find ideas in preaching books. In his book *Designing the Sermon*, James Earl Massey wrote about "opening men up"—it's a great passage that sparked a sequence of thoughts in my mind. In my reading, one sentence will often set off a chain of reflection. Whenever I read anything, I think, *How does this relate to my preaching?*

I also get ideas from talking with people. I used to play golf with the former president of a bank here in New York. He's a good man, although not particularly religious, and he told me one day he saw the stage play *Your Arm's Too Short to Box with God.* He told me how moved people were at a certain point in the play, and then he said, "But you know what bothers me about black people? They depend on Jesus to do everything."

I started thinking about that. Later I developed a sermon about that idea and sent him a copy. My thesis was that yes, black Christians do call on the name of the Lord often and depend on him greatly. But often they are the same people who are buying homes, sending their children to school, and making decent lives for themselves. They have done more concerning the practical things that matter than all of the social clubs, fraternities, banks, or other black institutions.

Once I have an idea rolling around in my head, I initially study Sunday's text without dipping into the commentaries. Only then do I see what others have to say about the passage. I might go to Joseph Parker's *Preaching Through the Bible,* Maclaren's *Expositions,* Calvin's *Exposition of the Scriptures,* one of Barclay's commentaries, or *The Interpreter's Bible.* Sometimes I look at the critical commentaries and research the original language.

I may find the Scriptures don't say what I thought they did; I have to be open to the possibility that I may have to change my idea. I am not free to flit about the Scriptures looking for favorite notions; I'm liable to become a Johnny-one-note. Even in topical preaching, I must stay true to Scripture.

The spirituality of the preacher

Perhaps one of the most important but often neglected parts of sermon preparation is our spiritual life. The apostle Paul says, "Lest that by any means, when I have preached to others, I myself should be a castaway" (1 Cor. 9:27 KJV). It's easy to get so engaged in the mechanics of preaching that one loses the vitality of it, the center.

I recently read in the book of Ruth where Naomi says, "I went out full, and I've come back empty." That's the story of life. It's also the story of preaching; we must keep ourselves full so we can empty ourselves in the pulpit.

But there are times when I have what my wife calls preaching plateaus, in which everything is flat country. That happened more when I was younger, when I'd hit preaching slumps in which the stream didn't flow, the wheels didn't turn for three, four, five weeks. I learned to look inward at those times and offer what I was passing through to God. I tried to believe by the promise of the Word that those sermons spoke to somebody who was having in some sense the same kind of experience.

When this happens, I often study the history of preaching. I don't see how any preacher can stay flat when he reads of Jean Massillon preaching the funeral of Louis XIV before all of the crown heads of Europe. From the nave of Notre Dame Cathedral, he looked out over that royal gathering for a moment and then said, "Brethren, in the hour of death, only God is great." Anybody who stands in that tradition must feel good about the calling.

Preparing to apply

In addition to finding a sermon idea and studying Sunday's text, each week I must spend time making the connection between Sunday's text and the world of my listeners. Kyle Haseldon, once an editor of the *Christian Century,* had a saying about the Scripture being the "revealant." There is no such word in the dictionary, but it's a good word: what is revealed, over against that which is relevant. The preacher's job is to see how these two things intersect and report on it. Karl Barth spoke about standing in the pulpit with the Bible in one hand and the newspaper in the other.

Sometimes this connection is easy to make, given my circumstances. Once I had to talk earnestly with the Lord about my nagging worries for my wife. She was in excellent health at the time, but after forty years together, I figured something would happen sooner or later. She had been so much a part of my life that it was almost unbearable for me to think of our separation.

I had to ask the Lord to deliver me from this terrible shadow. In thinking about this, I realized that these same worries affected others in my congregation. I had to open myself before God and, one Sunday, give voice to these fears in the light of the Scriptures. This is what the preacher is called to do.

Sometimes my sermons consciously address certain needs; other times, though, it happens mysteriously. The Word of God breaks through the preacher by the power of the Holy Spirit. Other times, in spite of the preacher, the people will be ministered to. Occasionally a parishioner will say at the door of the church, "You spoke to me; this was my problem, and you spoke to it," and the preacher didn't mean to speak to that problem at all.

Writing the sermon

I try to determine my introduction by Thursday night. By Friday night I like to come within a page of completing a full manuscript of my sermon, although I don't use it in the pulpit or memorize it. Some of the material is lost in actual delivery, but material I hadn't planned on comes to me while preaching. The one makes up for the other.

Sometimes, when the momentum is flowing, I'll write the conclusion on Friday at two or three in the morning. But if not, then I'll leave the conclusion for Saturday morning. On Sunday morning, I listen to spirituals and gospel music on my stereo. They help me get into a cadence, which is part of my background. Even before getting up, I often go through the sermon in my mind to see what grasp I have of it.

I read over my sermon three times: twice on Saturday, once to proof it because it has to be typed later and the second time for absorption. I'll also read it over before I leave the house Sunday morning. Once I get to the church, I see several people about the announcements, and then about 10:30 A.M. I seclude myself in my office and don't see anyone else until I go to the pulpit at 11:00. That is the moment of truth; all the apprehensiveness comes to a head.

On my way to church, I sometimes pass laborers on the street and wish I were doing anything except having to get into the pulpit again. But once I arrive and the music and hymns start, something happens. Bob Gibson, the great St. Louis Cardinals pitcher, said the hardest thing about baseball for him was getting to the ballpark and putting his uniform on. Once he did that, it was a joy.

I give many secular addresses on public platforms, but I never feel as tense about them as I feel about a sermon. Preaching is a different ball game from public speaking.

The delivery

Black preachers used to have a formula for delivering a sermon: "Start low, go slow, get high, strike fire, retire." I can't offer a formula for how I deliver a sermon; it depends on the sermon, on the mood of the preacher, on the mood of the congregation. But I can offer three components of my delivery that I monitor to help me, as Paul Rees once said, move people up as close to the heart of God as they can be moved and then leave them there.

Openings. A preacher has three or four minutes, hardly more than that, to interest people. If I miss them in those first three or four minutes, I'm finished. Their minds have gone off somewhere. There are thousands of techniques preachers can use to communicate more effectively: the rhetorical question, the incident out of life, the illustration from literature, the dramatic pause. The techniques cannot be used mechanically; yet they have to be planned by the preacher as a living part of the sermon.

Chemistry. Once I get into the sermon, I try to get close emotionally to the congregation. Any movement on their part, for example, bothers me greatly, because I have to feel they are right there with me. What I am delivering is not an abstract lecture, but a communication about a life-and-death matter.

In a black congregation, there is often a vocal response to the preacher, though not as much as there was once. I enjoy that. We had a Canadian guest preacher at Concord one Sunday when I was gone, Frank Zwackhammer, and Frank told me later he must have been laboring a point a little too long because one of our deacons said out loud, "All right, we've got that. Go on."

There's an invisible, mysterious interplay that goes on between pastor and people, and I can feel whether I'm getting to the people or not.

Words. T. S. Eliot spoke of his work as "a raid on the inarticulate." Preaching is a raid on the inarticulate and the inexpressible. Words are the currency in which the preacher deals; we must be careful not to deal with them loosely, because if they are debased or devalued, there's no other currency in which to deal.

A preacher should revere language. There is no excuse for sloppy language. Words must make definite suggestions, not only in their definition but in their sound. There are words that caress, words that lash and cut, words that lift, and words that have a glow in them.

But I'd like to add a caveat: words also can reveal the heart. A remarkably gifted colleague, Sandy Ray, was at Cornerstone Church in Brooklyn for thirty-five years. I listened to him year in and year out, and I never heard a false note or saw a false move. I never sensed that this man was playing to the galleries.

But I know also a preacher of enormous talent whose preaching, although attractive, has never achieved the force, the thrust, which I thought was in him in his student days. I listened to him two or three years ago, and I think I found out why—he's using fancy footwork, he's showing he can do it. I'm sure he doesn't realize it, but there's always half a smile on his face as if to say, "Watch, now, what I'm going to do."

In my early years I had a fascination for form and eloquence that was, I'm afraid, not heart deep. At one point, I wanted to take elocution to train my voice. My wife discouraged me from it, so I never did it. Her reasoning was that preaching never ought to be a finished thing, a polished performance. She was right.

Evaluating Sunday morning

I rarely feel satisfied with my preaching, even though I feel an enormous sense of relief afterward. Now and again, I get a foreshadowing of what my preaching ought to be, and I strive to preach that way all the time. That, of course, is impossible, so I have to make peace with reality. But I always push to give my best.

Arthur Gossip reports a mystical thing that once happened to him in a Scottish church. As he came down the pulpit stairs after preaching, he met a Presence who said to him, "Was that the best you could give me today?" Gossip said he went back in the vestry and wept.

That's a question every preacher has to ask himself, "Is this the best I can give?" If the answer is yes, that is all we can do.

We must, eventually, come to terms with the unique preaching gifts God has given each of us. When I first came to New York, I was privileged to be a colleague of some of the greatest pulpit figures of this century. They were all great men of God, but they were all different. Robert McClacken preached with a probing wistfulness. George Buttrick was a man in touch with the tides of current thought, yet always subjected them to the scrutiny of the Scriptures.

Paul Scherer was grand and expansive. One of his students asserted that when Scherer said "Good morning" to you, it was an occasion; his preaching was almost Shakespearean in its manner. Sandy Ray had a gift for observation of human nature, of taking simple things and giving them eternal meanings. He used to say, for instance, that some of us are ocean liners and we sail great waters; and some are little tugboats; but the only way the ocean liner can get to port is with the help of the tugs.

A preacher has to find what he or she is all about on the inside and work with that flow. Arthur Gossip used to say he would preach to himself, and then find out he had preached to all other people. Now a preacher can't become simply an echo of his own eccentricity, but one has to come to grips with self first.

When one has found that acceptance, that person has come into an incomparable authenticity. I have never known a preacher who did not have a unique power if he or she would allow it to shine forth. I had a student at Colgate-Rochester who stuttered—sometimes even when he preached he stuttered. But there was a force in the stutter that caused people to almost stand up in their effort to help him. It wasn't for effect; it would have fallen flat had it been that. But he could draw forth an interest in his preaching that few could do.

With all the doubts and uncertainties I've had, I'm more and more thankful the Lord made me a preacher. I remember reading a sentence from Wordsworth that led me to consider what I would do when my ministry faded "into the light of common day" as he put it.

Well, my preaching has long since faded into that light, but whenever I come down from that pulpit so weary that I never want to preach again, the Lord finds some way to revive me and usually makes my next ministry opportunity one of my most exciting ones.

13

The Tunes of Preaching

*The gospel playing in our lives for years has
created in us a distinctive sound.*

—FRED CRADDOCK

Everyone knows a sermon has points, but not everyone knows
a sermon also has a tune.

I applied the word *tune* to preaching a few years ago when I
began to wonder, *Why do I especially like certain sermons? What
makes certain ones really work?* There was an important ingredient in effective sermons that went beyond the normal consider-
ations of content. That ingredient, I realized, was the tune.

A sermon's tune—its mood or spirit—is not easy to define
precisely, but it's unmistakable. Hearing some sermons, I think
of seventy-six trombones coming down Main Street. Other messages make me picture a violin and a crust of bread.

We don't often think of the tune we'll play when we're preparing a sermon because our preparation tends to focus on the
content. But afterward, when we evaluate how we spoke it and
how people responded to it, *then* we recall the tune: the subtle
atmosphere that was projected, the mood that filled the sanctuary.

But not just sermons have tunes. So do preachers. I ask my
students to imagine what sound track would best complement
their preaching, and they give me answers ranging from Willie
Nelson's music to something majestic from Handel's *Messiah*.

In fact, when I open my ears, I find tunes all around me.
Churches have their tunes. Communities do, too. In Appalachia,

most of the tunes are somber: "We're Going Down the Valley One by One," "Tis Midnight, and on Olive's Brow," "The Old Rugged Cross." Pathos flows through these tunes.

If I want to preach to Appalachia a greater sense of Easter, I can't fuss at them for not jumping up and down the first Sunday I sound that unfamiliar refrain. Joy is a strange tune to their ears. They need time to catch the beat.

So I've realized I need to be aware of the tunes of preaching. My sermon, the text it's based on, my church, and my own personality—each has a distinctive "sound." A sermon's tune may not play well in every situation. The idea is to harmonize our preaching with the notes being sounded around us.

Your predecessor's tune

Preachers new to their church need to discover their predecessors' favorite tunes. It's especially important if the predecessor had a lengthy tenure because that preacher's style has defined the word *sermon* for that congregation. In the minds of the hearers, any variation from that tune struggles even to qualify as a sermon.

Suppose for twenty-three years my predecessor said each Sunday, "I have four things I want to say about the text this morning. In the first place . . . and the second . . ." and so on, and at the end summarized the sermon. That's a precise, ordered tune, like a military march. The congregation is accustomed to a methodical, logical sermon—major premise, minor premise, and conclusion—so when I come in singing another song, I can't expect everyone to ooh and aah. If I don't preach that way, I can expect, at least for a while, that the congregation will not accept my "talks" as sermons. They'll probably say, "Well, it just didn't seem like a sermon."

This is not reasonable. For many listeners, a change in *form* is equivalent to a change of *content*. Preach a narrative sermon, and the people who have been used to hearing Reverend Outline preach "One, two, three, four" will say, "Well, it was real interesting and all, but we like more Bible." You may have included more Bible in your sermon than he ever did, but the only way listeners have to register the different tune they heard—even when the content or theology of the sermon was virtually identical—is listing some vague problem with its content. They couldn't take their usual notes on the sermon, so they figure it must have had an unbiblical melody.

Now in a church I wouldn't try to imitate the previous pastor. Nobody preaches well enough to imitate, and no one can sing someone else's tune anyway.

However, I need to prepare the people to hear a new tune. And that takes time, just as it took me time to get used to new translations of the Bible. I first memorized Bible verses from the King James Version, so I *talked* about using other translations long before I was comfortable with them emotionally.

Second, I must respect how hard it is on a congregation when I change the *form* of the sermon. If the form is always new and different, congregations don't hear it as well. It's like hitting them with a hymn with unfamiliar words and tune. But if the basic form of a sermon remains predictable and clear, I am allowed to work creatively within it.

Most congregations can handle only one variable at a time. So if I am going to vary the form of my preaching, my message had better be familiar. Or if I plan to hit them with a novel message, my preaching style ought to be predictable.

That rule extends to the service itself. If I plan to preach a different kind of sermon, the rest of the service ought to be straightforward and predictable, and if I'm going to experiment with the service, I'm wise to preach my standard sermon.

Since visually and vocally I'm a new variable to the congregation when I first come to a church, I try not to add a lot of clever innovations initially. Once they get accustomed to my voice and appearance, then I can make some changes. Whether I like the waiting period or not doesn't matter. What they're accustomed to has shaped the ear.

The congregation's tune

I work not only with my predecessor's tune but with my congregation's. I analyze a congregation somewhat like I would a group of people going down a street. I ask myself, *What are they doing? Is it a parade? Are they just out for a stroll? Or is it a protest march?*

For some congregations, every Sunday is a protest march. Some issue must be taken on: arms control, taxes, poverty—whatever. They're marching to city hall, and you can almost hear the drumbeat of protest, protest, protest.

Certainly there are things to protest. But if you protest all the time, people get weary of that tune: *Here we go again to city hall.* It's not effective. I may thump my suspenders and say, "I'm a prophetic voice in this age!" but the point is, I'm not getting anything done.

Some congregations, however, are on parade; you get a sense of John Philip Sousa. It's triumphant. Every day is Palm Sunday, and everything is grand and glorious. But there are always people recently widowed or hurting or whose daughter is on drugs or whose job just disappeared. These people are not in the parade.

That means the music has to vary. Some sermons need the feel of a friendly stroll down the street, just a couple of you talking. Then the parades and protest marches provide a different beat, a new sound that catches one's attention.

The text's tune

The tune of a sermon also needs to be appropriate to the tune of the text. With some of the psalms, you're excitedly on the way to Jerusalem. With others, you're sitting in a trash dump, saying, "I just want to die." There are some where you're sitting in a circle with your kids. In some of them, you're all by yourself: "My soul is quieted within me."

So sometimes the biblical material itself may say, "Don't play the wrong tune here. This is a penitential psalm, so don't try to inspire people."

Once I listened to a pastor preaching on the Beatitude "Blessed
are those who hunger and thirst after righteousness, for they will
be satisfied." But he started hitting people with what was wrong
with them. "You're out hungering after this and thirsting after
that," he fumed, "when it should be *righteousness* you're after!"
He said some good things, but the words *hunger* and *thirst* did
not flavor the sermon, and as a whole it never came across as a
blessing. He turned a Beatitude into an exhortation and thus
changed the music entirely.

Later I asked him, "Do you have other words for *blessed?*"

"I don't like the word *happy*," he said. "I would rather just say
blessed."

"That's an important word in the Bible," I said, "but blessed
are those who live within earshot of the Beatitudes." I wanted
him to know that somehow the soft oboes of blessing needed to
be heard.

Your weekly tune

My personal experiences during the week—my work, my
prayers, my study, my attending all kinds of events—have set up
a certain rhythm, a tune, in my own life. And I may discover my
tune doesn't fit that of the text.

My tendency at times like that is to tell the congregation,
"When I chose this text with its stately marching cadence, it
echoed the way I felt. But this week I've had 487 committee
meetings, and everything is still hanging. I'm exhausted. Yet this
passage arrives so beautifully in Jerusalem that I wish it were my
experience today. So if you detect in my voice some longing,
some wishing, it's really there."

That's the course I take when my personal tempo is out of
sync with the text. It works better than saying, *Fred, get up to
that text!* That's often unrealistic. I say to people, "I'm down
here, and the text is up there. If anyone wants to try to reach up
to it, let's give it a try."

I want to understand my personal tunes, but unless they prove
unhealthy, I don't feel obliged to alter them. If I'm constantly

sucking melancholy out of every situation, however, I may need some help. But within the normal variations of my life, it's wise to recognize my own tunes and share from them.

Most often, people will be able to pick up our tunes. There will be days when we show up with a violin and everybody else brings drums, but most people can adapt. And next Sunday will probably be better.

Your dominant refrain

Although we will play variations on our theme, most of us settle into a dominant refrain. The gospel playing in our lives for years has created in us a distinctive sound. Congregations usually accept the theme to which their pastors return.

But it's dangerous to assume that ours is the tune everyone must play. In the best of circumstances, we know and the congregation knows that ours is not the only tune the gospel will play but is what the gospel plays best through us. Others will have their distinctive tunes as well.

Understanding individual tunes can help avoid a lot of heartache and jealousy. When we invite guest speakers, we can say, "We're bringing in a set of tympani, folks. You've been listening to this little ol' clarinet, but the gospel in this person's life sounds with extraordinary resonance, and you'll love it!"

That little speech helps keep people from saying, "This preacher is better than that preacher," because that's like saying a drum is better than cymbals. You can't compare them. It's also a good way to get people ready for a new minister.

Over time our tunes become like theme songs. Thirty years later, people will recall my ministry and say, "He was the violin we had way back before we brought in the trumpet." And once my tune becomes a theme song, I can talk about it at points where I know there will be dissonance, like at the beginning of a difficult sermon: "This is a tough one today, folks, so I'm going to bring out the violins."

Of course, overuse turns it into a ploy. But it's useful every now and then when I know my experience and theirs are at cross-purposes, or the text and I are on different wavelengths. And it sure beats getting mad because they are not in tune with me.

Tunes you can't play

There are many things I cannot do physically. I'm small; I weighed only 120 pounds when I entered the ministry. And I have a weak voice that doesn't project well. All the preachers I heard growing up, however, were big, tall fellows full of physical prowess. Their voices were full of thunder and lightning.

When I started preaching, I tried to be like them. I tried to be bigger than I was. As I struggled to get my voice and my body to do things they couldn't do, I must have looked like a cartoon character. Of course, it didn't work, and learning that was painful. Finally I had to accept my limited range and find some way I could use my weaknesses as well as my strengths.

One of the ways I have compensated for my shortcomings is to use the dramatic. People like stories, and stories evoke strong feelings, especially if in telling the story we experience it ourselves. Take the story of Hannah giving her child Samuel to the Lord to live in the temple. You can get inside that story and tell it in a way that travels the full range of your emotional capacity, even though you've never actually given up a child for adoption.

Storytelling allows for great emotional impact. Even if your voice or physical presence in the pulpit is not all that exciting, the story itself will do it. One of my students told me my voice is like the wind whistling through a splinter on a post. So even though I'm not exactly a prime candidate for the Met, if I can get the attention off my voice to the compelling melody of the story, people forget my limitations.

We are all limited in one way or another. I recently heard a New York actress with years of training do a dramatic presentation from memory of the Gospel of Mark. Her dramatic range was extraordinary, but even with her ability, the apocalyptic sections of Mark were too much for her. She could not climb that mountain, but she was comfortable enough with herself to do well on the foothills.

The Bible is bigger than her talent or mine. Luther said, "I cannot preach on Abraham offering Isaac. That is a demonstration of faith far beyond anything I have experienced. Why should I even attempt it?" Maybe he could have attempted it had he said, "I'm only pointing you to a mountain I have not climbed," and then shared in a humble, clear way. So sometimes I'll walk around the foot of the mountain and point to the top with no claims of having climbed it.

Fortunately, the Bible has such a wide range of possibilities that most of us can find a unique method to compensate for our inability to pull out all the stops. Sometimes I'll say, "Look, if we had the full orchestra here and not my thin clarinet, this would be the point for a full crescendo."

I can also accomplish the same effect by planning the flow of the worship service. For instance, a brief but magnificent doxological anthem following the last words of my sermon can accomplish what my voice alone is unable to do. I can supplement my tune by orchestrating other, more dramatic parts, such as scriptural readings, vocal numbers, or instrumental pieces. These added voices provide what I cannot achieve for any number of reasons.

Our apparent limitations can be transcended. My students are so concerned about the little things of preaching—how they look and what they should wear and all that. Three times in one sermon, I heard a minister with an artificial limb thump that leg and tell us not to think about it: "Now I don't want you feeling sorry for me because of this leg." I hadn't thought about the leg until he told me about it, but it was obvious the main thing on his mind was that leg. And that makes for a sorry tune.

On the other hand, I heard a preacher once who had been severely burned in an automobile accident. The tissue on his face, arms, and hands appeared practically melted away. When he first stood up, I thought, *I'll have to close my eyes.* But he was a man of extraordinary passion and love for what he was doing, full of interest and delight and humor. Before long I forgot about his appearance. It's like a well-dressed person; you don't remember what the person wore.

Beginning with the ear

Often I go into the sanctuary and sit in the pews to do part of my work on a sermon. There in the quiet, I ask myself, *How would this part sound? If I heard this tune in the sermon, what would I think?* I want to be sensitive to the tunes of preaching, to operate from the ear to the mouth.

Isaiah writes,

The Lord God has given me the tongue of a teacher,
that I may know how to sustain the weary with a word.
Morning by morning he . . . wakens my ear (50:4 NRSV).

Preaching, like music, begins with the ear. If I get the tune right, people will understand not only my words but will sing along.

14

Putting the Sermon in Its Place

The sermon is where we tighten the focus on our congregation, on our situation. It's where everything gets down to us.

—JOHN KILLINGER

The pastors of the church I grew up in didn't know much about worship. They invariably followed the pattern they had inherited from the past: two or three hymns, an offering with a prayer, special music, a sermon, an invitational hymn, and a benediction. Fortunately, the music was usually spirited, the prayers and the sermon were earnest, and we had a sense of being in the presence of God. That, after all, is what worship is all about. You can have the most cleverly designed worship program in the world and still fail if there isn't a sense of that all-important presence.

But I have learned, over the years, that a well-planned worship service can usually help people to know they are in the presence of a transcendent being. The Holy Spirit works in wondrous ways, I know. Yet I believe that the Spirit can work better on me as a pastor and preacher when I am in the quiet of my study, thinking about the Sunday service and the sermon I have to preach, than when I wait for our encounter on Sunday morning with hundreds of other people present. If I seek the Spirit's leadership in the planning of worship and the sermon, I am freer when the moment of encounter comes, and we can really "get down to it," as the jazz musicians say.

Worship and preaching are inextricably linked, whatever some preachers think. The entire worship experience is something we offer to God—*including* the preaching. The hymns and prayers and special music aren't mere preparation for the preacher's art. They are open communication between God and God's people. When the preacher stands to preach, it is like the moment in a choral concert when the spotlight shifts to a soloist. The soloist isn't there alone and doesn't sing in a vacuum. The soloist merely has a special part at a particular moment in the concert. It is the concert that matters most, not the soloist.

Conducting the tour

I don't plan worship and preaching independently of each other. It's almost as if they're in colloidal suspension until suddenly they both appear. Our church uses a fairly consistent format for worship, so I normally think about how to make each element of the service a part of a journey that we will all take together.

For starters, I assume people enter rather cold, unprepared, and we have to give them something in the beginning that will get them up and going. Many come to church frazzled, without a sense of high expectancy. This puts weight on those of us who plan worship to meet their needs and provide the kinds of surprises in which the gospel can be heard. My job as their tour conductor or storyteller is to help worship happen even if they didn't expect it.

Of course, the needs of individual worshipers vary greatly. That's why I don't usually follow a single theme in planning; if I do, I may suit a few persons and miss all the others. What I'd like worship to do is focus on God—on God's greatness, God's majesty, God's graciousness, God's abiding love—and let other things sort of cascade around that.

My sermons always follow a particular line of thought. Sermons don't do much if they're not focused. But they are always set in the context of a worship service that is general enough not to leave anybody out. Say I'm preaching on loneliness, for example. I'll try to make the sermon as wide as possible in order to speak not only to those who know they are miserably lonely but to those who are miserable but don't know it because they're lonely. And I'll set all our loneliness in the larger context of our loneliness for God, our need for the divine and transcendent in our lives.

I may mention loneliness in the morning prayer, but only as one aspect of the prayer. And one or two of the hymns may have something to say about loneliness. But in general the hymns will range over many other topics, and the responses will come from the large, catholic tradition that doesn't focus on a single theme. People who didn't come to church feeling lonely won't go away sensing that the worship wasn't for them, that they couldn't "dig" it because it was oriented toward something they weren't really feeling in their inner beings.

Even the announcements are part of the worship journey. I know a lot of pastors have relegated announcements to the beginning or end of a service because they want to keep worship "pure" for God. But I have always purposely kept announcements in the middle of the service as a moment when I can relate to the congregation in a light, friendly way. The personal warmth and humor of this time provide a brief rest for the congregation in the building intensity of the service.

Shakespeare, you remember, used comic interludes for this purpose. He'd have some very serious business going on—people plotting to kill other people, people being estranged from their children or parents—and he'd interrupt that with comic relief, something that permitted the audience to pause and catch its breath. Shakespeare knew his business. He realized that people can attain greater dramatic intensity, can go deeper into heavy stuff, if they have such moments occasionally to rest them along the way.

Recently I was introducing new members and their sponsors. When I came to the last sponsor, I couldn't for the life of me remember the man's name. I finally said, "And the next person you all know." I went on quickly with the announcements, and by the time I got through, I remembered the name. I apologized and made a joke out of this old man's not remembering names anymore. Everyone laughed. It was a human moment that rested us before we went on to more serious matters.

Tightening the focus

Preparing our people for the sermon is as necessary as preparing the sermon. I can feel whether the members of my congregation are ready for my message by the way they have responded in the singing, especially the doxology, which immediately precedes the sermon. The volume and enthusiasm are a key to their readiness. If these are high, I know they are ready to settle back and listen with eagerness.

I normally read the Scripture with a calm, gentle voice, trying to read it, as one old Scotsman put it, as though I were listening to it and not as if I had written it. In the quietness and mood of gathering intensity, now I'm ready and the congregation is ready. I can sense if that feeling is ever missing. Usually it isn't, but I am greatly put off if it is. I may in that case even request that the congregation sing another hymn, or perhaps a little chorus, something that will put a better edge on things.

The best way to ensure that people will be ready for the sermon, aside from the quality of the worship service itself, is to preach consistently the very best sermons of which we are capable. It's a lot like going into a restaurant to eat. If you've been there before and had a delicious meal, you'll be eager to go there again. But if the fare has been dull and tasteless, you'll not be happy to be there. If we set the very finest meals before our congregations Sunday after Sunday, they'll look forward to tucking their napkins under their chins and having another each time they come.

Our preaching, like any other element of worship, must be truly good to contribute to the sense of spiritual encounter that builds throughout the service. The sermon, as Theodore Wedel liked to say, is where the gospel gets transubstantiated. It's where the gospel becomes truly incarnate. The hymns and prayers represent the general church, the sense of worship in all the ages, and so does the Scripture reading. But the sermon! The sermon is where we tighten the focus on *our* congregation, on *our* situation. It's where everything gets down to *us*.

A worshipful sermon is one that begins somewhere in the human situation recognizable to the congregation and then leads them to a place where revelation occurs. I try to invite the listeners on a journey with me, and somewhere along that journey there's an epiphany, a manifestation of something higher than all of us. I can't say where it will be; it's unpredictable even when I'm writing the sermon. I've got a diverse group of people—a caravan, if you like—and I'm beckoning them with the storyteller's art to keep them intrigued, like Scheherazade of *The Arabian Nights,* and different people have their epiphanies in different places. Some people attain a sense of transcendence faster than others. Some people get there faster one day than they do another.

I almost always start a sermon with a comment or a story that is easy to get into, that is revealing of human experience. For example, when I preached a sermon on the third commandment, about not taking God's name in vain, I began with a comment from Ruben Alves, the Brazilian theologian. A friend once told Alves that not taking the Lord's name in vain simply means not using the Lord's name unless you're serious about it. I said that probably catches a lot of us, who are casual churchgoers not really committed to the Lord, who may use a little profanity now and then, and maybe even ministers who speak too glibly about the name of God. I wanted them to see that we are *all* guilty, even those of us who act and speak so piously around the church. We *all* treat God's name too lightly.

I usually design my sermons to reach a high moment near the end. I employ illustrations as resting places along the way—to provide breathers—and then keep working on the intensity until I reach a peak toward the end. But I don't stop there. I want to "cultivate the quiet close," as James Stewart of Scotland once called it. I taper off gently, hoping people can interiorize the sermon, and lead quietly into the devotional hymn.

A few times I have surprised my congregation with an altar call, with good results. We don't usually have such invitations in the Presbyterian tradition. In a way, that is good; we don't wear out the vehicle, the way it often seems to be worn in churches that exercise such a call every Sunday. But I do try to lead my people to a decision-making moment in every sermon, and hope they will make inward decisions that will change their lives. I try to lead them to this through the words of the sermon and then let them make their commitment to God during the last hymn, so that the sermon will continue to work on their lives when they go home.

But we can't program exactly where the gospel will be heard. We must simply preach sermons that have a lot of theological integrity and hope that people will enter some door along the way that will lead them down the hallways to the heart of what we're trying to do.

Preaching ought to be like a ball of yarn you can grab hold of any place and follow to its ultimate core, which in the case of preaching is a well-articulated theology. I hope that every sermon I write, whatever its text and whatever its showcase material, is true to a consistent theological center in my thinking. Every statement, every illustration, every aside, ought somehow to be traceable to that center, that core. That way, people can get to the center no matter where they take hold, no matter what door they enter.

Fully alert

As worship director, the pastor can make several mistakes. The first is in attempting to be too dramatic. Drama is important, and there is a discernible dramatic pattern to the unfolding of worship. But any good actor will tell you that restraint is a large part of high drama. The dramatic schema must be there, but it must not *appear* to be there. I remember Madeleine L'Engle lecturing once about writing. She said, "If I want to write about passion, I write it with ice, not fire." Restraint. Holding back. Not permitting a slobbering enthusiasm to substitute for the real substance of what we're doing.

Another mistake is inadequate preparation—not constructing the prayers with genuine care, for example. I didn't always write out my pulpit prayers. I grew up in the hills of south central Kentucky and had never seen anything but a Southern Baptist worship service before I went to Harvard and encountered George Buttrick. I wondered why everybody thought he was so important, because I hadn't even heard of him. But Buttrick transformed the way I saw things. He said that if you've got time to write out only the prayers or the sermon, write out the prayers. I understand now what he meant. The prayers are critical to the mood of the service. Their phrasing, their rhythm, their substance, may be easily missed if done extemporaneously, on the spot. You have so little time, in a prayer, to gather up people's unspoken thoughts and present them to God. Some people are good at doing it extemporaneously. But even those people would probably do a better job if they spent some time preparing their own spirits, then concentrating on the words and substance of the actual prayers.

Inadequate preparation also impairs the sermon. It isn't easy to spend the kind of time and sweat that disciplined preparation requires. I can understand why many preachers take the easy way out. And some preachers really thrive on the sense of discovery that occurs occasionally when they are up in front of a congregation preaching and they suddenly say something that is revelatory to them as well as the congregation. What they don't realize is that these moments would come a lot more often if they only applied themselves to their craft in the study. They wouldn't ever prepare a sermon without experiencing this sense of visitation.

I worship all week as I prepare my sermon, because I know I am doing it before God. I pray for understanding and illumination. I can be writing a sentence and suddenly some phrasing, some way of putting an idea, will flash out like a divine manifestation at me, and I'll say, "Thank you, God," and type furiously to get it down before it is gone. I'll continue to think about that all day and the next day and the next. And when I preach it on Sunday, I'll enjoy it again, and inwardly I'll thank God again for it.

When you really prepare your preaching week by week, you feel a lot like an athlete training for the big event. When you get into the pulpit, it's like taking the field. You feel your whole being poised for what you are about to do. Your body, your mind, and your soul are all alert, and the adrenaline begins to flow. You become an offering to God with your total being.

You're not free to do this when you're unprepared and have to think your way along through the entire sermon, stammering and stuttering.

Freshening the format

Accurate feedback is critical to the improvement of our worship. My wife has always been my most trustworthy critic. I'm sure, as Thomas Hardy put it, that she sometimes "tempers the wind to the shorn lamb," especially when she thinks I'm feeling particularly vulnerable or sensitive. But in general she has been a fine barometer of how things have worked in a service. We talk informally about everything—not just the sermon, but the hymns and the prayers and all the rest. I learn a lot from that, because she's a very discerning person.

Another way to ensure honest feedback is to invite a colleague who's sensitive to worship to give a frank appraisal. Consultants are useful in other spheres of our lives. Why not in our churches' worship? We ministers could do each other a lot of good by visiting each other's churches and offering our professional appraisals of what does and doesn't work well in the services.

But improving our worship doesn't necessarily mean we need to change our patterns. It isn't usually the format that people grow tired of; it's the routine, insensitive way the format is handled. There is genuine value in having worship patterns remain fairly stable, so that people feel secure with them. Constant fiddling with the format can be confusing and unsettling to them. The important thing is to find a sound liturgical pattern and then work hard at keeping its parts fresh and vital. That's why we should spend a lot of time on our prayers and sermons, and why our musicians should work so hard on their music.

In my churches, we have varied our formats occasionally in order to remind people that formats themselves are not sacrosanct. Worship is something we create for God. But because we create it, we can do it in other ways.

Some pastors are born innovators and offer something new to people every Sunday. One of my former students, for example, preached a sermon recently that was based on the thought of Paul Tillich. He knew his congregation hadn't read Tillich and possibly wouldn't understand Tillich if he quoted him. So he planned a fascinating sermon that actually began with him, the pastor, attempting to share Tillich's ideas. Suddenly a voice on the PA system interrupted him. "Hey, what are you trying to do to those people?" it asked. The minister stopped. "What do you mean?" he asked. "They can't understand Tillich," the voice said. "They don't care about what he said."

Appearing irritated, the minister continued. Again he was interrupted by the voice, protesting that people couldn't follow the abstract thought of a theologian like Tillich. "But," protested the minister, "I'm just trying to tell them that . . ." And he *explained* what he was trying to get across by using Tillich's ideas. "*That* they can understand," said the voice. "But that's what I was trying to say," said the pastor. "They can understand it the way *you* put it," said the voice, "but not the other way."

By the time the sermon was over, everybody had heard the message and understood it. People had also realized that it was the minister's own voice, prerecorded, they were hearing over the amplifying system. They loved the sermon, and wanted to know when they could hear another one like it.

Such experimentalism is good and is especially welcomed by some congregations, especially in collegiate settings. But it has been my experience that most congregations are comfortable with settled liturgical formats. What they want is fresh prayers, fresh sermons, fresh music within those formats. That is why we need to devote ourselves to creating meaningful worship, to keeping all these parts of the service crisp and new.

I have a friend who is a columnist for a large metropolitan newspaper. "I have the same amount of space every week," he says. "What I have to do is sit down at my computer and produce something that is interesting and readable, that will grab people's attention and make them think about an issue. Otherwise they won't read the column, even if they read it the week before. I may be forgiven if I botch up a column now and then. But if I do it consistently, people will stop reading me altogether, and the newspaper will jerk my column."

This is true with preparing the parts of the worship service. People will forgive occasional lapses. But what they want, week by week, is a sense of freshness and meaning in the parts of the service they are accustomed to. They may not take us off the job for not giving them what they want. But they will certainly not be happy if we disappoint them too frequently.

The player's temptation

Worship will always be different for me than for my congregation. It's the difference between a player on the field and a spectator in the stands. The person on the field is one with the crowd, in a sense, and yet is also conscious that he or she is making it happen for the crowd.

There's no getting around the fact that the attention of the congregation will be on the preacher, the way it is for the athlete. In fact, if I'm up there preaching and don't have their attention, I feel bad. But having people's attention the way we do can be a subtle form of temptation, and this has ruined a lot of preachers, who begin to preen themselves on being seen by others, on being the focal point of everything. They forget that God is our focal point, and they set themselves in place of God.

It is important not to succumb to a sense of showmanship in the pulpit. I think of Laurence Olivier, the famous British actor. Olivier could milk a part for everything in it. But he never became a showman. Not in the crass sense. He was an artist. The difference between a showman and an artist is that the showman puts on a show and everyone knows it, while the artist paints a picture and draws people into it so that they are no longer conscious of watching something, they become part of the process.

Phillips Brooks, the great New England preacher, once said that shy people make the best preachers. He himself was a shy man. Shy people interiorize a lot. They meditate and reflect. When they preach, they know how to get inside people's minds. They are more skilled at this than extroverts, who spend less time trying to understand what others are thinking and feeling. To perform well as preachers, shy people must be well enough prepared to subjugate fears and timidity. When the message begins to flow, they forget that they're shy.

We all face the temptation to try to make ourselves look better than we are. We learn to do this even when we are children. Ministers, being human and wanting the congregation's approval, are always tempted to present themselves as smarter or wiser or more compassionate than they really are, and sermons are opportunities for doing this.

I'm often asked, "Is it all right to allude to yourself in a sermon?" My answer is, "Yes, it's all right if you remember one thing: Don't try to make yourself look good." In fact, we can very profitably use personal allusions in our sermons if we use allusions that show us in a human light or in a bad light. This reminds people that we all stand under the need of God's grace, even the preachers.

It's important not to use the sermon to puff yourself. I have heard preachers who name-dropped, for instance. You know what I mean. "I was having dinner with Colin Powell the other night, and we were discussing Desert Storm." That sort of thing. It becomes tiresome and represents the preacher as a social climber or an egocentric person. If we are going to be autobiographical, we should aim at being truly honest about our feelings and show ourselves for the doubting, struggling, feckless creatures we really are.

The trick is to be transparent to the presence of God, so that as we draw people's attention, we really remind them of God, not of ourselves. When they leave church on Sunday morning, they should be saying, "Don't we serve a fantastic God!" not "Wasn't the preacher brilliant today?"

At the risk of reiterating what I have already said, one of the most important factors to me is the thoroughness of preparation, so that when I preach, I'm leading people on a journey that becomes more and more intense until they suddenly have their epiphanies, their meetings with God. If I have prepared as I should have, and have done my part right in the service, they have forgotten me by that point. Like a hypnotist, I'm a mere voice guiding them on a trip where they have a rendezvous with God.

Trying to be quiet

Even after many years in ministry, I am painfully aware of the distance between my spiritual life and where I ought to be as a preacher who dares to say anything about God. Like so many preachers, I fear that I may have even dulled my own sensibilities for the holy by speaking about it so often. That happens, you know. You handle the important things so frequently that you become inured to them. You trivialize them and forget how to fall down in awe and trembling.

Once I wrote Corita Kent, the famous nun who made those beautiful posters, and asked her to come to Vanderbilt University to lead some worship experiences for us. I received a postcard from her. All it said was: "Dear, I am trying to be quiet." It was a beautiful statement. It has haunted me for years.

The mere fact that you are put on a pedestal as the people's spiritual example is one of the most damnable things that can happen to you. You become a spokesperson with something to say on every official occasion—even some unofficial ones—and the speech comes easily to your tongue and lips. Eventually you are lulled by the sound of your own voice, by the high-sounding phrases of your own pronouncements. You begin to think, as other people do, that you know what you're talking about.

Rainer Maria Rilke, the German poet, once advised a young poet that if he ever became famous, he should "take another name, any name, so that God can call you in the night." I think about that. It is a liability to be well liked as a preacher. You may lose your own soul, your own sense of what is truly spiritual.

I like to hear some preacher speak who is just beginning his or her ministry—somebody who is still struggling with the issues. Then I think I have a chance to hear something authentic. I become wary of preachers who have been at it too long. We are inclined to pontificate, to speak as if we really understood. And that can be disastrous for us.

We should all be more like the little priest in Georges Bernanos's *Diary of a Country Priest*, who prayed, "Lord, send me back to seminary, for I am a danger to souls." That kind of sensibility would make better preachers and leaders of worship of all of us.

15

What Is Successful Preaching?

I know I can get a quick response if I preach to felt needs, but that doesn't mean I've preached successfully.

—STUART BRISCOE

Many years ago, during the Cold War, I traveled to Poland for several weeks of itinerant ministry. One winter day my sponsors drove me in the dead of night to the middle of nowhere. I walked into a dilapidated building crammed with one hundred young people. I realized it was a unique opportunity.

Through an interpreter I preached from John 15 on abiding in Christ. Ten minutes into my message, the lights went out. Pitch black.

My interpreter urged me to keep talking. Unable to see my notes or read my Bible, I continued. After I had preached in the dark for twenty minutes, the lights suddenly blinked on, and what I saw startled me: everyone was on their knees, and they remained there for the rest of my message.

The next day I commented on this to one man, and he said, "After you left, we stayed on our knees most of the night. Your teaching was new to us. We wanted to make sure we were abiding in Christ."

Nights like that make you want to keep preaching!

It usually isn't that easy to know whether preaching has been a "success." Most of us preach each week to largely the same people, people accustomed to our speaking rhythms and themes, who perhaps take us for granted. Our people rarely tell us more than "I enjoyed the sermon, Pastor."

But like any worker, we need to know if our aim is accurate, if our preaching is accomplishing its purpose.

We not only need it; most of us want this information. After shooting an arrow, we run to the target to see if we've hit the bull's-eye. We cherish any objective measure of results: letters of appreciation, people coming forward after the sermon, extraordinary comments afterward.

A tricky business

Objective feedback, though needed, is unreliable. If I judged the success of my preaching by the standard of my night in Poland, I would be mostly disappointed. We rarely see our listeners so visibly moved.

Furthermore, most pastors who complete an annual denominational report sense the discrepancy between what numbers say about a church and what God is doing in people's lives.

The question of whether our preaching has succeeded is clouded by many factors.

Who's evaluating? Recently I preached a sermon on work. Conscious that a number of people in the congregation were out of work, I mentioned they should not feel useless. "While you get your unemployment benefits, you could work at church doing something significant."

After the service a number of people thanked me for being sensitive to their situation and said they would like to be given something to do at church. But one woman objected to my "socialist attitudes." She said she knew I was British, and Britain was socialist (Maggie Thatcher would have been surprised!). "You have no business dragging socialism into the American church!"

What scores 9.9 with one person, in one tradition, in one part of the country, in one church, may take a nose dive elsewhere.

Individual needs also skew a listener's opinion. If a woman, devastated over her crumbling marriage, hears the sermon on "Why Be Committed to the Local Church," she may consider the sermon self-serving propaganda. If the preacher happens to deliver the sermon "What to Do When Your Marriage Is Falling Apart," she'll regard it as the greatest thing since the Sermon on the Mount.

If we look at success from God's point of view, some of the greatest sermons ever preached, by the prophets for example, have received a thumbs-down from the congregation. So who listens and how they listen make a huge difference.

What is good? After one sermon, a woman shook the pastor's hand at the door and went on and on: "That sermon was one of the most wonderful I've ever heard!"

The pastor, being necessarily humble, said, "Oh, it really wasn't me. It was all the Lord."

"Oh no," she replied, "it wasn't that good."

It's hard to know what people mean when they tell us about our preaching. Getting a "Not bad" from a hypercritical person may mean "Wonderful!" From a tactful diplomat it may mean "Horrible!"

The seen and unseen. I preached at a chapel service at Trinity Evangelical Divinity School in Deerfield, Illinois, and afterward a man with a European accent introduced himself to me. "I've been looking forward to seeing you again," he said.

"When did we last meet?" I asked.

"Twenty-five years ago, I was a student in the Bible college where you taught the book of Romans. Ever since, I've wanted to tell you how much that meant to me. The book of Romans changed my life. In fact, I now teach Romans at a church in my native Slovakia."

"Are you a pastor?" I asked.

"No."

The man's friend, standing beside him, interjected, "He is a leading nuclear physicist in Eastern Europe."

I ministered in Indonesia recently, and a woman who runs an orphanage in Java said to me, "I should have written you long before, but I just want to tell you how much your preaching meant to me when I was a teenager in England."

These two reports were happy exceptions, for I infrequently see the long-range impact of my sermons. We can't see into the heart, where beliefs, values, priorities, and devotions change, so a pastor's preaching may bring about significant spiritual breakthroughs that can't be quantified in the year-end report.

Felt needs and real needs. I know I can get a quick response if I preach to felt needs, but that doesn't mean I've preached successfully.

Needy people focus on symptoms, not diseases. A sermon on self-esteem may temporarily boost people's self-confidence, but if we fail to give an antibiotic for the underlying problems—pride or lack of faith—it's malpractice. Symptom-oriented sermons, like candy medicine, make people smile, but people go away as sick as ever.

I do address felt needs, but primarily as an entrée to people's real needs, for that's the seedbed of the most successful preaching.

Spiritual variables. God's Word always achieves its intended purpose, but wielding it is not an exact science. In some ways we resemble farmers who intentionally burn parts of their fields; fire breaks out in unanticipated ways. Sometimes after a sermon bombed, someone will say I helped him or her tremendously. And sometimes we help people in spite of what we said or what they heard.

I once preached a sermon from the King James Version about the Lord being our "shield and buckler." A woman wrote me saying she was greatly helped by my teaching on the Lord being her shield and *butler.* She was encouraged knowing that the Lord was standing at her shoulder ready to help!

We must never assume, then, that the sermon is ours to make or break. In the 1800s a famous organist traveled from town to town giving concerts. In each town he hired a boy to pump the organ during the concert. After one performance, he couldn't shake the boy, who followed him back to his hotel.

"Well, we had a great concert tonight, didn't we?" said the boy.

"*I* had a great concert," replied the maestro. "Go home!"

The next night, halfway through a fugue, the organ quit. The little boy stuck his head around the corner of the organ, grinned, and said, "We aren't havin' a very good concert tonight, are we?"

If God isn't pumping when we're preaching, nothing happens.

Seven signs

How a sermon is received, then, is but one criterion of a successful sermon, and not a reliable one at that. Instead, I put more emphasis on how a sermon is prepared and preached. I look for seven signs in examining my sermons. If I've fulfilled most or all of these criteria in a sermon, I've gone a long way toward preaching a successful sermon.

Let me summarize them briefly, illustrating them with a sermon that did, in fact, receive a favorable congregational response: "What About Shaky Marriages?"

God-centered. My primary concern in preaching is to glorify God through his Son. That's my concern even in practical sermons, like "What About Shaky Marriages?"

I bridged the practical and theological as I discussed the difference between the Greek words for *love:* "You can have all kinds of *philia* and *eros* and still not approach the love that makes marriage work best. The third word for love in Greek is *agape.* This word describes God's love for us." Later I said, "The Bible teaches that *agape* love is directly related to the work of the Holy Spirit."

At the close of the message, I said, "The Spirit of God begins to shed his love in our hearts. There's a fundamental spiritual dimension here that must never be shortchanged: the dedication to go on loving and being devoted to the One who is the source of all love."

The sermon focused on a human problem—shaky marriages —but I still wanted to point to God as the source of marriage-healing love.

Biblically based. A successful sermon comes from God's Word, not my or someone else's experience, not another book or article. A biblical text cannot be a pretext: I can't read the text, then ignore it for the rest of the message (the preaching equivalent of bait and switch).

With literature on marriage abounding, I could have easily based my marriage sermon on psychological principles. That would have helped people, I'm sure. But I wanted to go even deeper, so I based it on the characteristics of love described in

1 Corinthians 13. I took each quality of love—love is kind, love is patient, love rejoices in the right, and so on—and simply explained and applied it.

This doesn't mean that all my sermons are verse-by-verse expositions. Still, I try to ground every point in a clear inference from the text.

People directed. I delivered a series of expository sermons on 1 Peter some time ago. After a year of that, one staff member commented, "You're getting bogged down. People are losing interest."

I had sensed the congregation's interest flagging, but I had idealistically been thinking, *This is God's Word. It's eternal truth. As long as I explain it and help people apply it, fruit will result.*

When my colleague brought it to my attention, I realized I couldn't ignore the problem. If people are tired, bored, or distracted, my sermon will be hampered even if other factors are in my favor.

Over the years I've become increasingly aware that people were not made for the sermon but the sermon for people. Successful sermons help people with both eternal life and daily life, with both felt needs and real needs. They don't deal just with ideas, principles, and Scriptures, but with people, emotions, problems, families, money, work.

Furthermore, I've found that from the beginning I must communicate clearly that the sermon is for them. If I give twenty minutes of exposition and then try to tack on an application, I will have lost most of my listeners. So right in the introduction, I usually tell people how the sermon will relate to their concerns.

In "What About Shaky Marriages?" I began like this:

Clint Eastwood made a movie called *Heartbreak Ridge.* I'm not a Clint Eastwood fan, but there is a side story in that movie where Eastwood—the 24-year-veteran marine gunnery sergeant, Congressional Medal of Honor winner—has lost his wife: she's left him and doesn't want anything to do with him. This big macho man is quite pathetic. He doesn't know what to do, so he starts buying women's magazines. You have a remarkable picture of Clint Eastwood reading women's magazines to find out what on earth his wife really wants. The tragedy is that it's perfectly obvious to everybody else but not to Clint. Marriages are shaky. People involved in shaky marriages don't understand some very basic facts about marriage.

Intellectually competent. A successful sermon appeals to the mind by being logical and credible. It coherently interprets Scripture, and it develops in a way that makes sense to listeners.

To be intellectually competent, a sermon often must nuance thought and make subtle distinctions.

In my marriage sermon, in speaking on the phrase "Love is not jealous," I said:

> Now this poses a problem. We know that God is love, and we know that God is jealous. How can Paul say that love is not jealous?

> There are different kinds of jealousy. There's a holy jealousy committed to protecting that which is dear. I protect Jill. If people get after her, they don't just deal with her; they deal with me. If they get on her case, that's my case. If they criticize her for what she's doing, or for what she doesn't do, then I will handle that for her. (I'm getting ticked just thinking about it!) That is holy jealousy.

> There is a jealousy that goes beyond protecting and becomes possessive. That possessiveness becomes a power that dominates the other person with little interest in the other's well-being. In some marriages you'll find one partner or the other so committed to what they expect of the other person, they won't even listen to the other person's desires. Their jealousy has become destructive possessiveness. Love is not jealous.

Emotionally moving. Successful sermons address not only the mind but the heart.

In explaining the phrase "Love is not rude," I said:

> Rudeness despises people. Rudeness denigrates people. If it goes on long enough, rudeness destroys people.

You remember Archie Bunker. What angered me so much was Bunker's attitude toward his wife. He constantly called her "silly cow!" That woman, as portrayed in the program, was totally beaten. I don't think he physically abused her, but she lived with constant verbal rudeness and denigration, which for all intents and purposes destroyed her. She had come to the conclusion that she was a silly cow. Bunker was clearly limited in his love for his wife. Love couldn't possibly be rude.

Archie Bunker's treatment of his wife would offend most listeners; it would strike at an emotional level, as it did me, and that's one reason I used him as an illustration.

Volitionally challenging. A successful sermon also appeals to the will. It doesn't just spew information or inspire emotions; it calls people to live in a new way. How I put it was:

We are not to assume that *agape* love is simply the result of the Holy Spirit working on passive people: I stand around, and the Holy Spirit loves you through me. It doesn't work like that. You will notice that the Bible also speaks of *agape* as a responsibility. This wonderful passage in 1 Corinthians 13 concludes with the words, "Follow the way of love."

Unfortunately, whoever divided the Bible into chapters shoved that phrase into the next chapter, but after Paul talks about love, we are told to follow the way of love. The words translated "follow the way of" mean "to hunt or to pursue relentlessly"—to target a goal and fulfill it. *Agape* love is the result of the Holy Spirit operating within our lives, but it is also the result of making a commitment to target somebody with *agape* love and loving them relentlessly.

Practically comprehensible. A successful sermon is as clear and useful as the morning paper. My favorite Scripture about preaching is Nehemiah 8:8: "They read from the Book of the Law of God, making it clear and giving the meaning so that the people could understand what was being read" (NIV). I'm best at "making it clear and giving the meaning" when I show how a biblical principle looks in daily life. Here's how I did that in one passage of my marriage sermon:

> When things go wrong in an intimate relationship, as they inevitably do, we carefully recall and rehearse what went wrong. If we continue to rehearse in our own minds what went wrong, we will find ourselves resenting what went wrong. Resentment builds until we are concerned about revenge. Sometimes we have to recognize that resenting and revenge seeking have absolutely nothing to do with what the Spirit of God wants to work in our lives: a willingness to forgive as Christ has forgiven us. Love does not keep records.

Growing continuously

The above criteria are not the end of it. Successful preaching cannot be reduced to a formula. It's a dynamic process, and an essential part of the process is the preacher's growth.

It's easy to stop growing, of course. You've been churning out one or more sermons a week for years. It takes increasingly more work to make slight improvement. People respond well to your messages. The time may come when you say to yourself, *I've got this thing nailed down,* or *This is as good as I'm going to get.*

Some preachers resemble many NFL first-round draft choices, those naturally talented athletes who never reach their full potential. Success has always come easily, so they never had to exercise great discipline; they coast on their gifts.

Granted, in some facets of preaching, our growth will be limited or nil. I have never been comfortable preaching in large evangelistic settings where an "altar call" is expected, and I don't give invitations at Elmbrook Church. That's partly my personality; I am basically a shy, undemonstrative person who has never answered an altar call himself. I've been in situations where my hosts wanted me to give an invitation, and I tried, but I felt awkward.

But I work at growing in other areas. Warren Wiersbe observed in one interview that over the years my preaching has changed. It no longer is straight exposition, he said, but has become earthed where people live. Over the years I have worked hard at illustrating better.

I find continued growth comes best if I remember three things.

First, I want to build on my natural gifts. When Tom Landry, former coach of the Dallas Cowboys, saw running back Tony Dorsett play football for the first time, he turned to an assistant and said, "You don't coach that. You draft it." His point, of course, wasn't to quit coaching a talented runner, but that the best results come from working with talent.

Some preachers are gifted at evangelistic preaching, others at teaching. Others are relational in the pulpit, counseling people en masse. Others are natural exhorters, who can effectively challenge listeners to greater obedience. Some prefer expository preaching, others topical. Whatever your strength, major in it.

Enhancing strengths, however, still leaves room for experimentation with new things, for stretching ourselves. We don't know what we can do until we've tried.

In the sixties the last thing I wanted was to work with youth. "That's not my strength," I told people. "I can't do it." Eventually a friend more or less shamed me into helping him with a coffeehouse ministry to the teenagers of Britain.

My friend, a physician, had surveyed hundreds of school kids and found that they were interested in Jesus but totally disinterested in church. He said to me, "You have a gift for reaching kids with the gospel, but you aren't even close to most of them because you preach in church settings. So if we are going to fish for people, you and I need to go where the fish are. They're in the coffeehouses."

He was right. I knew it, so we went. Eventually I developed my own ministry called Coffeebar Evangelism, and people wrote me from around the world, asking how they could do it. Speaking to youth became the focus of my ministry.

I also try to learn from other preachers. Copying others is a mistake, but comparing and contrasting can benefit us in several ways.

First, other preachers show us possibilities.

In my upbringing, most of the things that went on outside the church were considered "worldly." I was interested in these off-limits subjects—sports, drama, and literature—but they played no role in my preaching. Then I heard Paul Rees, an evangelical leader of the last generation. He was not only interested and knowledgeable about such things; he talked about them in sermons. In him I heard a preacher who was not only interested in the culture but who found illustrations of biblical truth there.

Second, other preachers model preaching values. In my formative years as a preacher, I admired Alan Redpath and Stephen Olford for their fire. Their messages gripped them and me. John Stott's preaching has always challenged me to be clear, to lay out the Word in orderly fashion. The sermons of G. Campbell Morgan, Charles Spurgeon, and John Wesley strike me with their high regard for Scripture and their passion to get the Word out to people.

Third, I weigh feedback heavily. While I don't evaluate my own preaching in a structured way, I do pay close attention to what others tell me.

My wife, Jill, reminds me of my need to keep working at application, the weakest area of my preaching. That's because I wrongly assume others are like me. I learn through principles; give me the principle, and I'll figure out how to apply it. Jill reminds me that most listeners need specifics: "First you do this, second you do this, third you do that."

Though the comments of others can sometimes be unnerving, I find safety in this process. When preachers veer onto a tangent or fall into a rut, it's usually because they have secluded themselves from a trusted circle's healthy feedback.

When I was a teenager, a man asked me, "How old are you?"
"Seventeen," I replied.
"It's time you were preaching."
"I can't preach."
"Have you tried?"
"No."
"Well then, you can't possibly know you can't do it."
That's how I got started in the pulpit. And since then, I've

worked hard to preach effectively. But I've also learned to trust as well.

Farmers plow their lands, plant their seed, and then go home to bed, awaiting God's germinating laws to work. Surgeons only cut; God heals. I must give my full energy to doing my part in the pulpit, but the ultimate success of my preaching rests in God.

Section 2:
Changing Lives Through Worship

Worship is the gospel in motion. It remembers the saving event, proclaims that event, and enacts it. This is a non-negotiable. Worship is not about anyone else or anything else. The response of thanksgiving to God's saving deed is what lies at the heart of worship.

—ROBERT WEBBER, AUTHOR OF *Worship Is a Verb*

PART 5

Preparation

16

Can Worship Leaders Worship?

Pastors, as player-coaches, must both give instructions and follow them at the same time.

—BEN PATTERSON

Some of the things the apostle Paul said scare me. For instance: "I do not run like a man running aimlessly; I do not fight like a man beating the air. No, I beat my body and make it my slave so that after I have preached to others, *I myself will not be disqualified for the prize*" (1 Cor. 9:26–27 NIV, emphasis added).

That makes the hair on the back of my neck stand up—spiritually speaking, that is.

It is an occupational hazard of the ministry, is it not, to have spent our time and energy trying to get others to love, obey, and worship Jesus Christ, only to discover in the end that we ourselves have not. We have been so occupied with coaching other runners that we ourselves have never actually run the race!

Pastors have an extraordinarily difficult job, one filled with great spiritual peril. We are player-coaches. We must both tell others how to be Christians and be Christians ourselves. We must both preach what we practice and practice what we preach. The difficulty is the tension between the two. The great pastoral peril is to succumb to the temptation of being just a coach.

Nowhere is this problem more apparent to me than in the Sunday worship service. I can get so preoccupied with trying to get the congregation to worship that I don't worship.

It doesn't take much to get me to forget why I am there in the first place. Sitting as I do, up front on the platform, I can see

most of what is happening in the sanctuary. I can see if the
ushers are botching their job. I will notice if the junior highers
sitting in the back are nudging each other and giggling. I will be
more aware than I want to be if a young woman is imprudently
wearing a low-cut sun dress to worship. If the choir sings poorly
or an associate goofs a cue or the congregation seems half asleep,
then I am distracted or dismayed or disgusted or all of the above.

In any case, the player-coach becomes only a coach. His attitude and tone cease to be "Let *us* worship God," and becomes
"*You* worship God."

This peril presents itself in its purest form when I preach.
Every good preacher I know is a bit of a ham. He or she enjoys
standing up front and having people listen. There is nothing
wrong with that pleasure in itself. When pressed into the service
of God, it can make for effective communication. When left to
itself, it can sour and cause us to worship not God but ourselves.

I can't count the times I have felt the sweat running down my
back as I struggled to hold on to a congregation I felt was slip-
ping through my fingers. I was losing not only them but also my
focus on why I was there. If you'd asked me after one of those
services how the worship went, I would have said, "Terribly!"
Why? Because my sermon didn't cut it.

The same can happen in reverse when I feel the sermon
clicked. Then I believe the worship service was a grand success
because I performed well.

Both are cases of the worship leader ceasing to worship in the
act of leading. Instead of the sermon being itself an act of worship, it becomes a performance. In one case, a performance that
failed; in the other, a performance that succeeded. But in either
case, it was a performance *for the people.*

When I preach for God before the people, I am a player-coach.
When I preach for myself before the people, I am just a coach.

What do I do about this? I have developed a few mental and
spiritual exercises, none of which, alone or in combination with
the others, have been 100 percent effective in making me a worshiping worship leader. But they have helped.

Prayer

I pray specifically, throughout the week, that what I do on Sunday morning will be pleasing to God. I also ask God to let that singular desire be my motivation as I lead worship.

I try to make Sunday morning, before I enter the sanctuary, a time of quiet before the Lord. This is hard, because although I give thoughtful and rigorous preparation to my sermons, I cannot make myself come up with the final product before 6:45 Sunday morning. We worship at 8:00 A.M. If we worshiped at 8:30, I wouldn't be finished until 7:15. I'm not sure why this is so, but I think it has something to do with wanting the sermon, when it's delivered, to be "hot off the press" with all the late-breaking news items, spiritually speaking.

Whatever the reason, Sunday mornings before worship are often my least prayerful days of the week. I hope that what I have done Monday through Saturday will make up for that lack. I pray throughout the week with that in mind.

Good preparation

The more thought my staff and I put into planning worship during our Tuesday morning staff meetings, the better able I am not to worry about worship details on Sunday. The less worried I am, the more emotionally able I am to worship as I lead in worship.

I realize this may not sound helpful to pastors of congregations that prefer a distinctly nonliturgical, unstructured approach to worship. But I offer it, nevertheless, as an apologia for the great benefits of planned worship. I believe the Holy Spirit can speak as clearly on Tuesday morning as he can on Sunday. In fact, I think he can speak more clearly when the pressure is off and we are quiet and prayerfully thinking through the service.

Planning does not rule out the immediacy of God speaking in the present tense. My experience is that preparation provides a vehicle for these things to happen. It certainly helps enable the worship leader to worship.

Specific worship behaviors

I do a couple of little things during worship to keep me focused.

After the people are welcomed and before they are actually
called to worship, we have a few moments for quiet preparation.
Usually the pianist plays a reflective prelude. During this time I
make it a point to really pray. I studiously keep my eyes closed
—very important for not noticing all the things that may be
happening in the narthex!

When I sing hymns, I do something my friend David Mains
once suggested. I do not look at the congregation, but above
them. I imagine Christ standing there physically, and I sing the
words of the hymns directly to him. That in itself not only radically refocuses my attention on the reason for our gathering
together, but it can also be very moving. More than once I have
been moved to tears as I imagine singing directly to Jesus words
like "Be thou my vision, O Lord of my heart" or "My God, how
wonderful thou art, thy majesty how bright!" or "Alas, and did
my Savior bleed, and did my Sovereign die? Would he devote
that sacred head for sinners such as I?"

Attitude

I try to enter the sanctuary recognizing that the service is in
God's hands now. Of course, it was when we planned it on
Tuesday, too. But now I want to jump in and participate, mistakes and all, and entrust the outcome to the Lord. I don't want
to hesitate or worry. It is time to forget about how smoothly our
plans are progressing and simply worship God.

When I was playing high school football, we lost the second
game of the season—one we shouldn't have lost. Films of the
game revealed that many of us were hesitating at the line of
scrimmage because we were not sure who to block. All the next
week, we practiced firing off the line. The coach drilled us to
knock somebody down, *anybody!* "Do something, even if it is
wrong!" he shouted.

That may not be the most felicitous metaphor for worshiping

God, but it helps me. I want to go into worship . . . and worship! Even if I sing when I shouldn't, forget to pray when I should, or preach a mediocre sermon, I'm going to concentrate fully on God. If the sermon is weak, I want it to be zealously and earnestly weak! A. W. Tozer was right when he said it is not *what* we do that makes a thing sacred, it is *why* we do it.

Grace

Finally, I remind myself that only by the grace of God are we here to worship him, and it will be by his grace that our worship will be successful.

When we stop to think about worship, just who do we think we are, walking into the presence of the almighty and holy God, the Ancient of Days, presuming to invoke his presence and offer him anything—even the praise and thanks that are his due?

Annie Dillard once wrote:

Does anyone have the foggiest idea what sort of power we so blithely invoke? The churches are children—mixing up a batch of TNT. One Hasidic slaughterer, whose work required invoking the Lord, bade a tearful farewell to his wife and children every morning before he set out for the slaughter house. He felt, every morning, that he would never see any of them again. For every day, as he stood knife in hand, the words of his prayer carried him into danger. After he called on God, he feared God might notice and destroy him before he had time to utter the rest, "Have mercy."

Mercy! It is only by his mercy that we can walk into his presence and call upon his name. It is only by his mercy that we *may* worship at all. It is only by his mercy that we *can* worship at any given service. All our plans and preparation, all our prayers and meditations, are no more than widows' mites cast into the temple treasury. Only the Master knows if what we did was worship. Only his Spirit will make it worship.

Pastors, of all people, should be aware of what is at stake when the people of God come to worship him. There is no higher and nobler task. There is therefore nothing capable of greater debasement and sin. It was in worship that Cain purposed to murder Abel.

We talk disparagingly of the congregation "just going through the motions" in worship, and well we should. To do so is to become cauterized to the things of God. But what of worship leaders who are just going through the motions? Even motions of leading worship?

Is not the peril even greater?

Indeed, Lord, have mercy!

17

How I Prepare Myself

A pastor, of course, must do many things to prepare to lead people weekly in worship. But before I attend to technical matters, I've learned to attend to spiritual concerns.

—JACK HAYFORD

I was twenty-two when I took my first pastorate, a small congregation in Fort Wayne, Indiana. At best we averaged 47 people in worship.

We had one rough stretch. As some members moved and others went away for the summer, our average attendance over a five-month stretch dropped steadily, from 47, to 44, to 33, to 22, and finally, by the middle of August, to 11.

One Sunday morning only 8 people showed up. When my family came back for the evening service, nobody showed. No one.

I sat discouraged in the front row next to Anna, my wife, and our baby, who was lying in a bassinet.

I had already felt defeated after the morning service, but now I felt simply awful. *What in the world am I doing here?* I thought. If we had had enough money, I would have packed my family in the car and left town. But we didn't.

Sitting there, I made what I later realized was a crucial decision.

"Honey," I said to my wife, "you stay here with the baby and kneel. I'm going by myself to pray. If we don't pray right now, this will beat us."

While praying I saw a mental picture of the church building on fire—not burning up, but flames were going up from the building, and the cinders blew east of the church and came down on top of houses and ignited them. I felt as if the Lord was telling me he was still intending to bring his "fire" to that church.

I was strengthened and encouraged to stay at the church, and did so for another two years. I can't say the church exploded with Spirit-filled enthusiasm after that. In fact, it never became much larger than it was at its peak. But in those two years, we had a number of families from that housing development to the east start attending.

That incident reinforced for me the priority of prayer in ministry and especially in preparing to lead worship. A pastor, of course, must do many things to prepare to lead people weekly in worship, from preparing a sermon to putting hymnals in place. But before I attend to technical matters, I've learned to attend to spiritual concerns.

Worship distractions

Prayer helps my heart, mind, and soul focus on the meaning and direction of worship. I make prayer a priority because it dissolves the distractions of worship.

One leading distraction is the yearning for "successful" worship, which takes various forms.

A smooth service. During one recent Sunday service, I became angry. A group that was to make a special presentation didn't show up on time; it was rainy, and the van that was supposed to bring them was late. I became irritated and said a couple of abrupt things to a staff member who was on the platform.

Immediately, I felt rebuked. First, I realized that this group's tardiness wasn't anybody's fault, certainly not the staff member's. Second, I remembered that the strength of our service isn't in its smoothness; that isn't the source of its power. So I quickly turned to my colleague to whom I had spoken harshly and apologized.

Naturally, we want a smooth service. If things are disjointed, people can be distracted from focusing on God. But spiritual power in worship doesn't come from the smoothness of transitions.

An excellent service. Sometimes we get distracted from true worship by being preoccupied with the excellence of the choir, the preaching, or the special music. We even sanctify that yearning by saying that nothing we do for God should be less than excellent.

The greater truth is that while we ought to aim for excellence, God doesn't need our excellence; it doesn't enhance him a bit. It may make things more lovely, but it can also lead to pride. We become preoccupied with style rather than substance, with how things look and feel rather than with what truths they communicate.

Naturally, I'm not encouraging shoddiness, but we must keep excellence in perspective.

An effective service. Sometimes we're distracted from worship because we want to make an impact on people. Perhaps in the first service I will say something funny that I didn't plan, but that nonetheless makes a point in the sermon. I may be tempted to repeat it in the second service mainly because it's cute or clever and people will like it. If that's my motive, the spiritual vitality will be drained from it.

Recently, in the first service, as I came to the key point in the sermon, I became moved. I asked if we wanted to be a charismatic entertainment center or a body that transmits the life of Jesus to the next generation. I was surprised, in fact, at how moved I became. And I did something unusual for me: I hit the pulpit—hard!

I haven't done that ten times in twenty-one years of pastoring, yet on this morning, I did. But it came naturally, spontaneously, and it genuinely communicated my passion for the subject.

But what was I to do the next service? For me to mimic that would be disastrous. To do so would be merely to seek an effect, an emotional response, and not to focus attention on the truth of the message. Whenever we become unduly conscious of techniques and effects, we are distracted from the worship of God.

Attitude check

Developing a worshipful attitude is, for me, the most important thing I can do to prepare for worship. It's vital for me to nourish a real humility before God and to sustain a genuine childlikeness before the people I lead.

Our culture thinks there is something fundamentally immature about childlikeness. But true childlikeness reminds me that no matter how old or seasoned I become, when measured beside the Ancient of Days, I'm a mere child. In addition, I want to remain flexible and open to the Spirit, as a child is open (usually!) to the leading of loving parents.

Prayer is the key, for me, to nurturing a childlike spirit. When I regularly engage in three particular types of prayer, I develop an attitude conducive to leading worship.

Putting my spiritual garden in order

When I was a boy, each Friday night my father would give me a list of chores for Saturday. He usually worked on Saturday and wouldn't arrive home until after four o'clock. But then he'd walk with me and examine the work I'd done.

He was a perfectionist, although not an unkind man. He had been in the navy where everything was shipshape. So, he'd examine my yard work carefully. If I left a couple of leaves in a flower bed, he'd just point, and I would know to go over and pick them up. If he saw a weed I'd missed, he'd point it out.

For me this was a positive experience. I loved my dad, and I wanted to do well for him. When he looked at what I'd done, I wanted him to be happy. So when he pointed things out that I'd missed, I didn't mind. I would have done those things had I seen them, but I saw them only when he pointed them out.

King David wrote, "Search me, O Lord, and know my heart. Try my thoughts and see if there be some wicked way, and lead me in the way everlasting." When it comes to preparing myself for worship, that's my desire as well. I want my heavenly Father to walk with me through the garden of my heart and see if I've missed anything.

I do this by regularly engaging in cleansing prayer. This is different from my daily devotions; it's more intense. Sometimes I feel like I need a thorough cleaning, like a car radiator periodically needs to be flushed. It usually happens about once a month. I take a day and devote it to prayer and self-examination.

I don't have a specific agenda. I usually prostrate myself and "call on the Lord," as the Psalms put it. I'm not loud, but since I'm alone, in a closed room, I feel free to speak aloud. I try to let God stir within me. I don't think I'm finished just because I feel stirred or teary-eyed. I'm ultimately looking for a new perspective on myself, a revelation of pride or self-centeredness, or an insight into what God would have me do next in ministry.

During one of these cleansing prayers, for instance, I was feeling a vague hollowness. I couldn't put my finger on a glaring sin, but eventually I realized I felt empty because I had been squandering my free time. It wasn't an earth-shattering revelation, but I had to acknowledge that I had been watching an excessive amount of television. I felt the Holy Spirit was prompting me to prune this form of sloth.

Such prayer keeps my spiritual garden in order and allows me to lead worship in spirit and truth.

Getting in touch

For me, Sunday morning starts on Saturday night, and Saturday night begins with a special form of prayer. Almost every Saturday night at about 7:00 or 8:00, I go to the church, walk through the sanctuary, lay hands on each chair in the room, and pray.

Sometimes I'll walk down every row, sometimes I'll go down every other, but I'll let my hand at least slide over every seat. Once in a while, I'll sing a hymn or chorus as I walk. Sometimes I'll do this alone, other times with a few church leaders. Praying through the sanctuary usually takes about fifteen to twenty minutes, but it makes a profound difference in the next day's service. Specifically, it does three things.

I become open to God's power. Although God is present with me at all times, when I acknowledge his presence, I become more dependent on him.

As I walk along, I might pray, "Lord, you've given me gifts as a speaker. But I also know I can't touch all those people where they need to be touched. Only your Spirit can touch their spirits. I ask you to do that tomorrow."

Sometimes I will so feel the presence of God, I'll be moved to tears. Other times I won't feel a thing. At such times, I go to the back of the sanctuary, look over the room, and pray, "Lord, I am glad that you're here, even though I don't feel one thing. And I'm depending on your being here tomorrow."

I gain insight from the Spirit. As I pray through the sanctuary, I'm also asking the Holy Spirit, "What is the one thing you most want to do tomorrow?" By this time, we have the essential outline of the service, but we can still decide which element of the service we will highlight. That decision, then, flows from this prayer time.

Sometimes I feel grief for people who have been bereaved or anger that Satan's attacks have divided homes, abused children, or encouraged drug abuse. I believe these feelings are more than coincidence; they're burdens the Spirit gives. Often, based on this experience, I will return home and rewrite the introduction to my sermon or the opening remarks of the service.

People have told me that I have a knack for opening sermons, for getting people's attention. If that is true, I attribute it to these times when I walk through the sanctuary, pray, and literally place my hands on the chairs where individuals will be sitting the next day, spiritually standing with them, identifying with their lives and need.

I bless the people. I also believe I impart a blessing to people by touching the seats and praying. It's not magic; I believe that along with prayer, the Holy Spirit uses physical means (like human touch or bread and grape juice, for instance). I don't speculate on how God does it, and I strongly guard against any superstition that such a truth could breed. But I've found that God often integrates the visible and invisible realms to communicate himself.

We regularly receive letters from people who have visited our service. They say that as soon as they walked in the door, something began happening within them. They immediately sensed the presence of the Lord. What changed their lives was not the service or preaching, but their conviction that God was present. I believe our Saturday night prayers are part of the reason people sense that.

In the same way, the night before a baptismal service, I'll often go to the baptistery, get down on my knees to reach into it, and stir the water with my hands as I pray. I believe the Lord wants to make every baptistery like the pool of Bethesda—a place where people are delivered from the crippling effects of sin.

There is, of course, no handy formula, no set prayer that will guarantee spiritual results. Praying over the chairs on Saturday night is not a third ordinance. But for me, it has been a practice that has borne spiritual fruit on Sunday morning.

Praying the sermon

On Sunday morning, I, like many pastors, pray in preparation for worship. This prayer takes a different form: I pray through the sermon. Sometimes I look at notes as I do, but most of the time I simply think the thoughts of the sermon and pray about each one.

This fixes the sermon in my mind, but the spiritual goal is more important. I liken the process to Elijah's stacking the wood at the altar. What I'm doing in my study is stacking wood, and I'm asking for the fire of the Lord to come down upon the message and the congregation. I often pray something like, "Lord, I want to enter the service with my thoughts fresh and clear, and especially I want you to glow within me."

One Sunday I was praying through my sermon based on the woman at the well. The subject was missions, and the main text was Jesus' statement: "Whoever drinks this water will never thirst again." I was feeling a little empty because it seemed such an obvious thing that people need Jesus. Ninety-eight percent of those attending the service already believed in Christ.

As I was praying, suddenly I was stirred with the thought that many in the body of Christ, even though they know him, still go back and drink at the old watering holes. They find, of course, that it's no more satisfying than before. But the reason they go back is that they've become preoccupied with their thirst. If they would seek their satisfaction by satisfying other people's thirst, they wouldn't be thirsty for the things that used to attract them.

I can't convey in print what a difference that made in the service, but it became a powerful point in the message. It helped people identify with the woman at the well and to recommit themselves to satisfying others' needs and not just their own.

Leading worship and worshiping

During the service, there are a host of technical things to think about: how to make a smooth transition from one chorus to the next, when and how to get people to interact, how to signal the instrumentalists to cut a song short, knowing when and how to modify a sermon. The worship leader has so much to think about, there's hardly opportunity to worship personally.

At one level, of course, that can't be avoided, especially for the younger minister. For the first few years of leading worship, maybe pastors ought to make sure their need for worship is fulfilled in other settings, such as in private devotions or in visiting other churches.

But before long, you learn both to lead worship and to worship. Some of that is due to experience and some to thoroughness of preparation. When a concert pianist steps on stage, if his preparation has been thorough, he will be able to be engaged fully in his playing. He will do more than play a series of notes. In some sense, he is able to enjoy the music more than the audience, which has not put as much into preparing for the performance.

Likewise, the worship leader, especially if he or she is well prepared, can worship the Lord and also think about what's coming next.

Diminishing distractions

When I was younger, I'd struggle with carnal indulgence or a bad temper or idle away my time (for a while, I simply didn't take studying seriously). I also used to feel a heaviness on Saturday night and dread the weekend. I thought ministers were supposed to feel that. Later I realized I simply feared no one was going to show up on Sunday. I was afraid all my preparations would be wasted.

I still feel spiritually weak sometimes, but now it doesn't take as long to pray out of that kind of depression. That's nothing to boast about, of course; it's just part of the normal process of maturation in faith. And in preparing worship week after week, year after year, a lot of things become easier. It's also easier (though not necessarily easy) over the years to prepare myself in the most important way, putting myself out of the picture and trusting in the Holy Spirit.

18

Worship Worthy of the Name

Worship is seeing what God is worth
and giving him what he's worth.

—TIM KELLER

Dan Wakefield, a writer who moved to New York in the 1950s, was originally from Indiana. When he arrived in New York, he completely overturned his Baptist roots and became a bohemian. In one of his books, he describes how he wanted nothing to do with the values of middle America. He completely rid himself of religion.

Now, however, he's near sixty years old, ostensibly needing spiritual meaning, and attends a liturgical church. Why? Probably because to him, the church feels safe, it's connected with history, it doesn't feel like a fly-by-night operation, and it is more satisfying aesthetically.

Historic liturgy often appeals to a certain kind of person. It opens doors to the heart that the art of pop culture—drums and guitars—can't.

Personally, I like both. Each form of art opens different doors into my soul. But each form must have at its core true worship. It all begins with this question: What is true worship?

Instinct run amok

At our deepest level, we were created for worship. But this instinct has gone awry.

Jonathan Edwards spoke of religious *affections*—that core of our being that orients our mind, will, and emotions toward an object. Sin has caused our affections to stray, propelling us to worship relationships, achievement, work—everything but God. Alfred Adler would say we gravitate toward control or power or comfort or approval.

We obsess about those things, comfort ourselves with them, fantasize about them. Biblically speaking, those things are idols. Worship is pulling our affections off our idols and putting them on God.

The word *worship* comes from an Old English word meaning "worth-ship." I define worship as a private act that has two parts: seeing what God is worth and giving him what he's worth.

Job says, "I have treasured the words of his mouth more than my daily bread" (Job 23:12 NIV). When I treasure something, I longingly look at it, for example, in the store window and think about how great it would be to own it. I ponder its virtues, talk to my friends about how great it is. Then I go out and buy it.

Worship is treasuring God: I ponder his worth and then do something about it—I give him what he's worth. Every approach to worship must have those two elements.

Harnessed worship

The only difference between private and public worship is that in public worship, individuals are doing it in concert with others. In a team of six horses, each horse is affected by the speed and direction of the other five. The same is true of corporate worship—it's individuals worshiping God in harness.

If the minister is talking about the holiness of God, for example, I'm seeing God's holiness in concert with the congregation. Together, God's people are in harness, letting the worship leader guide them so they can respond to God individually by giving him what he is worth.

At Redeemer Presbyterian Church in Manhattan, we structure our service in cycles of seeing what God is worth and then giving him what he's worth. To begin the service, I often give a devotional that focuses on some aspect of God (seeing what God is worth). The following two pieces of music and time of silence for confession allow people to respond (give back to God what he's worth).

Scripture readings, exhortations, and sermons show people what God is worth. The offering, prayers of repentance and thanksgiving, and times of confession allow people to respond to God.

Of course, in any given service, not everyone will be worshiping. A good service is one in which a large number of those attending are seeing God's worth and responding. A poor worship service is one in which few people are. Unfortunately, there's no tangible way to tally the percentages. I've led services in which I thought few people were truly worshiping, but when I talked to my wife afterward, she sensed just the opposite.

I can, however, determine whether I have truly worshiped or merely sat through a religious activity.

In order for us to worship, our mind, will, and emotions have to be moved. They're all organically connected.

Merely learning a truth about God is intellectual education, not worship. For example, I can know intellectually that God is good but still be worried silly about something that's coming up this week. If the morning's sermon is on the sovereignty and goodness of God, I haven't worshiped unless that truth descends from my mind and touches my emotions and my will.

I worship, then, when I realize I've been trusting in my own abilities, not the sovereignty and goodness of God. When I pull my affections off the other things I've been trusting in—which is why I'm anxious—and put them on God, I will be touched emotionally. I may cry; I may not. It depends on what kind of personality I have. But the truth will affect my emotions.

My will is also affected when I decide to change the way I handle that threat next week.

Worship is grasping a truth about God and then letting that truth strike you in the center of your being. It thrills you, comforts you. That's when the truth has moved from left to right brain—from mind to heart. On the spot, it will change the way you feel. The whole brain, the whole person, is affected.

Mistaken emotions

Not everything we feel Sunday morning can be labeled true worship. Several emotions often are mistakenly associated with true worship.

Nostalgia. Some people are moved to tears by listening to "The Old Rugged Cross" and others by "The Wind Beneath My Wings." But those feelings are not necessarily worship. They could also be merely a sentimental connection; the song reminds people of a warm memory. This is one reason why people will say, "I can't worship if I don't sit in my pew," or "I can't worship because you rearranged the furniture," or "I can't worship if I don't know the hymns."

That's nostalgia, a fond sentiment that people often need because everything else in life is changing. But that feeling isn't worship, and there is no resulting impact on their whole lives.

Conscience clearing. Some people feel guilty because they haven't gone to church for a while, or they haven't been praying, or whatever. So because they're in church, singing a hymn and putting something in the offering plate, they feel better. Their consciences are clear. Perhaps that feeling is better than the sentimental feeling, but it's still not worship.

Aesthetic experiences. Other people may have only an aesthetic experience, which is still not worship. Even people hostile to the gospel can weep while listening to Handel's *Messiah*. C. S. Lewis said that his imagination was baptized when he was still an atheist because of excellent Christian art.

After preaching a sermon, I've had people say, "Your sermon was wonderful. It made me feel terrific, but I don't believe any of the things you said." They liked the logic, the delivery, the overall impact, but they couldn't believe it.

So you can withhold your intellect and your will and yet have an incredible aesthetic experience as you see the gospel presented in an artistic way.

Our emotions become a legitimate part of worship when, in response to a truth about God, we give something back to God: our money, our sin, our praise. Again, the three elements must be there: mind, will, emotion.

As it relates to worship, I'd rather use the word *moved* than the word *emotion*, however. I agree with Edwards, who essentially said that if we don't find that our affections have been moved from earthly idols toward God, we haven't worshiped. Our affections are more than just our emotions.

Some of us, myself included, are not emotionally expressive. That's just who I am. However, if I leave Sunday morning having had no emotional connection whatsoever, I haven't worshiped. I must allow my heart to be touched to worship.

Baptized art

In recent years, churches have emphasized excellence in worship, especially in seeking to reach non-Christians. In general, churches that focus on excellence tend to attract more non-Christians.

Non-Christians are attracted to the art of a tight-sounding worship band or string quartet. They are not, in general, attracted to the special music of Brother Joe's seventh-grade nephew, who gets up and plays "A Mighty Fortress Is Our God" on his clarinet. That music is meaningful for the members of Brother Joe's church, who know and love the nephew, and who know and love the truth. But those who don't have the relationship already are only made uncomfortable by the lack of excellence.

Aesthetics is a movement from the right brain to the left. Consequently, art is often a back door to truth. Clearly, people are brought to faith through great aesthetics. The power of the art draws people to behold it. After a while they begin to wonder if the ideas that inspired it are true.

As a general rule, the larger the church, the more important worship aesthetics become. It can be compared to the difference between two restaurants, both of which have great food. One restaurant is a dive, tucked away in a hard-to-find basement; its patrons are proud of the fact that not many people eat there. It attracts few new customers because nobody knows where it is unless you're told by an insider.

The other restaurant, however, places a premium on good advertising and a pleasant ambiance. It's easy to find, warm and friendly. Everything about the restaurant communicates, "Why don't you try our food?" I would go so far as to say that when planting a church, you determine its future size in part by the importance you place on aesthetics in worship.

But it's important to keep worship aesthetics in perspective. Frankly, I doubt that to God there's much difference between the classically trained soloist and Brother Joe's nephew. God is the one we want to please, and I doubt he judges on the basis of aesthetics.

To me, aesthetics are important because they remove the obstacle that bad art places in the path of the would-be worshiper. Effective evangelism has usually combined excellent aesthetics with communication. George Whitefield's preaching was great aesthetics: he had a gripping voice, and he could weave moving stories, causing the crowd to groan and weep. His oratory attracted crowds of five to ten thousand people.

Whether Whitefield's oratory, Willow Creek's drama, or Redeemer Presbyterian's more classical aesthetics—the object is to communicate a message that penetrates the head, the heart, and the will.

Easy access

Contemporary pop music is not the only art that attracts non-Christians, however. I'm always puzzled when I hear pastors suggest this.

Our largest service at Redeemer is not the one we started with the contemporary band (though that could change). It's the one with traditional hymns and string quartets playing classical music. Perhaps that's because New York faces Europe more than the rest of the country. I've found the people of Manhattan like formality. They're used to cathedrals, art museums, symphonies. Many non-Christians feel safe in a liturgical service because they know what's happening next. There are no surprises.

I've also found that many who come back to the faith often

choose a liturgical church. These people tend to be intellectuals: professors, writers, musicians.

At Redeemer, with services in historical liturgy and with drums and guitars, we say that we are not targeting either believers or seekers. Ours is a worship service calling everyone to respond to the truths of God. We just do it in the vernacular.

We attempt to make our worship accessible (which, in many ways, is also good aesthetics). The words of the liturgy must be beautiful and understandable, especially since in historic liturgy, the congregation recites aloud more than in free-church styles. Our bulletin is actually a booklet, several pages thick, that includes the words to the hymns and responsive readings and folk choruses. (American folk tunes, amazingly, blend nicely in high-culture worship.)

To worship in the vernacular, I explain more. For example, I'll say, "Let's read this passage of Scripture and then spend a few silent moments in confession," and explain what confession is. Or I'll say, "At the end of the sermon, I will be calling for a life commitment. Committing our lives to God means . . ."

However, in reality, you can do only so much education and so much evangelism in a worship service. Therefore, a congregation needs venues outside of Sunday worship for both.

Nonnegotiables

The pressure on a pastor to create a good worship service each week can cause me to react wrongly when a service doesn't come off the way I think it should. I'm a detail person, and occasionally, I cringe when a vocalist blows it or the microphone system goes haywire. That's not good. It indicates an overemphasis on aesthetics.

We recently moved from a smaller facility, where we packed out the place, to an auditorium at Hunter College that seats 2,200. Our largest service, however, draws 800. That has dampened our worship energy, because acoustically, our singing cannot fill the expanses of the auditorium.

That has been frustrating. We purchased an organ, which

helps, but we've had to accept the fact that until we fill the auditorium, our singing, aesthetically, will not meet our expectations. Some of our people were disappointed when we moved in, but we didn't have any alternative.

Yet, just as people can have an aesthetic experience and not worship, they can also worship without good aesthetics. I need to remember that. I'm committed to excellence but don't want to make it a nonnegotiable. Aesthetics are negotiable; truth is not.

Neither is the authenticity of the worship leader. Before Sunday, I must have been worshiping God throughout the week. I use daily Martin Luther's scheme of "garland" meditation, which he describes in a letter. I meditate until some thought of Scripture catches fire in my heart. I collect those thoughts, which stay radioactive all week, and use them in my worship leading the next Sunday.

This prepares me to worship in concert with the congregation. My people can sense whether I am worshiping or not. I believe the church needs to see me worship, to see my affections being moved by the truth of God.

19

Balancing Form and Freedom

Spontaneity offers no innate advantage over liturgy.
Liberty is where the Spirit is, not where the preacher has thrown
away his notes.

—PAUL ANDERSON

A woman who was visiting a liturgical service kept punctuating the pastor's sermon with "Praise the Lord!" Another woman finally turned around and said, "Excuse me, but we don't praise the Lord in the Lutheran church."

A man down the pew corrected her. "Yes we do; it's on page 19."

The conflict between form and freedom is not new, and we have both sides in our congregation. Some wish we would throw out the liturgy so we could be free to "move with the Spirit." Others are tired of innovations and want to return to the good ol' days when they knew what was happening and could follow the bulletin play by play.

Is it possible to have the best of both worlds? Yes! Order and ardor can be happily wed. The issue is not structure or freedom, but Spirit. God has no preference for formless spiritualism or Spiritless formalism—he rejects both. Spontaneity offers no innate advantage over liturgy. Liberty is where the Spirit is, not where the preacher has thrown away his notes.

Protestants have traditionally been better workers than worshipers. Pastors may spend fifteen hours on sermon preparation and fifteen minutes throwing the service together.

But God wants worshipers above anything else. Jesus told the

Samaritan woman, "He seeketh such to worship him." Karl Barth wrote, "Christian worship is the most momentous, the most urgent, the most glorious action that can take place in human life." If we agree, then worship must not be "the things we do before we get to the important stuff."

One glimpse into heaven reveals that it is of eternal significance. The whole book of Leviticus was written to teach a nation how to worship, an acknowledgment that at the center of life is the worship of God.

Like other Christian disciplines, worship requires balance. Here are some areas we try to handle appropriately.

Balancing praise and worship

Our family went to see "The Glory of Christmas" concert at the Crystal Cathedral in Southern California, and it was glorious! Dr. Schuller asked that applause be held till the end of the performance. After every marvelous piece of music, complete with drama (live camels and flying angels included!), my four-year-old daughter clapped vigorously. She knew it called for a response, and I could not convince her that silence was more appropriate (much to my embarrassment). With all respect to Dr. Schuller, I think Naomi was taking her cue properly from a joyful heart, not the rubrics of the evening.

Reading about the worship of Israel convinces me that God is no grouch. Dancers, singers, and instrumentalists combined to make worship a time for rejoicing: "Four thousand shall offer praises to the Lord with the instruments that I have made for praise" (1 Chron. 23:5 NRSV).

One of the men in our church said, "I used to think Cecil B. De Mille was overdoing it—trumpeters on this wall, heralds on that wall, and a chorus in every corner. But after reading the Old Testament, maybe he was downplaying it! I'd love to see a service with processions, banners, colorful vestments, and antiphonal singing."

David declared it legal to shout to the Lord; Pentecostals have gradually made it more acceptable.

And yet after entering his gates with thanksgiving and his courts with praise, there comes a time of needful quiet— worship. "Know ye that the Lord is God" is best done in silence. "Be still and know that I am God."

One of the Hebrew words for worship means "falling on one's face." Prostration before God says we are seeing something of his greatness in contrast to our frailty. In worship, Isaiah's "Woe is me" is more appropriate than Peter's "It's sure good to be here."

We realize in worship we ultimately have frightfully little to say to the Lord who inhabits eternity. In the words of the hymn writer:

O, how I fear thee, living God,
with deepest, tenderest fears,
And worship thee with trembling hope
and penitential tears!

A congregation that praises loudly without worshiping meekly has not experienced the awesome and terrible side of the Almighty. To celebrate his presence is one thing; to tremble before him, as the psalmist exhorts, is another.

Yet praise is usually the necessary prelude to worship. It is rare for people to drop to their knees after the opening prayer. The skillful leader woos the congregation into worship like the patient lover draws the beloved. The congregation is brought into the audience of God more by evoking than provoking. The leader who breaks in with a jarring "Okay, let's sing all the verses of number 317, and real loud on the last verse" doesn't realize that instead of exhorting, it's better to enter into the experience of praise and encourage others to follow by example.

Some congregations excel in praise, complete with guitar, tamborines, and drums. But having learned to make the joyful noise, let us also practice the blessed quiet. Noisemaking seems out of place when "the Lord is in his holy temple." Clapping after every choir anthem does not distinguish between the joyful moment and the sacred one. The holy hush is just as powerful as the jubilant hallelujah.

I've found most congregations are more adept at praise than worship. Where this is the case I have used times of planned silence. A sermon that has gripped hearts may need a moment to settle before the service moves on. We have discovered that words of confirmation and personal application often grow out of the soil of silence.

But we do not begin there. Our preludes used to be typically quiet organ meditations. People entered in silence and did not make a sound until the opening hymn. But starting with silence makes it harder for people to feel a kinship with one another. Too often the quietness betokens only unholy hush of mental inactivity.

We now sing songs of praise for fifteen minutes before the service "officially" begins. This change has brought a greater spirit of celebration and camaraderie. And, I believe, helps us balance praise and worship.

Balancing structure and spontaneity

Liturgical forms give worshipers a sense of continuity. Confessing the ancient creeds reminds us that the church is a lot bigger than we are and has been around a lot longer. Forms help establish community by creating church family traditions, so valuable for people whose present situations change by the minute.

Liturgy gives people identity. It links them with saints around the world and down through the ages who share a common confession. It helps guard against an individual piety and a proud contemporaneity. People who tend to be dazzled (and tyrannized) by the latest model Oldsmobile and computer appreciate coming to a Sunday service and finding some things don't change as fast.

Liturgy gives structure to worship, reminding the participants of the breadth of concerns in the hearts of the saints. You *will* have an agenda, whether it is planned years in advance or on the spot. Ritual provides a workable plan, which is often the springboard for spontaneity.

Liturgy is drama, and the better it is performed, the more beautiful worship can be. The psalmist who combined holiness and beauty ("Worship the Lord in the beauty of holiness") saw that ethics and aesthetics are friends.

Protestant worship often lacks aesthetically, because it has throughout its short history shown more of a propensity for freedom than form. But if actions do communicate better than words, if symbols are the language of the soul, then the forms of the faith can speak to our subconscious in ways that spoken propositions cannot.

But forms have their liabilities. We who want to worship God in the worst way often do. Rite easily moves into rote. Those active participants may learn the forms and stay disengaged throughout the whole process. The prophets denounced the priests who made rite more important than righteousness. Jesus had harsh words for them also. While their lips honored God, their hearts were far from him.

Spirit is replaced by technique, doing the rite thing the right way. The state of the art supersedes the state of the heart. Any sensitive worship leader appreciates the importance of mechanics, but when the how-tos get magnified, externals have replaced internals. Nothing made Jesus angrier. Liturgy void of Spirit is brassy.

So, we emphasize freedom and leave the rite—right? Wrong. Freedom without form imprisons us as much as form without freedom. What the Corinthian Christians lacked in maturity they made up with frenzy. Paul put an apostolic check on their emotional excesses and gave some structure and guidelines to their freewheeling worship. Freedom can be human-centered, superficial, or just lazy.

From an anthropological point of view, Mary Douglas argues that "the contempt of external ritual in modern western society has led to a private internalizing of religious experience." We miss the artistic, the mysterious, the subconscious, and the historical in the overly intense drive for the immediate. Enthusiasm may run high, but nervous systems cannot take that much stimulation for long.

Again, balance is needed. A Spirit-inspired free prayer does more than a cold form. But a well-crafted prayer that expresses the heart of the worshiping community does not have to be cold. Liturgy that breathes will not suffocate the saints.

A small directive can give worshipers just enough structure to set them at ease. A train on its track is going somewhere. Some might call that limiting, but those willing to be instructed make good team players. They can have their part and play their part and know it is a part, not the whole.

Theologian J. J. van Allman writes, "Liturgical beauty is a protest, not only against all aesthetic self-centeredness, but also against negligence, coarseness, casualness and in general against vulgar familiarity." Total freedom leads to heresy. Anything doesn't go. There are ways to approach God, and there are avenues that dead-end. Uzzah found that out when he touched the ark. Truth is a boundary in which the Spirit moves.

Worship is as much a matter of seeing as of hearing. We have so elevated the pulpit (sometimes as much as twenty feet in some post-Reformation sanctuaries) that we have created stiff-necked people who think they have worshiped if they took good sermon notes. For Israel worship was a dramatic production that invited the attendance of the majestic Lord of hosts. The more the senses are involved—seeing, smelling, tasting, touching, hearing—the more the people of God are doing liturgy. If the form has not created such action, we have not properly used it.

Ways we have sought to let the liturgy live in our church include combining the great hymns of the church with more contemporary worship songs, often without a break in between. When they are in the same key, one can flow beautifully into the other. The hymns have a theological richness often missing in modern songs. On the other hand, the songs of today have simple Scripture texts that are quickly learned. They enable people to worship freely without props.

We also include well-known liturgical responses as a part of our informal prayer and praise services. By doing this we are telling the people we like to bring out the treasure of things both old and new.

Balancing the timely and the timeless

God is a progressive. While the saints are singing, "Gimme that old-time religion" the Almighty is declaring, "Behold, I do a new thing." He is not the old fogey some might picture him—*we* are the experts at maintaining the status quo. We routinely turn movements into monuments, institutionalizing them so we can control them.

We don't do well with change, though we desperately need it. Those trained by Jesus to be people of the Spirit rather than people of technique will be alive to the now, "The Spirit blows where it wills," and sensitive people are eager to catch the direction of the wind.

The New Testament has two Greek words for time, *chronos,* or linear time, and *kairos,* which is opportunity. Hebrews thought more in terms of *kairos* than *chronos.* The opportunity presents itself and must be seized. It is the fullness of time. All times are in God's hands. He orders the times and seasons, and his creation must be sensitive to his action and respond appropriately.

If we are only alive to the *chronos* (and in our church, the clock is in clear view), we might get out at the scheduled time, but fall short of God's opportunity. Sensitivity to the moment does not preclude planning, but it may prompt the minister to change his direction because of some nudging he believes is from God.

When God comes into the midst of his people, we should know it and be able to respond to it. To be locked in to the bulletin at that time is to be absorbed with the menu rather than to enjoy the food.

There are times in liturgical worship that cry out for free expression. That's why we often allow people to tell how God is working in their lives. To miss this is to leave worship unfulfilled.

And yet the past has volumes to say to the present. Faith is related to history. The God who acts is known because of the God who has acted. History and encounter are cousins. Remembrance and realization meet in worship.

James Dobson, Christian psychologist, writes that "our generation has the idea that history first began when the Beatles hit the Palladium. Such thinking alienates us from yesterday and creates a rootless society."

The strength of the contemporary is that it speaks our language. The major liability is that it appears (and may be) shallow. It has not stood the test of time. The danger of time-dated material, however, is that it is so distant it seems unapproachable. Gregorian chants make fine songs for monks, but not for kids in Levi's and sandals, or so it seems. People like one or two antiques around the house, but they don't get much use.

Can we blend the two together? We try by offering a *variety of musical styles.* To throw out Bach because half the church is under thirty is to cheat the young. Those who appreciate "good" music will get it elsewhere, but few youth will ever go for Baroque unless we make use of it.

Contemporary music reaches their ears. Still, there is a side of God they are less likely to know. When President Kennedy was assassinated, several radio stations abandoned their normal programming and played three days of powerful classical music. Rock 'n' roll was judged inappropriate for the situation. It could not speak what had to be said.

So we use both hymns and worship songs. Music shapes theology. Of the 287 Old Testament quotes in the New Testament, 116 come from the Psalms, the hymnbook. The theology of today's songs will shape the minds of our children. Luther said, "Music is the handmaiden of theology." His enemies said, "Our people are singing their way into Luther's theology." We make sure our music is saying what we want it to—then use it generously.

We also *mix free prayers with written prayers* of the great saints. This way, people grow to appreciate "the older members of their family."

Balancing leaders and laity

Worship in the New Testament drew from the sacrificial system as well as from the postexilic synagogue service. The Lord's

Supper took the place of the Passover as the dramatized act of redemption. The indwelling Spirit made every believer a priest and gifted member of the body. According to New Testament theologian Ralph Martin, Pauline worship stood on three legs: the didactic, the eucharistic, and the charismatic. Word and sacrament were blended with the sovereign activity of the Spirit.

By the time of Constantine, the freedom of the Spirit had been replaced by form. An increasing division between the people and the priest left the laity with little to do but watch. They did not share in Communion, now a Mass. Long cathedrals magnified the separation.

The Reformation recovered the truth of the priesthood of all believers. The Scriptures were given to the common people, singing by all was encouraged, prayers were spoken in a language all could understand, and sermons were preached to build up the people of God.

And yet how much new ground have we won since 1517? Does the Spirit blow as it wills in our services? Do we have a new trinity, as some suggest—the Father, Son, and holy Scriptures? On Sunday morning are we entertaining spectators or training participants? Is it a one-person show or a gathering of the called? Church was not meant to be a place where the minister ministers and the congregation congregates. Worship is not something done for the laity but by them. Our goal, according to A. W. Tozer, is more than believing—it is beholding. Actively beholding.

While the apostle did put the clamps on the Corinthian "charismaniacs," he did encourage considerable liberty by the individual worshipers (1 Cor. 14:26–33). How much freedom are pastors willing to risk? Do they want the person in the pew healed of spectatoritis?

A revolution in communication has put the pressure on pastors to do their stuff on Sunday. Some feel guilty if they do not run a three-ring circus for people who are paying well to see a good show. God deliver us!

But we do need pastoral leadership in worship. Paul's admonition about the need for "distinct notes" (1 Cor. 14:7 NRSV) came in the context of corporate worship. Tending the flock includes giving them the best we can when they are all gathered together. The more secure the leader, the more we are able to draw the people into worship and take them where the Spirit is moving.

One way I've tried to live this out is by letting the proclamation of the Word be shared by a variety of people, although I do most of it. I work with people individually and as a group to prepare them for speaking assignments. When I preach, I often use members to share testimonies as an illustration of my main point.

I've also found that the more people are free to respond to the initiative of the Spirit, the less nudging they need from the pastor. In our church, the teaching through the years has created an expectation that God will indeed move through the people and not only the pastor.

The end of worship

Most of us spend too much time with people, too little with God. We enjoy the *koinonia* in the outer court; we are less comfortable entering the Holy of Holies. We ride more on the good ship fellowship than the more important one called worship.

Yet the cure of countless physical and spiritual maladies is found in approaching His Majesty.

When have we worshiped? For some, it is when people have raised their hands or clapped joyfully. For others, when they have contributed to inspired singing or heard a powerful sermon. For still others, when the service has moved smoothly without any hitches in the sound system, the ushering, or the music.

For Israel, however, it was meeting with God. Being in the Presence might bring quietude or exuberance, weeping or joy, repentance or reflection. But worship meant coming to God on his terms and encountering him.

One morning God moved among us in a special way. A woman came out the door with tears in her eyes. "I've never

worshiped before," she exclaimed softly. "I've been to hundreds
of services, but today I worshiped."

And that, of course, is the reason for all our attempts at balance—to enable people to enter the presence of God to worship.

PART 6

Prayer

20

Prayer-Fed Preaching

If we have it, people will know it; if we don't, no homiletic skills will take up the void.

—RICHARD FOSTER

What is it about prayer that links it to preaching?

Why would a person like Martin Luther set down as a spiritual axiom that "he who has prayed well has studied well"? Why would E. M. Bounds, the great Methodist preacher and pray-er of a century ago, say, "The character of our praying will determine the character of our preaching. Light praying makes light preaching. . . . Talking to men for God is a great thing, but talking to God for men is greater still"?

In touch with God

Prayer gets us in touch with God, causing us to swing like a needle to the pole star of the Spirit. It gives us focus, unity, purpose. We discover serenity, the unshakable firmness of life orientation. Prayer opens us to the subterranean sanctuary of the soul where we hear the *Kol Yahweh,* the voice of the Lord. It puts fire into our words and compassion into our spirits. It fills our walk and talk with new life and light. We begin to live out the demands of our day perpetually bowed in worship and adoration.

People can sense this life of the spirit, though they may not know what it is they feel. It affects the feeling tones of our

preaching. People can discern that our preaching is not the performance of thirty minutes but the outlook of a life. Without
such praying, our exegesis may be impeccable, our rhetoric may
be magnetic, but we will be dry, empty, hollow.

We are told that when the Sanhedrin saw the bold preaching
of Peter and John, they perceived them to be men who had been
with Jesus. Why? Because they had a Galilean accent? Perhaps.
But more likely it was because they carried themselves with such
a new spirit of life and authority that even their enemies sensed
it. So it is for us. If we have it, people will know it; if we don't,
no homiletic skills will take up the void.

What does prayer of this kind look like? What do we do?
Intercede for others? Perhaps, but primarily we are coming to
enjoy his presence. We are relaxing in the light of Christ. We are
worshiping, adoring. Most of all, we are listening. François
Fénelon counseled, "Be still, and listen to God. Let your heart be
in such a state of preparation that his spirit may impress upon
you such virtues as will please him. Let all within you listen to
him. This silence of all outward and earthly affection and of
human thoughts within us is essential if we are to hear his
voice."

Add to those words this perceptive observation of Søren
Kierkegaard: "A man prayed, and at first he thought prayer was
talking. But he became more and more quiet, until in the end he
realized that prayer was listening."

Prayer involves what the devotional masters often called "rec-
ollection." It cultivates a gentle receptiveness to divine breath-
ings. We do not do violence to our rational faculties, but we
listen with more than the mind—we listen with our spirit, with
our heart, with our whole being. Like the Virgin Mary, we ponder these things in our hearts.

Perhaps one meditation exercise will illustrate how we prac-
tice centered listening. I call it simply "palms down, palms up."
Begin by placing your palms down as a symbolic indication of
your desire to turn over any concerns you may have to God.
Inwardly you may pray, "Lord, I give to you my anger toward
John. I release my fear of the dentist appointment this morning.
I surrender my anxiety over not having enough money to pay

the bills this month. I release my frustration over trying to find a baby-sitter for tonight." Whatever it is that weighs on your mind, just say, "Palms down." Release it. You may even feel a certain sense of release in your hands.

After several moments of surrender, turn your palms up as a symbol of your desire to receive from the Lord. Perhaps you will pray silently, "Lord, I would like to receive your divine love for John, your peace about the dentist appointment, your patience, your joy." Whatever you need, say, "Palms up." Having centered down, spend the remaining moments in complete silence.

There is no need for hurry. There is no need for words, for like good friends you are just glad to be together, to enjoy one another's presence.

And as we grow accustomed to his company, slowly, almost imperceptibly, a miracle works its way into us. The feverish scramble that used to characterize our lives is replaced by serenity and steady vigor. Without the slightest sense of contradiction, we've become both tough with issues and tender with people. Authority and compassion become twins and infiltrate our preaching. Indeed, prayer permeates everything about us. It is winsome, life-giving, strong, and our people will know it.

In touch with people

Some of the richest times in my pastoral ministry came when I would go into the sanctuary during the week and walk through the pews praying for the people who sat there Sunday after Sunday. Our people tend to sit in the same pews week after week, and I would visualize them there and lift them into the light of Christ. I would pray the sermons on Friday that I would preach on Sunday. Praying for their hurts and fears and anxieties does something inside you. It puts you in touch with your people in a deep, intimate way. Through prayer our people become our friends in a whole new dimension.

In our congregation in Oregon was a little fellow who underwent two serious brain operations. The times of prayer we shared during those six weeks built a bond between us that was

like steel. Twice I stayed in that hospital all day with his mom
and dad waiting to see if Davey would live or die. Davey was
only five years old, and he had Down's syndrome, but I value
him as one of my closest friends. And would he listen to me
preach! No children's church for him; he would perch himself
up on that pew, eager, attentive. I do not know if he ever understood a word I said, but I would preach my heart out because I
knew Davey was listening. If we have prayed with our people—
really prayed with them—they will listen to us preach because
they know we love them.

People in touch with us

Prayer gets our people in touch with us. I want my people to
know they have a ministry of prayer to give me. My people
know I want them to come into my office and pray for me. I do
not want them to feel the only time they can see me is when they
have some need or problem. They can come when things are
going well. I tell them I love to have them come and give me a
booster shot of prayer. It doesn't need to take more than a few
minutes, but it lets them know they count with me and they can
help me.

Obviously, there are times when we should not be interrupted, but there are other times when people should know we
would be delighted if they would come in and pray.

People need to sense our confidence and spirit of authority,
but they also need to know us in our frailty and fear. They need
to know that we hurt, too. We need their help. The religion of
the stiff upper lip is not the way of Christ. Our Lord knew how
to weep. In his hour of greatest trial he sought the comfort and
support of the three, and he went through that night in
unashamed agony. Many times our stiff-upper-lip religion is not
a sign of piety but of arrogance.

Beyond that, it is important to help our people understand the
ministry of prayer they can have for and in our worship services.
I would meet every Sunday at 8:00 A.M. with all the platform
people and remind them that perhaps the main ministry they

would be having that morning would be to pray for the people. They were in a unique situation to see people—those who seemed burdened or hurt or angry. They could pray for them; they could pray for me. Sometimes I would have people sit on the platform for no other reason than to pray. One dear brother would sit through both worship services every Sunday bathing the people in prayer, praying for the power of Christ to conquer, praying for truth to prosper. When you know someone is doing that, you can really preach.

Prayer is an essential discipline for preaching because it gets us in touch with God, it helps get us in touch with our people, and it helps people get in touch with us. As John Wesley said: "Give me one hundred preachers who fear nothing but sin and desire nothing but God, and I care not a straw whether they be clergy or laity; such alone will shake the gates of hell and set up the kingdom of heaven on earth. God does nothing but in answer to prayer."

21

The Cleansing Power
of Public Prayer

*After a week in the world, worshipers may need our prayers
as much as our preaching.*

—GORDON MACDONALD

Years ago, I became friends with a man who'd retired after many
years as a reporter and editor for a major newspaper. Over the
years he told me stories from his journalistic career—many of
them humorous, others indescribably sad. My friend was a reluctant but frequent observer of human cruelty, greed, exploitation,
and immorality. When I mentioned that fact to him, he did not
disagree.

"After you've been in the news business forty years," he said,
"you tend to develop a cynical and suspicious edge. You've heard
every kind of lie, you've seen every species of corruption, and
you've been witness to the sleaziest sorts of performances by folk
the public thinks are saints and heroes."

I asked him how he maintained his spiritual life amid such an
environment: "Don't you feel sometimes as if you're living in a
cesspool? How do you avoid becoming polluted inside?"

"I'm not sure I've always kept spotless," he responded. "By the
end of the week, I've often felt like a dirtied-up human being.
That's why when I head into church on Sunday I need something to clean me up—a spiritual bath."

This friend did more than anyone else to confront me with
what it means to pastor on a Sunday morning. I realized his
plight, while somewhat dramatic, was basically the same as that
of most people who come to worship. Whether they know it

or not, they also come out of a world saturated with evil. All of them need a bath. I began to wonder whether we provided it.

Garbage-pail prayers

Years after being alerted to this question, I preached at a worship service led by a friend, Bishop George McKinney of the Church of God in Christ. It was clear he knew something about spiritual baths and the daily lives of worshipers.

Bishop McKinney appointed two elders to stand at the front of the sanctuary. One held a basket so worshipers could step forward and deposit written prayer requests. The other elder stood guard over a garbage pail. Into it worshipers were invited to pour their sin: either a written confession of attitudes and actions or the actual implements of evil from which people wanted to part. The pail often held syringes, pills, marijuana, stolen goods, and once, the bishop told me, a sawed-off shotgun.

Most of us are usually too subtle or cautious to adopt the bishop's methods. Perhaps we take too lightly the spiritual weight folk bring to the sanctuary on Sunday and, sadly, too often permit them to leave carrying the same baggage.

What to do with the "dirt" our people bring to church? As a preacher, my first instinct is to ask what my *sermons* might do for such a person. But one day it occurred to me that the "bath" is not necessarily in the preaching (although that is important), but probably during occasions I frequently neglected: the *prayers*.

It took me a while to realize the value of prayers offered during worship, perhaps because people were quick to comment on my sermon and only rarely mentioned the prayers. But as I got to know people deeply, I realized what they longed for (though sometimes were unable to express) was not so much for me to instruct them but to earnestly pray for them, to help lift their heavy burdens. They come each week wearied, muddied, and bloodied. Perhaps the most refreshing thing I can do for them is offer heartfelt prayer.

I realized I had never been taught, either formally or by example, how to pray effectively in worship. My public prayers all too often were little more than strings of religious phraseology. They were extemporaneous but over time developed a ritual quality of their own. Long-term attenders could almost predict what I would say. Painfully, I realized few people were even listening to the prayers in a service; it was a time for minds to wander, drifting back to attention when they heard "and we ask this all in the name of him . . ."

How had I come to that conclusion? Dare I admit, my own experience? I had to muster all my concentration to listen to prayers myself. It was eerie to ponder the probability that on occasion, a thousand people might be present when a person was praying aloud, and that *no one was involved in a word said.*

Perhaps this is one reason that in nonliturgical congregations we see increased interest in scripted prayers. The ones supposedly spoken "from the heart" seem to have little thought (and therefore content) behind the heart. Even my friends in liturgical churches, however, admitted that well-crafted prayers didn't keep them or their congregations from sometimes approaching public prayer in a perfunctory manner.

That's why I decided to ask some hard questions about the meaning and placement of the various prayers in a worship service. I wanted to be sure that each time we addressed almighty God, we did so with the proper intent and content.

In worship, I discovered, there are at least six kinds of prayer to be offered on behalf of the people. The unknowing leader may confuse the six, mix their purposes, and diffuse the effectiveness of that "bath" my friend came to worship to receive.

The invocation

The first prayer of worship, usually called the *invocation*, has only one purpose: to invite and then acknowledge the presence of God among the assembled worshipers. To invoke is to request God's openness to the words and thoughts of the people. The prayer is to set aside this as a special time, a hallowed time unlike any other during the week. Holy activity is about to commence: worship, humankind's most important event.

The invocation is not a prayer for people or the issues of the present age, nor a rehearsal of the theological knowledge of the one praying. Rather it is a humble acknowledgment that those gathered look heavenward with thanksgiving, asking God's presence in what is about to be said and done.

My friends in liturgical churches say all of this in the concise "In the name of the Father, the Son, and the Holy Spirit, Amen." While I may use a few more words, our invocations focus on the same thing:

> We invite your presence, our Father, through the kindness of Jesus Christ. Having finished a week of work, of study, of play, we're here to worship, guided by the Holy Spirit. We have joined together to express our appreciation for the ways you have safely and lovingly led us . . .

The pastor's prayer

Another prayer of the worship service, perhaps the most cleansing of all, is often called the *pastor's prayer*. In my pastorates, it became the one prayer of worship I steadfastly refused to delegate as long as I was in the service.

I deem the pastor's prayer on a par with the pastor's sermon. If the sermon is the pastor's opportunity to hold up the Word of God to the people, the pastor's prayer is the opportunity to hold up the people to God. It is not unlike those occasions when Moses interceded for the people of Israel. And it is the congregation's opportunity (and, I believe, privilege) to hear their pastor pray for them.

As a pastor I often invited my congregation to join me in the kneeling posture for this prayer. I made kneeling an option, recognizing that some would have physical difficulty kneeling in a church without kneeling benches. I knelt on one knee myself and led the congregation from that position.

Kneeling or standing, I found it important to pray this prayer away from the pulpit. Usually I knelt at the head of the aisle.

That proximity to the people provided a point of contact for us all. It made my sense of praying more real, and I suspect the people felt more keenly that I was one of them.

The pastor's prayer usually has four parts. In traditional liturgies, some of these parts may be separated into prayers of their own.

The first is an acknowledgment of God himself and his involvement in our personal and congregational life. We need to be reminded who God is—his attributes and actions. It is a time to reaffirm the majesty of God, to be reminded of the smallness of our world in contrast to his infinite dwelling place.

All week long our world appears larger and larger as it seeks to intimidate, dominate, and exploit. It would be easy for my journalist friend to arrive at worship with the unspoken notion that reality is rotten and undependable. He, like others, needs to be reminded of another reality, that God is not sullied by the machinations of a sinful race.

Thus, a pastor's prayer needs to center on at least one aspect of God and our response. Majesty, holiness, kindness, and power are merely a few examples.

> Lord, in a world dishing out more than ample amounts of harshness, your kindness is a special reality to us. You treat us not according to what we deserve, but according to what we need. You give us gifts and capacities to enjoy the world you created; you give us abilities to love and receive love, to be able to forgive and forget. And most of all, you give us your Son, Jesus Christ. You are a kind God, our Father, and we love you.

In contrast to such an affirmation, the second part of the pastor's prayer is usually clear confession that we are sinners, that our past week was marked with attitudes and actions that grieve the heavenly Father. This confession concludes in affirmation of God's forgiveness for all who are humble and contrite in spirit.

It is no accident that Isaiah felt an immediate urge to confess his sinfulness the minute he visualized the glory of God in the temple (Isa. 6). There is an unbreakable link between the two experiences. We help people by offering opportunity to face frankly one's sin and resolve the matter with God.

This is a special and most poignant part of worship. As pastor, I speak to God on behalf of my friend the reporter, leading him and others into God's presence with a realization we are contaminated with the sin of this world. Together we need cleansing; we need to know we are once again clean. For me this moment is both tender and exhilarating.

In Bishop McKinney's church, the choir sang a lively soul song after people had had a chance for repentance and forgiveness: "Jesus heard my prayer, and everything's okay."

This part of the pastor's prayer is not something to pass by lightly. It admits our bent toward rebellion and the importance of the Cross in realigning the believer with the Father. Regarded properly, this can be a moment of liberation, of straightened accounts, for many who have come in desperate guilt and shame for failures in previous hours.

> Who of us here, Father, would not quickly admit we have disappointed you on many occasions this past week? The thoughts and attitudes we have often nurtured are things for which we are truly sorry. We repent of them. Some of us could quickly admit to deeds done or not done of which we are frankly ashamed. Some of us have come here today, Lord, bearing resentments and jealousies that would be terribly embarrassing if others knew about them. We confess these, Father. We need liberation from our sins. Thank you for hearing our personal confessions.

The third aspect of the pastor's prayer looks outward upon our world of revolution, starvation, disasters, elections, and achievements—the macro events people hear about throughout their week. Somehow my prayer must put these things into an eternal perspective and model how to pray in light of such events. All of us need to be reminded regularly that each world event concerns the Father and therefore must concern his children. Not to pray for these matters is to infer by silence that what happens in the sanctuary has no relevance to affairs during the other six days of the week. As a pastor, I found it important to make sure that on the way to church each Sunday morning I heard the latest news broadcast to be sure my prayer agenda was up to date.

> A part of our world hurts today, Lord. Men and wo men who think and feel just like us have no homes, no food, nothing to provide for their children's welfare. Father, many grieve today over the loss of loved ones in a tragic accident. Presidents and prime ministers engage one another today, Lord; they desperately need wisdom . . .

The final part of the pastor's prayer centers on the needs of the people themselves. I have rarely come to this point of the prayer without remembering the story Henri Nouwen tells of the abbot of a Trappist monastery who met his monks as they returned from the fields each evening, dirtied and wearied. As they approached, he would raise both arms to receive them and cry out, "Are any of you in trouble?" It was a time for each to pause, to reflect upon anything amiss within the heart or among relationships, and to find relief in God's promised kindness and grace.

The pastor's prayer, therefore, is a prayer for those who are in trouble and know it—for the worker who fears the loss of a job, for the person facing a doctor's appointment and potentially bad news, for parents raising children who do not seem to like them, for the single woman who is desperately lonely, for the teenager worrying about his sexuality. Mentioning such needs each week helps people in the pews sense their individual needs are being offered up, even if not specifically mentioned. Here we hold up arms for those in trouble. If we speak in tenderness, in hope, in authenticity (meaning real words describing real situations), and with urgency, the people will know they have been spiritually bathed.

> Father, some of us came here in deep pain: the pain of the body, the pain of wounded relationships, the pain of pure, unrelenting fear. Father, some of us badly need help and encouragement . . .

Wise pastors also intercede for various ministries in the congregation, not all of them at once, of course, but one each week perhaps.

The pastor's prayer can often be concluded by a song by the congregation. Some of my most memorable occasions were when we sang the Lord's Prayer without instruments. The sense of being welded together before the throne of God lingered with me for many days afterward.

In smaller congregations, parts of the pastor's prayer can be shared with the congregation in what is sometimes called "conversational prayer." When our sanctuary was smaller, I occasionally invited worshipers to stand and read one (I carefully held them to one) verse of Scripture that exalted the living God. What often happened was a beautiful mosaic of verses that directed our thoughts to many aspects of God's being and purposes.

Equally memorable were invitations to the congregation to stand and speak *one* sentence of praise to the Lord. I found it important to give specific instructions ahead of time in order to fend off the one or two folk who might dominate the occasion. On the other hand, those not used to public prayer were encouraged to participate, since the requirement was only one sentence.

Dedication of gifts

A third prayer of the worship service usually comes before or after the offering.

Recently I sat in a congregation where the offering was received by ushers, an equal number of men and women. Afterward the ushers walked to the front and held the plates high above their heads to offer them to the Father. We sang the Doxology and then were led in prayer by one who understood the money in the plates symbolized our week's labor. It was a touching moment.

What was this prayer doing? It was applying meaning and value to our work. We were saying, "We offer you, Father, the first fruits of our work." The pastor who prayed used words that let us know he was aware that we had worked hard, that the dollars in the plate had not come easily, that to give them was an act of cheerful obedience. I was impressed that the pastor who dedicated our gifts took them seriously, not as income for the church budget or benevolence program but as the fruits of our work.

> Some of us who are here today, our Father, are tired and bruised because we've had a hard week of work. But we have done our best at jobs that are sometimes exciting, sometimes boring. We have joyfully brought the evidence of our labor, and we present to you today a portion of what you have made possible for us to earn . . .

The prayer of illumination and submission

Scripture is not fully appreciated without the illuminating work of the Holy Spirit searching the heart, applying truth, bringing people to conviction. Thus, another possible prayer in the worship service is the prayer of submission to the Word of God.

In some liturgical services, it is common for the congregation to sing a hymn before the sermon. During the singing, the preacher kneels and prays for himself. As he consecrates himself to the work of the Spirit, the congregation become aware the preacher works under divine accountability and what they are about to hear is God's living Word for them.

This same preacher may call the congregation to prayerful attention as he opens the Scriptures. In this brief moment, all are commended to the work of the Holy Spirit and are caused to listen in submission to the Scriptures.

> The time has come for us to open the Scripture, Lord, to listen to your voice as it comes to us through the inspiring work of the Holy Spirit. Give us an ability to hear what is important and to place it into our experiences. We submit to your insight and guidance . . .

Prayer of decision and invitation

Assuming that a sermon connects God's Word to a worshiper's life, it is appropriate for the worship leader to end a sermon with a reflective prayer, focusing on the desired response. Silence is helpful here, giving the listener a chance to think through what he or she will do about what has been said.

Occasionally, I have used this time to give an old-fashioned invitation—a call to convicted people to walk to the front and kneel as a public act of commitment. But I never give such an invitation unless I have explained the procedure *before* the sermon. In a culture unaccustomed to revivalistic tradition, the idea of leaving your seat before the service is over and going to the front of the sanctuary is foreign. People need to know what will happen—that someone is prepared to join them and pray for them. This allows people to think through their response as the sermon is preached.

If not an invitation to personal prayers of commitment, then a sermon can end with a brief, reflective prayer, one that calls the listener to a point of closure. This prayer should not be a review of the sermon's major points but a petition that God's Word might be clear to each worshiper and properly applied to life.

All of us—beginning with myself—are startled with the richness of these truths, Father. They call us to something higher and more powerful than we've ever known. We need to do something about what you've said us today. Help us to discover what that could be . . .

The final ascription

Sometimes called a *benediction,* this is the concluding prayer in most worship services. All too often it is merely a signal that a service is almost over; people use the time to put away hymn books, grab coats, or even get a head start to the parking lot.

We are not merely closing a service with prayer. Rather, we are offering a final affirmation of blessing upon people and thanksgiving to God for having been present.

The prayer should be brief. It need not rehearse the events of the morning but simply acknowledge God's faithfulness and pronounce his blessing, as the traditional biblical benedictions do. Few things are more moving than for a pastor to raise his hands in blessing over the people and pray them Godspeed in their journeys. It is the final word to the children of God as they reenter the world. It should be encouraging, tender, and affirming, reminding them that they go with the covering hand of the Father and Shepherd.

> Father, we ask your blessing as we leave this place. We have done our best to tell you that we love you, that we're grateful for your kindnesses, that we want to know more of you. We return to our homes and places of work with confidence in your promised care and guidance. Our expectation is that you will help us seize the hours before us to advance the work of your kingdom.
>
> *(And speaking to the congregation)* Now may the love of Christ, the grace of the Father, and the power of the Spirit rest upon you throughout the days ahead. Amen.

What my friend the journalist means when he says he needs a spiritual bath is that he is in need of someone who knows how to pray for him, especially when he doesn't feel he can pray for himself. In the corporate prayers during worship, I have an opportunity to provide that sense of cleansing. But it will take time to plan, to think through my prayers, and to make sure each contains what both he and God ought to hear from me, the intercessor. Perhaps then he can return to the newspaper business on Monday ready to take on life in that world with a bit of kingdom power.

> Holy Father, may those of us who are pastors and spiritual directors come to increasing appreciation of the rich privilege of holding the people up to you. Give us the insight that helps us understand their needs. Give us the faith that causes us to be confident in the power of intercession. Give us a vision of yourself and your majesty, and ourselves and our brokenness, that causes our prayers for the people to have reality and power, we ask in the name of Jesus. Amen.

22

How to Light the Fire

I never want to let fear of the unexpected cause me to
institutionalize lukewarmness.

—Jim Cymbala

After I had been pastor of Brooklyn Tabernacle for about a year, the church had grown to fifty people, but we were facing problems: little money, few people coming to faith in Christ. One Tuesday afternoon I sat in my cubbyhole office on Atlantic Avenue, depressed. I knew that later that day, fifteen people, at most, would come to church to pray. *How could God call me and my wife to this city not to make a difference?* I wondered.

I walked into our empty little sanctuary and recited to God a list of my problems: "Look at this building, this neighborhood. . . . Our offerings are laughable. . . . I can't trust So-and-so. . . . There's so little to work with."

Then the Holy Spirit impressed upon me, "I will show you the biggest problem in the church. It's you."

In that moment I saw with excruciating clarity that I didn't really love the people as God wanted me to. I prepared sermons just to get through another Sunday. I was basically prayerless. I was proud.

I fell on my face before God and began to weep. "God, whatever it takes, please change me. I would rather die than live out some useless ministry of catch phrases."

That was a turning point for me and the church. In the weeks and months that followed, I continued to seek God, and my sermons began to have a sincere urgency.

"God wants to change us," I said from the pulpit. "If we'll let him work in us, all things are possible. We can be a church that makes a difference, that helps people find Christ."

The Brooklyn Tabernacle began to turn around, and twenty years later, we are still learning about the tremendous power of prayer. Every Tuesday evening many hundreds of people come together simply to pray.

Sensing our need

That experience (and many others) taught me that when we don't pray, it's primarily because we don't sense our need for God. Revivals have resulted not merely from a message of revival but from a dissatisfaction among Christian leaders. Revival won't come until we come to the end of ourselves.

For me, that moment came when I sensed that despite the soundness of our doctrine, our congregation didn't match up to the model given us in the Word. I would read in Acts that "the Lord's hand was with them, and a great number of people believed and turned to the Lord" (11:21 NIV). Then I would think, *Our doctrine is sound, the people are sincere, so what's wrong? Is it our hearts?* We may have to scrap everything, go back to zero, and ask, "God, what do you want to do in this church?"

When Barnabas came to Antioch, he "saw the evidence of the grace of God" (Acts 11:23 NIV). I longed for a church where people would be struck not by how clever the sermon is or how big the facility is but by the grace of God.

The good news is, once a minister has been given this seeking spirit, that desire is contagious. Hunger for God is contagious. Our attitude *will* communicate to people.

Before we begin to teach, we need to realize our own need and cry out to God. That is the fountainhead from which the waters flow.

Pointing out the disparity

Preaching remains one of the key ways we can inspire people to pray. It's possible, though, to preach in such a way that people leave more defeated and discouraged. I want to challenge listeners and give them confidence to draw near the throne of grace. To implant a positive motivation to pray involves two significant steps, and it's important not to stop after the first one.

The first step is to help people face reality. Preaching can become a searchlight to help people see the disparity between who they are and who God calls them to be. I might do that by reading Romans 12:11, which says, "Never be lacking in zeal, but keep your spiritual fervor, serving the Lord" (NIV). Then I might illustrate that kind of zeal in Acts 2: "They devoted themselves to the apostles' teaching and to the fellowship, to the breaking of bread and to prayer. . . . And the Lord added to their number daily those who were being saved" (vv. 42–47 NIV).

To bring home the disparity between that zeal for prayer and many Christians' lukewarmness, I might ask, "Isn't something wrong when many church members spend countless hours watching television but struggle with going to church one hour a week?"

It's crucial that all this be said in love, not anger. I know a pastor who burns with desire to see the church be all it should be. The more I heard him preach, however, the more I felt he was angry with his members, mad at them for what they weren't doing.

D. L. Moody got it right when he said, "If love doesn't prompt it, it isn't worth anything." But if the words are said with love, by this point in a sermon many will sense their need.

Pointing to the promises

I can't leave people there.

They would walk out of church disheartened. To stop at this point is legalistic preaching, for it tells people what they should do—"pray more"—but does not lead them to the promises of God. I want people to know that we all can humble ourselves and go to the throne of grace, where we'll find strength to pray—that we'll find grace and mercy to help us in our time of need.

After pointing out the disparity, we must point to God's promises. This is the essential second step.

The great Puritan preachers like Thomas Hooker let the law savage people but then quickly brought the balm of the gospel. What lifts people are the redemptive promises of Christ.

God doesn't call anybody to do anything without promising the grace to do it, and God's grace flows through his promises. The new covenant is characterized by promises of what *God* will do. "I will wipe away their sins; I will put my law in their heart; I will put my Spirit within them." Such promises draw us to God. They inspire us to trust him to do the work.

In one recent service, I had pointed out our need to pray through Isaiah 64 (NIV), which begins, "Oh, that you would rend the heavens and come down." That's crying out to God for our need, which has accompanied all revivals.

I then pointed to the promises of God: "Later Isaiah says, 'No ear has perceived, no eye has seen any God besides you, who acts on behalf of those who wait for him.' We have to wait for God. After we've given him the problem and still don't know what to do, we need to spend time with him. When we do, we will find he acts on behalf of those who wait for him."

Such a promise of God lifts people and motivates them in a positive way.

Providing opportunities for response

Even passionate preaching won't achieve its purpose, though, if we don't give people a chance to respond. It's counterproductive to stir people with the Word of God and then say, "Amen. Now, remember, tonight there's a potluck dinner." The difference between a lecture and a sermon is that the sermon calls for response. Allowing for that response is especially important in moving people to God in prayer.

At a convention, I heard a preacher deliver a powerful sermon, and when he finished, the congregation gave a prolonged standing ovation. He got embarrassed and kept nodding his head as the people continued to applaud. Finally, the leader of the meeting returned to the microphone.

I felt bad for that leader and felt the Holy Spirit must have been grieved. Since when does someone preaching about Christ get a standing ovation? The kind of response I'd rather see is people expressing their need to God so that God can refill them with power. The sermon is not a centerpiece but an arrow pointing them to the living Christ.

How people will respond varies with each congregation. But somehow we've got to fight the temptation for everything to be strictly orderly and over on time. We have to find ways that allow people to respond, to pray, to repent, to ask, to wait. The mere presentation of truth is not going to change anyone. God is the one who makes the changes, so we must provide opportunities for people to "come boldly to the throne of grace."

Opening to the unexpected

God is a great God, and he often does the unexpected. As we see our need and begin to call on God in prayer, we never know what may happen. We have to learn to be open to the unexpected.

Once I was preaching on the love of God, and I ended with an appeal to non-Christians: "For those of you who don't know the Lord," I said, "what will condemn you is that you reject God's love. He reached to you until the last breath you had, and he was saying, 'Come to me.' "

As I made this appeal, I closed my eyes. A man in the back of the auditorium got up and started walking down the aisle toward me. What I didn't see, because I had my eyes closed, was that he had drawn a .45 revolver and pointed it at me. My wife, Carol, was playing some background music, and she yelled, "Jim!" twice—but I didn't hear her. It was too late for the ushers to stop him, and he walked up on the platform.

This man walked over and threw down his gun on the pulpit. Then he panicked and began to run off the platform. I sensed his inner cry, "Jesus, help me," so I ran after him down the steps. Right in front of everyone he fell, crying, and ushers came to get him under control and to pray with him.

I went back to the pulpit and held up his gun, which I didn't know was loaded. Who knows what to do in a moment like that? There was pandemonium, yet also a sense of God's presence.

Then I realized what had happened inside this man. He'd had this gun (and was planning to use it after the meeting, I learned later), but as he heard of God's love, he thought, *I've just got to get this gun off of me, and I might as well give it to the preacher*. He had never wanted to hurt me.

I held up the gun and said, "Look what God's love can make someone give up." As I said that, people began getting up out of their chairs and coming forward to repent and pray. I didn't even call them. They just came because God had unexpectedly shown his love. We baptized more than twenty people from that one meeting.

I never want to let fear of the unexpected cause me to institutionalize lukewarmness. Our God hasn't run out of love and power. As we pray and cry out to him, and invite others to do so, he will move in our midst. If we will call on him, he will do what he has promised to do.

PART 7

Praise

23

When Worship Styles Clash

Pastors who attempt a broad range of musical tastes can find themselves in the cross hairs of some musical vigilante.

—GARTH BOLINDER

They were a thirty-something couple with a long history in the church. I knew them well—I thought. Imagine my surprise when, one morning after worship, they cornered me.

"That taped music has to go!" they snarled. "Whose idea was it, anyway?"

Before I could mumble a reply, they abruptly walked away.

I didn't get to tell them the music was my idea (whew!). After all, our organist was sick, our substitute possessed questionable ability, and besides, we had wanted soft preservice music to encourage contemplation. Why not play a gentle Windham Hill–type praise tape as people entered for worship? I thought it would set the mood for worship—background music is, after all, a way of life in our society. The actual worship service included only live music.

What's the big deal with taped music anyway?

As any pastor knows, musical style is perhaps the biggest force driving people's emotional response to worship. Many churches are a maelstrom of musical tastes, personality types, and worship preferences.

In an era of cultural diversity, how can one church find and develop its voice? With so many options available and so many individual preferences, how do we decide what will be our accent?

Our church grappled with this issue. It was fantasy to deny or avoid the issue of diverse worship styles. So we faced the issues —and we faced the music. Here's what we learned.

Choose reality over fantasy

Our traditionalists tend to believe that *real* music is at least one hundred years old or composed by a musical Ph.D. They are good people, often the backbone of the church. Some represent decades of faithful membership and service. Their commitments are strong, and so are their opinions.

Others are more contemporary but just as emphatic. They can act as if music more than ten years old is out of touch. Influenced by popular culture, these good people are at home with jazz, rhythm and blues, or rock 'n' roll. Hearing the truth of God declared in *their* musical voice enthuses them like traditional music never will.

We had people at both ends of this extreme—and in between. So we couldn't ignore the problem. We began by taking several steps to clarify the issues.

We asked the hard questions. Should our worship be for churchgoers or the unchurched? Should we use an organ or synthesizer, guitar, and/or (gasp) drums? Should we sing hymns, praise songs, or both? Do we focus on the theological or the relational? The intellectual or the emotional? Do we use hymnals, bulletin inserts, overheads, slides, faxes, or modems? (Who knows what the future holds?) Where does drama fit in? Must age boundaries prevent some from enjoying others' music? How can we deal with passionate people who threaten to leave if we change—or don't change—the music?

We admitted that our culture is saturated with musical options. With television, radio, cassettes, and CDs, today's options are an endless musical smorgasbord. And the sheer quantity of music can keep the most narrow musical appetite gorged for a lifetime.

Just as people channel-surf through stations to find *their* music or program of choice, we've found people "church-surfing" to find if our style of worship music fits their preference.

We became intentional about worship style rather than reactionary. We surveyed our church to find out, among other things, the music Hillcrest people listened to. "Classical" and "popular contemporary" tied for first place, "Christian" came next, followed by "country western" and "rock 'n' roll." We did get some write-ins for "rap," "grunge," and "alternative." A fairly accurate musical profile of the congregation emerged.

We also asked what type of music people preferred in worship. The top vote-getter was "more contemporary music." Then came "more congregational participation." Next came "stay the same," followed by "more hymns" and "more traditional music."

These responses confirmed that we were (and still are) a diverse congregation. Some desire worship that is predictable and dignified. Others prefer worship that is spontaneous and emotional.

The reality was that we were a congregation with wide and varied tastes. Our differences wouldn't go away by wishing. Admitting these things was the first step to getting past the illusions.

Choose vision over vacuum

Knowing we had a congregation with eclectic tastes didn't solve our problem. We had to decide on a course of action. The action began one day at breakfast with one of the younger musicians in the church. He issued a challenge.

"Garth, I know you have a heart for worship," he began, "and a music ministry that reaches all types of people—both inside and outside the church. But few know your passion. Some think you're trying to invade their musical turf with new and threatening sounds. Others think you're going too slow and capitulating to the status quo. You have to communicate a vision for worship and music that reflects your heart and passion."

He was right. I knew we weren't on the right musical track, but then I'd never articulated a direction others could follow. So

I began to pray for wisdom. How could our music mesh with our church personality and who I was as their leader?

The temptation to imitate was strong. For all the conferences, tapes, and articles I'd encountered, however, I felt we could not merely import someone else's successful style. Better to do what we could with what we had, right where we were. Above all, we had to be authentic.

I looked into Scripture and church history. I reflected on my own musical tastes. I analyzed the culture we were trying to reach. (Having teenage daughters was a great help here!) I considered various forms of worship we might incorporate. In short, I prayed for a vision so I could lead the church in worship.

According to Jack Hayford, "The leadership of the worship life of a church ought to be essentially pastoral—it is the pastor's role to lead people in worship."

When I felt God had showed me where we should be going, I communicated that vision to my staff. There was some disagreement, but their evaluation helped refine the vision. Next I consulted the elder responsible for worship and music. His suggestions helped clarify the presentation I made to the Council of Elders. Finally, we took it to the entire congregation. (See "A Vision for Worship" at the end of this chapter.)

Though a few voices dissented, most affirmed our direction. This vision proved valuable, giving us a sextant as we sailed into new musical waters.

Choose principle over personalities

Music can be incendiary. Martin Luther wrote that music is effective in driving the devil away. Maybe that's why the enemy seems to make church music the target of so much opposition.

Strongly held musical tastes run deep. Unfortunately, what is deep is not necessarily wide. One person's musical appreciation often is exclusive (and sometimes hostile). Such hard-held opinions limit both the power of music and the power of God.

Pastors who attempt a broad range of musical tastes can find themselves in the cross hairs of some musical vigilante. Antagonists can be young or old, charter members or newcomers, classically trained or raised on rock. Musical passion is not confined to one group. But when that passion is expressed in ways that are, shall we say, less than edifying, we encounter trouble.

One week two couples, separately, came to see me. One held more traditional views and the other more contemporary. Yet both informed me that they were probably going to leave the church. Neither couple felt they were hearing enough of their preferred worship voice. They wanted their own style of worship, even if it meant excluding someone else's.

That's when I found our vision for worship so helpful. When persuasive and persistent people object to the direction we're going, I can feel intimidated. But with clearly defined, well-focused principles guiding our worship, I can point to the vision our leaders have endorsed. It gave me leverage and confidence when facing off with strong personalities.

By choosing principles over personalities, we found that the exit door for the disgruntled few became an entrance door for many more.

Choose stretch over status quo

The God of all creation, in whom we live and move and have our being, isn't dull. Consistent? Always. Monotonous? Never!

Why is it, then, that we prefer to stay on one worship track, taking a sentimental journey and eventually forming a musical rut?

Let's be honest. Stretching beyond our personal musical and worship bias can be risky. Stretching usually hurts at first. But regular stretching causes muscles, even musical ones, to limber up and eventually get stronger. A fan of contemporary music, for example, may have to stretch to embrace a Bach cantata. The person who prefers classical may have to stretch to worship with a praise band. But the exercise can bring spiritual conditioning.

Some churches intentionally settle into one particular musical groove, one that fits their ministry niche. Others, however, settle into an unintentional rut, jealously protecting their comfort level. But when status quo is job one—whether contemporary or traditional—we usually find myopic vision and hindered mission.

We tried to make our diverse preferences a strength rather than a weakness. We wanted a tapestry of musical forms woven together. So our vision for worship seeks to blend our church's marvelous musical heritage with more contemporary expressions.

I regularly remind our folks, "Today's classical music was yesterday's contemporary music." Each generation finds expressions in the cultural forms of its day. Then it adds its own contributions to the worship repertoire.

Gerrit Gustafson writes in *Worship Today:*

> The church of the future must become transcultural. The evangelical church must learn to sing spiritual songs; the charismatic church must rediscover hymns, the traditional church must begin to sing a new psalm. The young church must respect the older church and vice versa. Bridges of cooperation and counsel must be built between black and white churches. The stagnating pools of our cultural prejudices must be flooded by the river of His divine purposes. . . . If worship styles have been the source of divisions among us, let's turn the tables and allow God's design for worship to be a source of unity among us.

But I found I needed help in implementing that kind of vision.

Choose pacing over power

That help came from the church leaders. In our attempts at innovation and balance, more than one elder looked me in the eye and said, "Garth, I appreciate your vision and passion, but you've got to work on your timing. Wait for the rest of us to catch up with you."

I had to learn the art of teamwork. (Again!)

Several months ago we were holding our annual stewardship dinner. We had planned our opening music to be upbeat. As the evening arrived, however, our church chairman expressed some concern. As people began entering, he came with an urgent look on his face.

"Garth," he said, "I don't think this will work. We've tried so hard to bring everyone along, but now, on the night when we're asking people to make commitments for the new year, we're jeopardizing everything with this music."

I thought the music was great. The musicians had practiced long and hard. Should we pull the plug just to appease those who might be offended? Would we alienate our musicians? Or should we let the music roll and risk an uproar among many faithful supporters?

By now, hundreds of people were streaming into the banquet room, and the program was about to begin.

At such moments there's not much time for contemplation. Our chairman waited, watching me. It was time to call an audible.

My decision had nothing to do with music style. Rather, I decided on the basis of our team style of leadership. We needed to be on the same page. Even though I thought the music was fine, I sensed his anxiety and respected his intuition. Since I was committed to lead from unity rather than division, I submitted.

I told our music minister to drop the opening musical segment. Disbelief with a mixture of "Are you kidding?" and "How dare you!" filled his eyes. He didn't argue, however, because he, too, was committed to being a team player. After he told the musicians that most of their numbers were being dropped, I figured I'd have to pick up the pieces later, so consequently I didn't enjoy much of the dinner. Every time I glanced over at the musicians' table, I could see their frustration.

Midway through dessert I felt a tap on my shoulder. It was Steve, our music pastor. I couldn't imagine what he wanted—except maybe to tell me he was turning in his keys on Monday. Instead, he asked if it might be possible to put the canceled music at the end of the program. That way, those who liked the music could stay, and those who didn't could leave.

I thought his idea was brilliant. After the closing prayer, our musical team presented their "opening" musical segment. Some people left, but most stayed, enjoying the music and the fellow-ship in an informal but fitting finale to a wonderful evening.

This incident illustrates the built-in tension always close at hand. Our commitment to lead in partnership helped me trust another church leader's intuition, even though I thought it meant we'd lose ground. By our willingness to lose a little, how-ever, we moved closer to winning it all.

Choose instruction over obstruction

Paul's advice to young Timothy (I wonder if those two liked the same music?) includes these words: "Don't have anything to do with foolish and stupid arguments. . . . Instead . . . gently instruct" (2 Tim. 2:23–25 NIV).

There will always be those who oppose anyone initiating change. Rabbi Edwin Friedman warns in *Generation to Generation* that sabotage is the one thing any effective pastor can count on. This seems especially true in areas of music and worship. The emotions are volatile. Personal tastes obstruct vision and values.

Rather than fighting, how about instructing? A true God-given vision doesn't fear controversy. It welcomes the opportunity to grow. In our case, we've been pushed to learn what true worship is all about.

Ongoing instruction has also pushed our leadership to review our motives: Is this vision God-given? Or just a personal pet project?

I've become more aware of my own musical motives. I've had to check whether the changes we were making really reflected a desire to please God and bless his people or merely a desire to be on the cutting edge.

This process has kept us in touch with Scripture, our people, and God.

Look up, not behind

Few of us will ever develop a music ministry inspiring media attention. We move ahead doing what we can, where we are, with what we have, to worship the living God in spirit and in truth.

We keep at it . . . where we are. Oswald Chambers said, "Never say, 'I am of no use where I am.' You are certainly of no use where you are not!"

But we have something to look forward to. It's the place, to paraphrase C. S. Lewis, where the music is "further up and farther in." All music on earth is a tin-eared echo of the music of heaven. The promise of what yet will be should keep us from pride that elevates one style over another, from excluding people with another point of view, and from giving up when musical dreams don't quickly come true.

Heaven sets the tone, steadies the rhythm, and creates the harmony for worship here on earth.

Recently, though, I wondered if we weren't getting close. Our worship included an organ prelude, a multigenerational orchestra, and a band (with keyboards, guitars, and drums). We had hymns, Scripture songs, and praise choruses.

Behind me a new believer sang newfound truths of the faith in a majestic hymn of praise. Firstgraders to my right quickly grasped the repetitive words of a praise chorus, though most of them couldn't read. An older widow nearby sang softly, eyes closed and tears glistening on her beautiful face. Teens sang to a familiar beat, but with words that went to their hearts.

Frankly, I can't say that we've reached our goal. Nor can I say that everyone enjoyed all the music that Sunday morning. But I can say I was thrilled to hear the sound of different voices who, though not always together, were together. I set aside my presermon anxiety and joined in the worship.

And I couldn't help wondering how it all sounded to the heavenly Audience to whom we were singing. Someday that's going to be all that matters.

Practicing for it now, I suspect, may be worth the effort after all.

A VISION FOR WORSHIP

Hillcrest Covenant Church developed the following statement to guide their worship. Not wanting to imitate other churches, nor suggesting others imitate them, they tried to articulate their own calling and identity as a church. The following condensation, perhaps, can serve as a starting place for others.

Our mission is to bring spiritual reality into the life of each person as they participate in corporate worship. We desire that every person, both believer and seeker, have a living encounter with Jesus Christ as they worship. Corporate worship is at the core of our life as a church. Therefore we will diligently plan worship that will:

Seek to please God first.

Be committed to excellence in all we do.

Be Great Commission driven . . . creating a worship environment to which we will want to bring unchurched friends, and to which they will want to return. (Examples: use words that are understood by all, provide a balance of traditional and contemporary praise music to appeal to different preferences, welcome visitors with personal greetings.)

Be thoroughly biblical in all we do . . . from the sermon to music.

Be practical in order to help people in their daily lives.

Integrate worship forms with a strong emphasis on praise. Integrate various forms such as drama, art (banners, bulletins), and music to bring worshipers closer to God. Praise songs during gathering time help break down barriers and focus attention on God.

Allow the entire congregation to participate. (Examples: hymn and praise singing, responsive Scripture readings, serving each other in Communion.)

Be bold, innovative, sensitive, reverent, relaxed, and joyful . . . open to creative ideas (new or traditional) . . . flexible and patient.

Equip people for spiritual warfare.

Allow people to be free and confident as they meet with God, without fear of being judged by others.

Build up the Body of Christ, surrounded by prayer as the Holy Spirit meets with us each week.

To accomplish this vision, a worship planning team will intentionally craft worship events to be thematic and authentic. The worship/music ministry will constantly evaluate and seek always to be improving. Our desire is that all our worship, both corporate and individual, give "blessing and honor and glory and power" to him who sits on the throne forever and ever.

24

Helping People Sing
Their Hearts Out

*Our most important choir is made up of the men and women
with untrained voices who sit in the pews.*

—HOWARD STEVENSON

One of the most magnificent and impressive "choirs" I ever heard had never been rehearsed. It was the vast audience that gathered in Anaheim Stadium one night during the 1985 Billy Graham Southern California Evangelistic Crusade.

I had been selected as the chairman of the local music committee and so assisted in the recruitment and direction of a 10,000-voice crusade choir, the largest crusade choir ever assembled in North America, according to Cliff Barrows. A magnificent sea of voices stretched along the entire third-base line.

Yet as mighty and moving as that choir sounded, the most powerful music that night came not from the third-base line, but from the huge 85,000-seat stadium.

The sound still echoes in my mind, a memory that remains electrifying and overlaid with emotion to this day. As Cliff was leading the stadium in singing the gospel song "At Calvary," I slowly walked out to center field, behind the platform at second base, and standing in the middle of the stadium, I watched the moon rising over the second deck as the power of that great hymn cascaded over me.

"Do you hear this, Lord?" I heard myself saying. "Do you hear the praise of these people?" I was thrilled as I listened to the unified testimony and thanksgiving that filled the air.

To this day, whenever I sing the words of that hymn, I see

again the image of that great, golden moon and hear those tens of thousands of voices singing: "Oh, the love that drew salvation's plan! / Oh, the grace that brought it down to man! / Oh, the mighty gulf that God did span at Calvary." I have spoken so often about that event that a friend framed those words for me, and I display them in my office.

That experience confirmed for me again the depth and impact of congregational song. It gathers strength in numbers and unlocks a deeper dimension of our souls, lifting our entire selves to God. Music is one key to the "heart dimension" of worship, whether we are gathered in a stadium, large church, hundred-seat sanctuary, or home Bible study. Singing has the power to help us freely express our feeling for God.

That's why an important part of our task as worship leaders is to involve the entire congregation in the ministry of music. Although the chancel choir, the soloists, and the instrumentalists are all vital contributors to the music of worship, our most important choir is made up of the men and women with untrained voices who sit in the pews.

Obstacles to effective singing

Effective congregational singing doesn't happen automatically whenever people gather. Consider some obstacles we face.

A shrinking body of commonly accepted congregational songs. On occasion, when I have directed music at another church or conference, I have begun leading a hymn I assumed was a familiar song, expecting the audience to join in. Instead, I often have found that most of the group are unfamiliar with part or all of the song.

In some churches, unfortunately, the great heritage of hymnody, which represents the praise and prayer of the church of many generations, has been abandoned. At the same time, praise choruses, with a more transient life, have become popular. In addition, regional favorites may dominate a church's singing.

We live in a time when sacred music is more available than at any other time in history. Yet, ironically, our congregations are growing increasingly unfamiliar with our rich musical heritage, a heritage that could bind Christians together.

A *spectator orientation.* Singing, which can be such a joy, is fast becoming a spectator sport in our culture. Music has become something we listen to, not something we open our own mouths and participate in. For example, college music programs find fewer and fewer freshmen who are trained and experienced candidates for their school's choral offerings.

Having just entered my seventh decade, I recall my days as a youngster when I sat in the front row of a storefront Presbyterian church, singing hymns and gospel choruses at the top of my voice, singing every stanza and every part. And we sang outside of church, too. My public high school chorus was filled, and our rehearsal was listed as part of the regular weekly schedule of classes. It was a natural part of growing up to learn melody and harmony—soprano, alto, tenor, and bass.

My upbringing may have been a little unusual, but it would be nearly unheard of today—the age of Walkmans, concerts, videos and audiocassettes, compact discs, FM radio, and ever-present headphones and speakers.

The proliferation of these spectator media makes me sometimes wonder, *How will the next generation ever learn to sing?*

Misunderstanding the role of music in worship. In churches, sometimes the power and efficacy of music are unconsciously belittled or underestimated. We've all seen music used as filler: "Let's sing a song while the latecomers are seated," or "We have a little more time; let's sing that last stanza again." Other times music is considered merely a warm-up act for the sermon.

When music is demeaned like this, worship is diminished and congregational participation undermined. People won't fully participate—heartfully, soulfully—if they see the leaders treat music as an appendage to worship.

We often don't ask or expect enough of the art of music. It can reach, touch, and move people in countless ways. Underestimating it is like using a genie, with nearly limitless power, merely to do a few household chores for us.

It's been a joy for me to work with a pastor like Chuck Swindoll, a gifted communicator who also has a deep love and respect for the ministry of music. We sometimes receive comment cards (from visitors, I assume) that read, "Too much music. We came to hear Pastor Swindoll." But Chuck knows music is as essential to worship as the sermon is, so we give plenty of time to it. Whenever the congregation is singing, Chuck is never distracted, never reading his notes. He, too, is singing enthusiastically, modeling how singing should be regarded by all.

Lack of time. If a good sermon needs time to develop and drive home a point, so does authentic worship. Worship needs at least fifteen to twenty minutes to build. In our church, we normally devote thirty minutes to worship—congregational singing, special music, and Scripture readings.

In order to devote that kind of time, we strive to eliminate as many nonessentials as possible. We want to give maximum time to worship and congregational singing. We know sermonettes produce Christianettes, and we don't want to find out what shortened worship produces.

Poor acoustics. Strong congregational singing requires the support and encouragement of the room itself. Ideally, the room should capture and blend voices when people sing. Unfortunately, many sanctuaries are lacking in one way or another. In ours, for example, the quality of the sound varies from place to place and from service to service, especially when the room is only half full.

There are ways to compensate for various acoustical problems, but the technical dimension of acoustics is too complicated to go into here. Suffice it to say that it's an issue not to be ignored.

Creating a comfort zone

In music, as in most endeavors, there is strength in numbers. The average person in the pews is reluctant to project his or her own voice unless surrounded by a host of other voices. Most people don't think of themselves as singers, and they tend to be afraid of their voices. This can be a handicap in smaller churches. But with the right leadership, even this difficulty can be overcome.

One key is to create a comfort zone for the congregation, an atmosphere devoid of tension, where a spirit of warmth and friendliness pervades, where people are not embarrassed to "make a joyful noise to the Lord."

How do you create this kind of comfort zone? First, by your own personality. If you are friendly, warm, accessible, and confident, your congregation is more likely to respond in kind. I find that smiling often and speaking in pleasant, personal terms break down many barriers.

Second, by having proper accompaniment. People sing more confidently when surrounded and upheld by a full sound; they won't feel they stick out. When strong accompaniment provides an introduction that clearly establishes the tempo, intensity, and key, people sing the first lines more boldly.

Choosing the right instrument to accompany also helps. It would be difficult to render the strength and majesty of "A Mighty Fortress Is Our God" with a guitar, or even two or three. On the other hand, a meditative response like "He Is Lord" would go well with the more intimate sound produced by guitar strings.

Third, by selecting songs, at least in the beginning, that are easy to sing and well-known by the congregation. A good hymn doesn't need much direction. Examine a great piece like "Holy, Holy, Holy," and you'll find a straightforward succession of quarter notes, a simple rhythmic construction. But within that disarming simplicity are the beauty, strength, and majesty of the piece.

Fourth, by putting some songs in a lower key. I find many songs in our hymnals are written a step too high. When I select a hymn, I scan it for high notes. I try never to force a congregation to sing any note higher than D or E-flat, or an octave plus one above middle C. If a song is written higher than that, I ask my accompanist to transpose accordingly.

Fifth, paradoxically, by giving people permission not to participate. For various reasons, some people hesitate to join in sometimes. Often, when I'm introducing a new song or chorus, I'll have the choir sing it through, and then I'll say, "You may not know all the words yet, but feel free to join in and hum along. If you don't know the phrases, just listen to the words, because that's part of worship, too." Then we'll sing it two or three more times. When we give people permission simply to listen, they often gain the confidence to join in, and by the third set, most of the congregation is singing.

Sixth, by lightening the spirit of the group. This may mean injecting a little humor. However, humor can be tricky, even deadly, if it falls flat or is misunderstood. We've all seen music leaders try to perk up a lackluster hymn by good-naturedly chiding the congregation: "That was really lousy, folks! Let's try it again." Or, "Let's smile when we sing, okay?" Or, "Think about the words." We walk a fine line whenever we scold or lecture the congregation, even in good fun. Some people can pull it off, and some can't. Those who can't usually only dampen a congregation's desire to sing.

Instead, I lighten the group spirit by moving to a song with rhythm and life. I often reserve a song such as "This Is the Day" for that purpose. I'll say, "Let me sing to you, and then you answer, phrase upon phrase." Then I'll begin, "This is the day," and the congregation will echo, "This is the day." And I'll continue, "That the Lord has made," and go back and forth with the congregation, having fun with the song. A song like that can help people loosen up and relax, and they'll sing more heartily after that.

Joy is close to every other strong emotion, and once we've unleashed joy through our singing, we can move quickly as a group to any other emotion on the spectrum. We can be laughing one moment and deeply moved to compassion or touched with grief the next. If we've done our job in creating a comfort zone for joyful expression in song, the Holy Spirit has greater freedom to move among us, speak to us, and change our lives.

These are seemingly mundane concerns, yet they are crucial for powerful congregational singing. I see hymns as sacred folk music. Hymn leading is not a place for technical artistry, but for simplicity, for enthusiasm, for involving everyone in the worship experience.

Capturing and focusing the mood

Many people live emotionless lives, at least on the surface. In the routine of life, few of us are touched at the deepest point of our spiritual selves. Music is an emotional art form, communicating much more than the message of the words. Sacred music, especially, taps our deepest spiritual and emotional levels.

As a worship leader, I'm privileged to bring inspiration to people. My job is to take people to emotional and spiritual heights, to show them the vistas and ranges of their faith, to lead them beyond the merely cerebral level of Christianity.

I need to remember that people bring to worship a wide range of experiences, tensions, needs, and moods. One woman carries a heavy load of sorrow, the man next to her a burden of guilt. The family in the next pew had a shattering argument on the way to church. Behind them are a man thinking about a business deal that went sour, his wife, who is planning next week's dinner party, and their teenage daughter, who is daydreaming about her boyfriend. Worship leaders must find some way to focus the minds and hearts of these individuals so that, with true unity, they may lift their praise to God.

Congregational singing is one of our best tools for doing that. And visualizing worship as a funnel helps me channel that singing to a unified end.

The opening of the service is like the wide mouth of the funnel, wide enough to include the emotions and experiences of everyone in the congregation, whatever they are. So we begin with broad themes, with songs that deal with unassailable truths such as the power, sovereignty, immortality, and unchangeableness of God.

With each successive selection, as we move down the funnel, we narrow our focus more tightly to the theme or desired response of that service.

The selection of hymns has a powerful influence on the overall mood and worship experience. I like to think of the array of congregational songs as my toolbox. As a craftsman selects a hammer to drive a nail, and a screwdriver to set a screw, I use certain songs for certain tasks.

Some hymns fill us with religious awe: "A Mighty Fortress Is Our God." Other hymns touch us with the love of God: "Amazing love! How can it be that Thou, my God, shouldst die for me?" Yet other hymns quiet our hearts and call us to prayer: "Take from our souls the strain and stress / And may our ordered lives confess / The beauty of thy peace." And still other hymns soften our hearts and make us receptive to God's Spirit: "Just as I am, I come, I come."

By the time we get to the narrow end of the funnel, we can insert deeply personal songs—songs that call for an individual response or make some deep subjective impact. This would be the place for "Have Thine Own Way, Lord," "Open My Eyes That I May See," or "May the Mind of Christ, My Savior." Or we might choose two or three brief praise choruses that focus on our love for God— "Father, I Adore You" or "I love you, Lord, and I lift my voice"—simple, expressive, personal songs that people can offer to God without opening a hymnal.

Congregational singing, even though it's done with hundreds of other people, can be a powerful personal expression.

The funnel directs the emotional flow of the worship experience, prepares us for the ministry of the Word, and allows us to express response to God.

A checklist for congregational singing

Music ministry and juggling have this in common: you have to keep a lot of things in the air at the same time. Spiritual sensitivity, personal preparation, attention to group dynamics, thoughtful song selection, and full-bodied accompaniment are just a few of the ingredients that contribute to powerful congregational singing. Here's a mental checklist I use to keep our congregational singing effective.

Are the songs meaningful? Every worship leader needs to have the gentle and engaging sense of an educator. When I occasionally introduce a song by briefly describing its history or giving a new perspective on the theme, singing becomes more meaningful for the congregation.

I use a hymnal with a good set of indexes. I use the topical index to match our song selection to the theme of the service. Hymns that refer to specific Scripture passages can be found in the Scripture-allusions index. When that passage of Scripture is read before, after, or even between verses of the hymn, the singing becomes more significant.

Am I enthusiastic? I want to let people know worship is enjoyable. Excitement is infectious.

Am I cultivating eclectic tastes? I try to vary my choice of music. Since people speak different musical languages, we give people a variety of ways to express their worship. We avoid an either/or approach to traditional and contemporary music. We try to be both/and. The simple and spontaneous praise songs can find a powerful counterpoint in the strength and steel of hymnody.

Am I avoiding the routine? I want to keep worship fresh and alive. I'll use the metrical index to discover what familiar tunes will fit a new set of words (or vice versa). That's a great way to introduce new material and yet still have enough familiarity that people will participate.

Periodically, I'll teach the congregation a chorus that's not in the song book. Or we'll sing a cappella. Or I'll sit at the piano, talk a little about the history of the song or tie its theme into the sermon, and then lead them into the song. Or we'll try something visual or dramatic to introduce a song.

Am I explaining enough but not too much? The essence of every art is understatement. I don't want to draw the congregation's attention to every clever seam in our program; we want it to appear seamless. Likewise, we don't explain the significance of every song, even though there is one. We let our congregation discover many of the nuances of our worship.

Am I alert to the emotional energy of the congregation? I continually monitor how well I'm doing at creating that all-important comfort zone, capturing and conveying the mood of the music, funneling our congregation, and drawing all of our people into a unified experience of worship.

In the harmony of pitch, rhythm, and lyrics, the congregation comes together, breathes together, and feels together. There's something indescribably moving about a group of diverse individuals who become united by the Holy Spirit and energized by infectious enthusiasm, and then open their mouths and offer songs to God.

I dearly love choral singing; nothing challenges me more. Nonetheless, over the years I've been convinced again and again that our most important choir is the one in the pews.

25

A Structure Runs Through It

Both free-flowing praise and traditional hymns can be included in an extended time of worship.

—BARRY LIESCH

Some musicians, not to mention some longtime church members, find the move to worship choruses in today's churches threatening.

Organists, for example, can have difficulty getting the proper feel for choruses with a pipe organ, and they fear they will eventually find themselves on the periphery of the music ministry.

Others, raised on traditional hymns, find choruses repetitive and boring, the free-flowing praise format undisciplined and aimless.

At the same time, still others find the "hymn/announcements/ hymn/offering" order of service disjointed and distracting. And some younger musicians don't identify with the style of hymns and gospel songs, and they contend that hymns and choruses don't mix.

All are legitimate concerns. Can they be allayed? Yes!

I'm not out to persuade anyone to adopt any particular style, but I believe we benefit by understanding and occasionally blending the strengths of diverse styles. If we become more comprehensively skilled, we are more valuable instruments for God's kingdom.

Worship choruses won't disappear in the foreseeable future, nor will the call for hymns. Finding balance, to appreciate both expressive praise songs and traditional hymns, is possible. Both can be included in an extended time of free-flowing worship.

What is the rationale for this style?

Eddie Espinosa of The Vineyard in Anaheim Hills, California, likens free-flowing praise to sitting down to a leisurely meal around the family table where you linger and enjoy fellowship and warm conversation with one another.

He also likens it to a physical workout. Just as a sustained period of exercise benefits the cardiovascular system, sustaining worship for fifteen to forty minutes gives worshipers an uninterrupted, spiritual workout that strengthens them.

Both head and heart can be focused on the Lord. Extended worship allows time to offer the whole self (mind, will, and emotions) to God without distraction.

But leading such a worship experience requires a leader to understand the direction of the stream and how to channel the flow.

Five phases of a worship workout

Eddie Espinosa and John Wimber, pastor of The Vineyard, developed a five-phase pattern for their "worship set."

In their worship services, the choruses were short, and their worship set was long. Rather than singing songs in random order, they recognized the need to smoothly link the many choruses and provide a sense of progression.

They identified five different kinds of choruses and how they could be linked into a sequence. The five phases are (1) invitation, (2) engagement, (3) exaltation, (4) adoration, and (5) intimacy, with a summarizing close-out.

Espinosa finds scriptural support for the five-phase model in Psalm 95 (NIV):

Invitation: "Let us sing for joy . . . shout aloud."

Engagement: "Let us come before him with thanksgiving."

Exaltation: "For the LORD is the great God . . . the mountain peaks belong to him."

Adoration: "Come, let us bow down . . . let us kneel."

Intimacy: "For we are the people of his pasture, the flock under his care."

You can also arrange your chorus and hymn repertoire into these phases. Here are some guiding principles:

- worship that has a goal and direction
- worship that respects the psychological dimension
- worship that reflects the character of God (both transcendence and intimacy)
- lyrics that point to function (singing "about" and later "to" God)
- mixing of hymns and choruses (richness, variety)
- smooth transitions (linking both pieces and phases)
- avoiding distractions (not "jumping around")
- common tempos
- common words
- common keys
- adequate preparation yet open to the leading of the Spirit

Let's look at each phase in more detail.

Invitation

The invitation phase is a call to worship. It accepts people where they are and begins to draw them into God's presence. Most people need to wake up, warm up, and be energized before they're ready for the spiritually strenuous work of true worship.

The usual feeling in the invitation phase is celebratory, up-beat, and praise oriented (but not necessarily so). It may be accompanied by hand clapping. The lyrics are directed to the people, not God, telling them what they are about to do.

The chorus "Don't You Know It's Time to Praise the Lord?" is a good example of an invitation song:

Don't you know it's time to praise the Lord,
In the sanctuary of his Holy Spirit?
So set your mind on him. . . .

Notice how the lyric does the inviting and focusing without our having to resort to verbal scolding ("Can we have quiet!") or exhortation ("Put the worries of the world away and give attention to God"). The music can do that without the leader's having to lecture.

"The skillful leader woos the congregation into worship like the patient lover draws the beloved," says Paul Anderson, a Lutheran pastor in San Pedro, California.

For a vigorous call to worship with hand clapping, the Hebrew chorus "The Celebration Song" would be excellent, whereas a more mellow call could be "Let's Forget About Ourselves and Magnify the Lord and Worship Him," or "Come, Worship the Lord."

Traditional churches could use hymns during this phase and conclude with a scriptural call to worship. In the invitation phase, the leaders continue until they have made contact with the people and everyone is focused.

The invitation phase is particularly helpful for churches meeting in high school gymnasiums or other structures where worship symbols such as a Communion table, an open Bible, stained glass windows, banners, or other visual worship enhancements are absent.

Here's a list of song possibilities for the invitation phase. The assigned categories are not rigid; a song may serve in more than one category. The list includes both choruses and hymns:

"We Bring a Sacrifice of Praise"
"Don't You Know It's Time to Praise the Lord"
"I Just Came to Praise the Lord"
"Let's Forget About Ourselves"
"Spirit Song"
"Come, Worship the Lord"
"As We Gather"
"This Is the Day That the Lord Has Made"
"Come, Christians, Join to Sing"
"Praise the Savior, Ye Who Know Him"
"My Faith Has Found a Resting Place"
"Let's All Go Up to Zion"
"Come We That Love the Lord"

Engagement

In the engagement phase, people begin to turn their attention directly to God, not to one another. Often the lyrics are addressed specifically to God.

A good example of this kind of engagement is the traditional hymn:

> Come, Thou Almighty King,
> Help us Thy name to sing.

A more contemporary song that can serve in the engagement phase is "I Will Sing of the Mercies of the Lord."

Espinosa likens this phase to the engagement period before marriage, for the congregation is now attentive, serious, ready to fully focus on the wonderful attributes of the Beloved.

Some church cultures may be able to skip the invitation phase and begin here. Here are song possibilities for the engagement phase:

"Our God Is an Awesome God
"How Majestic"
"Rejoice in the Lord Always"
"He Is the King"
"Great and Mighty Is He"
"The Celebration Song"
"I Will Sing of the Mercies of the Lord"
"I Shall Prepare Him My Heart"
"O Worship the King"
"All Creatures of Our God and King"
"Guide Me, O Thou Great Jehovah"
"Come, Thou Almighty King"
"O for a Thousand Tongues to Sing"

Exaltation

In the exaltation phase, the people sing to the Lord with power, giving meaningful expression to the lofty words of transcendence—words like *great, majestic, worthy, reigns, Lord,* and *mountains.*

Musically, we generally use greater pitch spans than in the other phases. The high notes bring out a dynamic response and project a sense of God's greatness. If the people stand throughout the invitation, engagement, and exaltation phases, their response will be stronger.

Traditionally, hymns like "All Hail the Power of Jesus' Name" and "Immortal, Invisible, God Only Wise" are examples of exaltation.

Contemporary songs like "Majesty" and "Our God Reigns" are also appropriate.

These songs of praise prepare people for the more personal aspects of worship. Here are the song possibilities for the exaltation phase:

"All the Earth Shall Worship"
"Let There Be Glory and Honor and Praises"
"All Hail King Jesus"
"We Exalt Thee"
"Our God Reigns"
"Thou Art Worthy"
"Majesty"
"Crown Him with Many Crowns"
"Immortal, Invisible"
"Rejoice, the Lord Is King"
"How Great Thou Art"
"All Hail the Power of Jesus' Name

Adoration

In the adoration phase, people are usually seated, the dynamics gradually subside, the melody range may reduce to five or six notes, and the key words may be *you, Jesus,* and terms of personal worship and love, as in the chorus "We Worship and Adore You."

In the exaltation and adoration phases, two sides of God's character receive expression. Exaltation focuses on his transcendence (his wholly "Otherness"). The adoration phase focuses on his immanence (his closeness to us).

Here are some song options for this phase:

"We Worship and Adore You"
"Glorify Your Name"
"His Name Is Wonderful"
"I Love You, Lord"
"Emmanuel"
"Lord, We Praise You"
"Father, I Adore You"
"Praise Song"
"Fairest Lord Jesus"
"My Jesus, I Love Thee"
"Be Thou My Vision"
"Jesus, Priceless Treasure"
"Majestic Sweetness Sits Enthroned"
"Of the Father's Love Begotten"
"How Sweet the Name of Jesus Sounds"
"He Hideth My Soul"

Intimacy

The last phase moves from immanence to intimacy. This is the quietest and most personal expression of worship, with God addressed in terms such as *Abba*. The choruses "In Moments Like These" and "O Lord, You're Beautiful" reflect the tone of this phase.

This is the "kiss" of worship. One meaning for the Greek word for worship, *proskuneo*, is "to turn toward to kiss." Kissing requires closeness, which comes only if properly prepared for in the preceding phases.

While the lyrics in the exaltation phase may emphasize the corporate "we," in this phase they now take the personal dimension of "I," as in "Father, I Love You."

Sometimes it's a good idea to change the wording of familiar songs to make them fit this intimate phase. For instance, "our" can change to "my" in the lyric, "Marvelous grace of *my* loving Lord; grace that exceeds *my* sin and *my* guilt."

"Him/his" can be changed to "you/your" in " 'Tis so sweet to trust *you*, Jesus, just to take *you* at *your* word."

Musically, this usually means a softer mood. Percussion may not suit the intimacy phase.

The worship set ends when the people stand for a close-out chorus or hymn—"My Tribute," for instance—that leads out of intimacy and helps people adjust to the next event in the service.

Musically, I like big, summarizing pieces for the close-out. Textually, I prefer songs of dedication, aspiration, and exaltation, or songs related to the pastor's theme or the next item of the service.

Here are two sets of song possibilities, one for the intimacy phase and the other for closing out the entire set:

"O Lord, You're Beautiful"
"Turn Your Eyes upon Jesus"
"My Delight"
"Alleluia, Alleluia"
"As the Deer"
"Sweet Perfume"
"Holy Ground"
"In Moments Like These"
"Jesus, I Am Resting, Resting"
"Jesus, the Very Thought of Thee"
"Children of the Heavenly Father"
"Close to Thee"
"O to Be Like Thee"
"Savior, Like a Shepherd"
"I Need Thee Every Hour"
"In the Garden"

"We Are One in the Spirit"
"In My Life, Lord, Be Glorified"
"Holy, Holy, Holy"
"Shine, Jesus, Shine"
"He Is Able, More Than Able"
"Thank You, Lord, for Saving My Soul"
"Our God Reigns"
"It Is Well with My Soul"
"My Tribute"

"To God Be the Glory"
"And Can It Be"
"Our Great Savior"
"May the Mind"
"Fairest Lord Jesus"
Great Is Thy Faithfulness"
"Because He Lives"

A model worship set

We don't want to stumble or break our stride while running. Overall, think of the tempos the following way: invitation and engagement (running), exaltation (jogging), adoration (walking), and intimacy (stopping, silent communion, gazing).

Here's what a twenty-minute time of worship singing could look like.

Congregation stands:
Invitation
"We Bring a Sacrifice of Praise"
Key: D
Engagement
"Rejoice in the Lord Always"
Key: D
Exaltation
"Rejoice, the Lord Is King"
Key: B/C
"Crown Him with Many Crowns"
Key: C

Congregation is seated:
Exaltation/Adoration
"Glorify Your Name"
Key: B-flat/C
Adoration
"I Love You, Lord"
Key: F
Intimacy

"As the Deer Pants for the Water"
Key: C

Congregation stands:
Close
"Fairest Lord Jesus"
Key: D-flat/D

Granted, hymns *are* more difficult to incorporate into the model. Their wide range of thoughts introduced from stanza to stanza tend to spill over into more than one phase. On the other hand, choruses, usually containing only one major thought, tend to fall into a single phase easily.

When hymns are included in the set, organists can share in the worship. The organ can be particularly effective during a hymn of exaltation or the close-out.

Flexible strength

If you think of emotional development, the five-phase progression has a balanced, graduated arch with a high point in the middle.

If you use the five phases as a handy frame to guide your worship thinking, feel free to be flexible. Employ it to guide the entire worship service before the sermon, or use it in place of a prelude. Use it at the beginning or at the end of your service. Or use it for an entire Sunday evening sing-along.

You can also be flexible about time. You can follow the same progression in either long or short worship sets, with any number of hymns or choruses in any one phase. Prayers or readings can be included between phases.

I've experimented successfully with short sets (ten minutes) toward the middle of the morning service that focus exclusively on adoration. It works especially well when the set emerges out of a time of prayer, or in the Communion service.

The exaltation and adoration phases seem to form the core of the model. A good place for Scripture reading is between these phases.

I suggest beginning conservatively when introducing free-flowing praise into a traditional service format in a conservative church. First include one chorus as a "response to revelation." Extend that to two, then three continuous hymns/choruses. As your skill increases and the people become accustomed to the change, gradually lengthen the set.

One benefit of the model is it keeps us from jumping back and forth between categories in a worship set. Such jerking about is disorienting, results in a lack of direction, and distracts from the spiritual focus of the service.

It resembles a home decorated with clashing colors, furniture, and paintings. The five-phase model integrates the service and the people into a glorious house of worship.

"The glory of God is a man fully alive," said Irenaeus, "and the life of man consists in beholding God." I have found that free-flowing worship often helps a congregation behold God better than we have before, and Irenaeus is right: there's life in that.

26

A Dramatic Addition to Worship

Drama helps satisfy the desire within all of us to be understood, even in our secret parts.

—Steve Pederson

Two decades ago the use of drama in worship services was relatively rare. When it was used, drama was usually limited to a children's Christmas pageant or disciples in bathrobes and sandals appearing at the Easter sunrise service.

That was then. This is now.

Today, dramatic presentations in Sunday morning worship services are becoming as common as praise choruses or keyboards. Crossing geographical and doctrinal boundaries, the use of drama has mushroomed in recent years. There's no question that the media have helped create a taste for drama. People today are so bombarded with images and fast-paced appeal that we have to speak that language to be fully understood.

Drama is one of those "cultural cues" the church needs to read and take advantage of in reaching people. It has become an attractive option to those asking, "How can we do a better job in reaching people, both the churched and the unchurched, in a creative fashion, without compromising the gospel?"

For too long the church has relied on talking heads and robed choirs to reach people. Given the changes that have taken place in our culture, those two strategies won't work as well as they did in previous generations.

Worldly entertainment?

Drama in church is not without its critics. Some say it's "too worldly" to use in worship. But that criticism stems from a misunderstanding of the nature of drama itself. Art, at its core, is make-believe, though our job in drama is to make it seem as true to life as possible. We use the techniques of drama—movement, positioning, and scripting—to give it an air of reality.

People often ask how someone can take on the character of an unsavory individual without becoming like the person he or she is playing. They fear, for example, that if a woman plays the part of a prostitute, her own morals will become corrupted. They see it as tampering with sin and becoming "of the world."

The performers, though, don't actually believe they are the person they're playing; they're disconnected from their character. More often than not, they are just trying to remember their next line or whether they're at the right spot on the stage to maximize lighting. So there is little danger of their assuming the character and personality of the person they are depicting.

Those watching the drama also understand what's happening. They agree to engage in what art critics refer to as a "willing suspension of disbelief." They consciously pretend it's real.

Another concern is that by having a man and a woman play the role of husband and wife, we're playing with fire. Perhaps there is a danger, but I'm careful about the people I choose to act opposite each other. I know their spouses, I know the strength of their marriages, and I try to be sensitive to the situations I place them in.

Yet another concern is that drama is more entertainment than worship, and *entertainment* is a bad word in many churches today. It has suffered from guilt by association: we tend to think of it as tawdry, cheap, or titillating. When drama becomes showy, calling attention only to itself, it is wrong.

But entertainment itself is not evil. Entertainment can move us powerfully and touch us deeply with truth. When it paves the way for the pastor to deal with a significant, deeply felt issue, entertainment can be a positive addition to the service. It can be used to create a response of adoration or thanksgiving or confession, as a hymn or song might do.

Satisfying secret desires

I was a professor at Northwestern College in Orange City, Iowa, when Willow Creek contacted me to direct their drama ministry. Frankly, I was not all that excited. My initial reaction was, "No, I don't think so." The little drama I had observed in church settings I didn't like.

Most churches tended to define drama too narrowly. Either they would limit it to retelling biblical stories and dressing all the characters in bathrobes, or worse yet, they would attempt to preach a sermon through it, wrapping up everything with tidy answers in an eight-minute sketch. The drama didn't reflect reality as most people experienced it.

But after a closer look, I found the type of drama Willow Creek used to be appealing. Rather than trying to raise and answer all the questions through the sketch, they were content to raise the relevant issues, to show the tensions. Then the pastor addressed the issues in the sermon. So rather than using drama to solve the problem, Willow Creek wanted to expose the pain and get the audience to identify with the characters.

Drama creates identification by helping the audience see themselves in the characters. That's why we use primarily contemporary drama based on real-life experiences. The characters talk, act, and look like normal people. The audience members then realize the characters are dealing with the same problems found regularly at home, at work, or in marriage.

In that sense, drama helps satisfy the desire within all of us to be understood, even the secret parts of who we are.

Drama is people revealing their hidden parts, enabling us all to understand better the human condition. It creates a beginning place for the Holy Spirit to work in people's lives.

Hidden talent

Drama that works well begins with qualified leadership. At least one person with a working knowledge of the craft must be willing to lead the charge. The person doesn't need a Ph.D. in theater, but he or she does need to be gifted in the area of drama.

If the person lacks training, the church could invest in sending a promising person to a local college to take courses in directing and acting. I've seen too many church productions where some basic elements of good directing were absent. Bad drama is worse than no drama.

You don't need a large performing company to produce consistently good drama; you need a leader and a few good people. It can, in fact, involve only one or two performers, and one sketch takes only five or six hours of rehearsal. At Willow Creek, we rehearse twice a week, once on Tuesday evening and then on Saturday afternoon.

Many people who visit Willow Creek assume we use professional performers. That's not the case. Most of our actors have had little or no prior drama experience.

One of our best female performers had never acted before. She came to what was her first audition when she dropped off a friend. She happened to be standing in the hallway when someone invited her to try out. She ended up making the drama team while her friend did not. Today she's not only a terrific actress but also a top-notch writer. You don't know whom you might have in your church.

What's most universal

Two principles have helped us make drama an effective component of worship.

First, each sketch needs to work well with the pastor's message that follows it. A sketch that raises questions that the sermon doesn't answer later on creates a problem. A great deal of coordination between what the pastor is planning to say and what we're preparing to present on stage is necessary for success.

Second, each drama must be personal and address a specific

issue. One of our most powerful presentations involved a grown man going back to his boyhood school. There he is confronted by the painful memory of the day he and a few of his friends tied the class sissy to the radiator and then pulled his pants down. When the bell rang and the class entered, the victim was left standing there naked, alone, and humiliated.

The memory is particularly painful because the kid who was picked on committed suicide as an adult, and the man recalling the event had for years assumed some responsibility.

When I first read that script, I hesitated. The whole incident seemed too close to the edge to produce in church. But when we performed it, the audience reaction was immediate. They seemed to put themselves into one of three groups: (a) those who had picked on others, (b) those who had been picked on by others, or (c) those who had stood silently by as others were picked on.

Once after we performed the sketch in Europe, a missionary approached me and said, "That sketch was the most powerful dramatic experience I've ever had."

"Really?" I asked. "What made it so powerful?"

"I grew up in a Christian boarding school," he replied. "Things happened in that school that I've never shared with anyone. When I saw the sketch, I wept as it all came back."

What's amazing is that this was only a seven-minute sketch, not a major production. It just goes to show the truth of the statement, "That which is most personal is also most universal," which I have hanging above my desk. That's one reason why I urge our writers to write from their own experience.

One of our writers wrote a script that portrayed an angry father, criticizing his daughter for the way she was raising her kids. I read it and thought, *Wait a minute. This is too much. This guy seems too vindictive and mean.*

But I went ahead with it and was literally overwhelmed by the response. Numerous people approached me and said, "That was my dad."

Checking the thermometers

Measuring drama's effectiveness is not easy. I typically watch people's reactions, and I also place "thermometers" in the congregation who tell me how they think we did. If people didn't laugh at a line I thought they would, I make adjustments. If something falls flat the first service, I won't hesitate to change it before the second one.

Audience reaction, though, is an inexact science. When we touch on sensitive topics, such as abortion, we know we may get mail. We make a concerted effort to be realistic, and that offends some people. Others are upset because the sketch itself isn't more polemic. But again, our main purpose is to raise issues that the pastor will answer.

To avoid offending some people's sensibilities, each director needs to be attuned to his or her congregation. Respecting your audience, not trying to push them as far as you can, is important. Artists are often unwilling to make concessions to people's sensibilities.

If I were launching drama in a church, my first sketch would not be on a highly sensitive issue, such as homosexuality. I'd start with a sketch that contains clear gospel content, such as a mime we do entitled "The Lane of Life." Introduce it on a Sunday evening, or as part of a youth night, or at an alternative service.

In our efforts to be honest, however, we do face hard calls. When I have questions, "Is this word proper?" or "Is this subject matter too volatile?" I run the piece by others. If we still aren't sure, we'll take it to a pastor or an elder. The beauty of a team decision is that we all share the responsibility for the calls we make.

Identifying with pain

Through the years, our drama has evolved. I'd say it has become more sophisticated, less like a skit (we prefer the term *sketch*) and more substantive. We also use more serious drama than we used to. Today we do sketches we couldn't have done five years ago. That doesn't mean today's dramas contain vulgar language or offensive content—far from it. But the audience has grown and matured in its willingness to consider difficult and sensitive topics.

A turning point came with a piece entitled "Great Expectations." The story focused on an infertile woman who had been waiting to adopt a baby for years. She was just three hours from picking up the child when the birth mother changed her mind. It went on to depict the woman's anger at God. The sketch raised the question, "Why does God dangle a carrot in front of our nose only to yank it away from us?"

So many people identified with the pain of this couple. We've used it numerous times in various settings. We've learned that serious drama, when done well, can be even more effective than lighter sketches.

PART 8

Presence

27

The Crux of Communion

*The decisions we make about Communion have
no small influence on others.*

—CRAIG BRIAN LARSON

Communion has been a theological battleground for centuries.
For today's working pastors, however, many of the issues sur-
rounding Communion seem more practical than theological.
They're often questions about how to make the service as mean-
ingful as possible for those who should and should not partake.
Questions include:

- What spirit do we want to surround Communion? Celebration? Solemn reflection?
- Who can take Communion? What about the person who "does
  not discern the body and blood of Christ"?
- How do we train people in their understanding of Communion? How do we work with people who feel unworthy to
  come—though we think they should?

To get answers to these and other questions, I talked with
respected pastors from a variety of theological traditions. Their
varied answers provide a menu of choices to help better set the
Lord's Table.

A varied focus

When I asked what spirit these pastors want to surround Communion, I found unanimous agreement on one thing: the need for variety.

"I don't find in the Bible a singular heart-set with which to approach Communion," says Bob Shank, pastor of South Coast Community Church in Newport Beach, California. "There are times when it's appropriate to take Communion contemplatively, with a deep sense of quiet reverence and awe. Other times it's appropriate for the family to be together around the table with a sense of release and joy, recognizing what Communion looks forward to and what it has done to paint our present differently. The one thing the Bible does say is we are never to do it frivolously."

Tim Keller, of Redeemer Presbyterian Church in Manhattan, sees the sacrament as an extension of the ministry of the Word. The spirit of Communion "depends upon the subject of the sermon," Keller says. "The sacrament is every bit as variegated in its hues and colors as the sermon would be. The sacrament can be administered as an evangelistic event, a repentance event, a fellowship event. The Lord's Supper means all those things. I don't think you can possibly do all those things every time you do the Lord's Supper, any more than you can do all those things every time you preach."

For that reason most pastors plan ahead to pursue a single emphasis for each Communion service. Gary Fenton, pastor of Dawson Memorial Baptist Church in Birmingham, Alabama, says they focus most often on one of three things: joy over our forgiveness, reflection upon the great sacrifice of Christ, or a renewal of our salvation experience.

Although he pursues a single theme, Daniel Brown, a Foursquare pastor in Aptos, California, has a dual focus. "We want to focus on a dimension in Communion that is ageless and traditional. But we also seek a present dynamic. I point people to some aspect of how God wants to provide today."

When Christianity is exclusive

The issue of who can take Communion invited diverse responses.

Dawson Memorial Baptist follows a simple approach that Communion is for those who have accepted Christ as their Savior and Lord, and they leave the question of who partakes up to the conscience of the individual.

The issue of who decides who is qualified is a sticking point for other churches, however.

"The Bible doesn't say how we are to ensure that people taking the Lord's Supper are eating and drinking worthily," says Tim Keller. "Presbyterians have decided a person shouldn't be self-accredited. Instead a person should have his or her testimony heard by a church, which will judge whether the profession of faith is credible. People have odd and often deluded understandings of what it means to be a Christian, so others need to check it out.

"In effect this means a person must be baptized or a member of some church, not necessarily ours, to take Communion with us. That's an inference from the Bible that I couldn't prove directly, but we are trying to safeguard the table by telling people they can't be self-appointed."

Since all churches require that those who take Communion meet certain conditions, some people present in the service will be excluded from participating. That idea doesn't always go over well in our tolerant, inclusive society. How do church leaders explain that without unnecessarily alienating seekers?

Daniel Brown stresses to the congregation, "It's the Lord's Table and not ours. He's the One who made the bread and cup possible. Anyone who has a relationship with Jesus Christ can partake of Communion. If you don't have a relationship with Christ, partaking of Communion would be at best a meaningless exercise, and at worst it could be a kind of mockery or sacrilege. If you don't yet have a relationship with the Lord, just be at ease and wait to partake until you do."

To unbelievers, Gary Fenton presents Communion as a learning time. "This service is an opportunity to observe and sense the reality behind the symbols."

Churches that emphasize ministry to seekers have a unique challenge. Bob Shank's church has no formal membership, and they expect and encourage the presence of not-yet-committed people in their ranks. Therefore they celebrate the Lord's Table in settings where they expect the family of God to be together, which primarily is their Wednesday night service.

Even so, seekers are present. Shank therefore explains to the congregation, "Communion is for those who are clear about their relationship with Christ. They have experienced on the inside something they are about to experience on the outside. While the church in most of its meetings is very inclusive, Communion by God's definition is exclusive."

Then Shank invites those who are not yet believers to do one of two things: "One, feel completely free not to participate without any sense of being uncomfortable. Or two, recognize that this is a moment when a personal expression of faith can happen for the first time."

Shank says that Communion can almost be seen as "walking the aisle." For that reason the church intentionally schedules several Communion services during the year in settings where they expect seekers to be in attendance, such as at Christmas services.

Redeemer Presbyterian gives people who are not taking the Lord's Supper spiritual exercises in the bulletin, skeletal prayers they can use during that time. "We invite everybody to do business with God," Keller says to the congregation. "We are not excluding anybody. You who are not yet believers should not partake, but we invite you to do business with God."

Keller says there are three groups of people in a Communion service: Christians who are communing, Christians who are not communing because they know they are holding on to certain sins, and non-Christians. All three groups need to be led spiritually about how to draw nearer to God during Communion.

Keeping Communion holy

The Lord's Supper is a holy sacrament. I asked pastors what responsibility church leaders bear in keeping it so. The consensus was that pastors must articulate the standards. Beyond that only in the most extreme circumstances would a pastor be responsible to enforce them.

Bob Shank feels pastors are responsible to officiate at Communion or ensure that those who do officiate understand the full meaning of Christ's work on the cross. The Lord's Supper is the moment when the chief undershepherd in a local church is responsible before God and the congregation to make sure that Communion is understood theologically and personally.

Daniel Brown feels an additional obligation to ensure that Communion is meaningful to participants. "My responsibility is to make sure that Communion never becomes rote," he says, "just a repeated set of words or activities. For me that means showing people how Communion is relevant for their lives today, that Jesus died for them. At Communion I might talk about how Jesus can soothe our painful memories, forgive us for our bitterness, or heal us of the wounds others have given us. Every time we do Communion, I try to focus on some particular need. To me that keeps it holy and powerful."

Recognizing the need for keeping Communion holy, what do pastors do and say prior to Communion to keep people from being too casual?

At Dawson Memorial Baptist the table used for the Lord's Supper is only in the sanctuary on the Sundays when they have Communion. There are a single loaf and the chalice in the front. When the table and elements are in place, people know the service is special.

"At times I will explain that historically the Lord's Supper has been taken to extremes," says Fenton. "In the early church it became such a celebration that they lost its meaning. On the other hand, we can make it such a solemn occasion that we miss the joy. I tell people the Lord's Supper is to be an event in which there is joy with dignity. Although in other services I may at-

tempt to find a common bond through humor, I deliberately
avoid that on the days of the Lord's Supper."

At the Coastlands Church, Pastor Daniel Brown feels doing
something different is one way they communicate the significance of Communion. They are an "electronic" church, with syn-
thesizers and electronic drums and guitars, but during Communion their worship team moves to the acoustic piano. From the
piano they lead worship without amplification. That changes the
atmosphere and mood.

Who's in, who's out

The question of how someone partakes of Communion in an
unworthy manner brought general agreement that the real issue
is understanding and attitude.

"We take Communion in an unworthy manner," says Gary
Fenton, "when we do not remember or understand the significance of the event. I don't think it has much to do with the
character of the person, the recent acts of wrong behavior, as
much as it does with not understanding Christ. If a person does
not understand grace, he or she takes it in an unworthy manner
because it is a grace event. It's a visual reminder that salvation is
by God's gift of Jesus Christ, rather than through our own
works. Salvation is through his blood and body."

Bob Shank believes that taking Communion in an unworthy
manner means approaching the table in a frivolous manner,
minimizing the cost of what is behind it and what it reflects.

But according to Tim Keller, there is a sense in which our
current behavior is an issue. He tells the congregation, "If you
know not only that you are sinning but that you are planning to
sin—if you know, for example, that you're doing something ille-
gal or immoral and you're not going to change—then you should
not participate."

Some people are unworthy to partake of Communion. Others
who should partake feel unworthy. A legalistic background can
cause many to refuse the invitation to the Lord's Table.

All of our responding pastors agreed that when sincere believers feel unworthy, the problem is, they don't understand grace. For a believer in Christ to feel unworthy to take Communion is a contradiction in terms. If someone confesses their sin, he or she has forgiveness in Christ. The purpose of Communion is to remind us we stand in our relationship with God not on the basis of how worthy or perfect we are but on the worthiness of the Lamb.

"If you have sinned horribly, but you are repentant," Tim Keller tells the congregation, "then you need to come. Not to come because you feel unworthy is a denial of the gospel. What you're really saying is, Jesus Christ is not a sufficient offering to bring you into the presence of God. You feel you have to bring at least three good days with you, or a couple of weeks of decent behavior. That's a total denial of the gospel."

Table training

With the diversity of church traditions surrounding Communion, we can assume there is a fair amount of confusion on the subject among the people in the pews. How can churches train people to rightly understand Communion?

Our pastors agree that preaching sermons on the subject is not the answer. Turnover in churches is simply too high. Membership classes offer a fitting opportunity to cover the subject, but they reach a limited population. So constant training is vital; each time the church receives Communion, pastors feel obligated to give a mini-teaching on the subject—in terms that even an uninitiated person can readily understand.

Tim Keller, who has preached a sermon on Communion only once in five years, says that soon on the days they serve the Lord's Supper, they will put an informative insert in the bulletin so the pastor doesn't have to cover all the ground verbally.

At Dawson Memorial Baptist, where they serve Communion approximately once a quarter, Gary Fenton presents a children's sermon each time on the Lord's Supper.

"That's the best means I've found of presenting it to adults as well as children," says Fenton. "We use three symbols to help the children (and indirectly the adults) understand the symbolic meaning of the bread and the cup: a wedding band, an American flag, and a hymnal. 'If I lose my wedding band,' I say, 'I'm still married; if a person does not take the Lord's Supper, it does not mean he or she is not a Christian. The flag is not America; it only makes us think of America. A hymnal has no music or sound in it; but when a trained person looks at the notes, she's able to produce the sound. In the same way, the bread and the cup we hold in our hands do not make us a Christian.' "

In most Communion services, there will be some present whom we might call seekers, or unchurched, some of whom might consider the rite odd. How can pastors explain Communion to them?

Bob Shank assumes that when seekers are present in a service in which Communion is being served (they normally serve Communion on Wednesday night), it is not that person's first encounter with their church. Seekers understand that things like baptism and Communion are germane to church life, and they aren't surprised by them. "I've never had a seeker come to me and say, 'I know nothing about Communion and it shocks me that you do it,' " says Shank.

He carefully explains the meaning behind the bread and cup, he says, in inclusive rather than exclusive language, never using a term like *propitiation* without explaining what it means.

Putting seekers at ease about what will happen during Communion, believes Daniel Brown, is vital. He assures them that it's his job to make sure they don't stand out or feel awkward, that he will always give them signals about what to do.

For example, he will say, "When everybody else in your row stands up to file up to the front, if you stay seated, people will trip over you coming and going. So the best thing for you to do is stand up with everybody else and file up front. If you don't take any bread when you file past me, I'm not going to say, 'Hey, buddy, you forgot to take the bread.' " Such comments help disarm seekers.

One hundred or more first-time visitors attend Redeemer Presbyterian every Sunday. At first Tim Keller thought that would present major obstacles to serving the Lord's Supper.

"I discovered an amazing thing, though," says Keller. "When the Lord's Supper comes around, the unbeliever is forced to ask, 'Where am I?' Communion is a specific and extremely visible way to see the difference between walking with Christ and living for yourself. The Lord's Supper confronts people with the questions: Are you right with God today? On which side of the line are you?"

One woman came up to Keller after a service and said, "I've been coming here for three months. I thought I was a Christian when I started coming, even though I hadn't gone to church since I was a little girl. I haven't come here every week, so somehow I missed other Communion services. When I got here today, I read the things about Communion in the bulletin and realized that I wasn't sure I was a Christian."

She decided she wanted to make sure. She gave her life to Christ as the bread and cup were being shared. She participated in Communion and told Keller that she felt her whole life changed.

"I don't think there's any more effective way to help a person do a spiritual inventory," says Keller. "Many seekers in the United States will realize they are non-Christians only during the Lord's Supper. At our church we may begin doing the Lord's Supper more often because we're realizing what a powerful evangelistic tool it is."

What's right, what's wrong

It seems that all churches take unique positions about the logistical issues surrounding Communion, such as who serves and how. Regarding such practical issues, there is no right or wrong; the deciding factors are personal preference and what values a church wants to emphasize.

At Dawson Memorial Baptist Church, the elements are kept in the back of the sanctuary, and servers always come from the back rather than stand up front. Only a single loaf and the chalice are at the front. Fenton feels this emphasizes the individual faith that each of us must have in Christ.

At South Coast Community Church, they don't fit Communion into a conventional service. Rather, in an evening in which there is no preaching, Communion is "the capstone of a service that celebrates our relationship with one another in common worship," says Shank. "We're hearing from God through the Word; we're hearing from our neighbors in our shared worship; we recognize our common creed with the appropriate celebration of the Communion."

Tim Keller likes passing trays through the auditorium instead of having people come forward. That way the person who serves you is the person on your right or left. It's a way for the people to minister to each other. One way they try to communicate that they are one body is they allow more than officers and leaders to pass the trays. They encourage all kinds of people to participate in the passing out of Communion.

"Theology is so rich," says Keller. "There's always some tension between expressing the unity of the church and the purity of the church. When you stress the one, it tends to narrow you on the other. We've decided to emphasize the unity of the church."

At the Coastlands, by contrast, people file to the front where Daniel Brown serves the people one by one. He holds a basket of broken matzo bread, and as people take the bread, he welcomes them, by name if possible, and speaks a blessing upon them.

This affords Brown a brief, personal touch. People in the congregation report they appreciate this approach for an additional reason. "Members sit and watch each person come," says Brown. "Many in the congregation find themselves thanking God for individuals as they go by. It gives us a family feeling."

A visual reminder

The decisions we make about Communion have no small influence on others.

"I grew up a preacher's kid," says Gary Fenton. "I despised the Lord's Supper. I found no joy in it. If I didn't take it because I felt unworthy, that brought pain. If I did participate, I always had questions about whether I was worthy, and I left feeling down. I always walked out of church feeling like a failure.

"Early in the ministry I found as a pastor I was dreading the Lord's Supper. I did it every so often because we were supposed to. But in the late 1970s, I began to understand the Lord's Supper as the visual reminder that salvation is by grace, not law. I made a commitment that the Lord's Supper would never be legalistic or boring.

"Since then, Communion has become one of the high moments of worship for me. It is one of my favorite services of the year. My adrenaline runs high. I love to prepare my Lord's Supper message!"

Communion—with appropriate preparation, it stands as one of the highlights of a church's life.

28

Worshipful Weddings

As pastors we have the best seat in the house; we witness point-blank the tender exchange of a loving couple's commitment before God, their family, and friends.

—R. KENT HUGHES

Almost everyone has a wedding story to tell, and it's usually slapstick. From the twenty years I have performed weddings, I have my share.

I've seen grooms so wobbly-kneed they had to be propped in a chair to finish the ceremony.

On other occasions, despite my traditional caveat to the wedding party not to lock their legs lest circulation be cut off and someone pass out, that warning seems only to function as a "sure word of prophecy." At one of those times, a garden wedding, the groom's brother crashed into the ivy during the prayer and did not wake up until after the kiss. The next week I dramatically warned another wedding party, using my fresh illustration. The result? The bride's brother passed out, also during the prayer, and actually bounced on the slate floor, again missing the nuptial salute! The best-laid plans . . .

Another time the groomsmen and ushers were shorted a couple of bow ties by their tuxedo service, which created a comical Laurel-and-Hardy foyer as they frantically exchanged ties as their duties came up.

Weddings, because they are idealized and romanticized, provide ample occasion for such "disasters," which invariably become fond memories as the years pass. "Remember when Uncle Joe hit the ivy?" "Yeah, it was great!"

Yet for the most part, weddings are wonderfully uneventful, and the pastor's participation a pleasant remembrance. As pastors we have the best seat in the house; we witness point-blank the tender exchange of a loving couple's commitment before God, their family, and friends. We see the flushed cheeks, moist eyes, trembling hands, and the nuanced gestures of this most sacred time. It is an immense privilege.

What are the important principles in planning and carrying out this privilege? How do we minimize the follies and maximize the sacredness? The key is to remember—throughout the planning, the rehearsal, and the ceremony itself—that the Christian wedding is a *worship* celebration. As we will see, this has several practical implications.

The planning session

Early in the preparation stage, usually about four months before the wedding, I invite the couple to my office to plan the ceremony, urging that both attend, if possible. I normally schedule thirty and no more than forty-five minutes for this time.

With coffee in hand and after we have visited a few minutes and prayed, I briefly outline the theology of Christian marriage. I emphasize that a wedding ceremony is a time of worship, of reverence, because in Christian marriage the man and the woman commit themselves to God as well as to each other (Rom. 12:1). I point out that while their human relationship will be showcased in the ceremony, it is not to be a show, for worship cannot be so.

Personally, I'm glad we seem to have passed the period when each wedding had to be a self-conscious production, with colored tuxes, bride and groom singing to each other, and lots of pressure on everyone to perform for the crowd. Lance Morrow, in a 1983 *Time* essay titled "The Hazards of Homemade Vows," warns against making the ceremony a display case for unbridled creativity:

> Some couples remain tempted by the opportunity a wedding offers for self-expression. It is a temptation that should be resisted.

. . . If the bride and groom have intimacies to whisper, there are private places for that. A wedding is public business. That is the point of it. The couple are not merely marrying one another. They are, at least in part, submitting themselves to the larger logics of life, to the survival of the community, to life itself. . . . At the moment of their binding, they should subsume their egos into that larger business within which their small lyricisms become tinny and exhibitionistic.

Also, while it is nice to have the vows memorized, generally I discourage couples who want to recite them from memory during the ceremony. The stress of the wedding day is enough without this added pressure. I want the couple to relax, to enjoy the event, to *worship* as effectively as possible.

So I make sure the couple understands these implications of planning the ceremony as a worship service.

But at the same time, I emphasize that worship does not mean the ceremony has to be somber. We're celebrating a wedding, not a funeral. I remind them that Christ saw weddings as occasions of great joy. In fact he performed his first miracle at a tiny wedding in Cana, changing the water to wine, a symbol of joy. Thus the wedding is worshipful and joyful celebration—and that is what I hope to help them achieve. Here, I always stress how honored I am to participate in such an event.

Next I give them a Wedding Ceremony Planning Sheet (see end of chapter), which outlines a typical ceremony. I explain this is simply a suggested outline—the order is negotiable, as are the contents. If there are other elements they prefer, they will probably be okay, if appropriate for worship.

The planning sheet, I've found, has a calming effect on the couple. The typical bride and groom are intimidated by the ceremony. It seems so arcane, so mysterious. The planning sheet immediately puts them at ease and acquaints them with their options as to special music, hymns, and personal innovations. Most couples become visibly relaxed and enthused.

From the pastor's perspective, it provides a quick, clear explanation. Normally, it takes no more than ten minutes to walk the couple through the planning sheet. I figure this approach has saved me hundreds of hours over the years.

After we discuss the content, I reconfirm the times for the wedding and the rehearsal, double-checking my own calendar and having my secretary do likewise with the church's master calendar. I then lay out the schedule of events. My rule of thumb is that the sanctuary should be clear forty-five minutes before the ceremony. For example, a schedule for a 1:00 P.M. wedding would be:

10:45–11:15 A.M.: Party arrives and dresses.

11:15–12:15 P.M.: photographs.

1:00 P.M.: Ceremony begins.

The rehearsal is normally best held the night before, for the convenience of out-of-town participants. My recommendation is to set it early, about 6:00 P.M. Because people are notoriously late to rehearsals, I ask them to be there fifteen minutes before we plan to begin. This means the rehearsal dinner can begin at a reasonable time. It also means a busy pastor can get to bed at a reasonable hour—maybe!

I also advise the couple on who should attend the rehearsal: the wedding party (groomsmen, bridesmaids, flower girl, ring bearer, and ushers), both sets of parents, the organist, other musicians, and the vocalists.

When the schedule is agreed upon, I ask the couple to repeat it back to me.

The next item I arrange is the appointment of a wedding coordinator. A wedding coordinator is by no means a big-church luxury; this person is essential if the pastor is to be a good steward of time. Many smaller churches I know have a volunteer wedding coordinator. But if such a position is not possible, it will still be to your advantage to appoint someone to help coordinate the rehearsal and wedding—traditionally an aunt, a relative, or some friend experienced with weddings.

This person performs three important functions. First, she advises the bride as to the church's policies regarding music, the use of candles, photography, the sound system, dressing rooms, and even the cleanup expected. She can be of help in suggesting florists, caterers, dinner sites, and the myriad other details involved in a wedding. Second, she presides at the wedding rehearsal along with the pastor. Third, she coordinates the wedding plans, and thus takes much of the pressure off the bride and wedding party.

Finally, I suggest to the couple that a nice way to spiritually prepare for their wedding is to read the Psalms in reverse order as a countdown to their wedding day. For example, if there are ninety days until the big day, read Psalm 90, then the next day Psalm 89, and so on. My wife and I did this before our wedding, and we enjoyed these poetic expressions of praise. Couples have told me, "It was great to know we were both reading the same things each day."

The session is concluded with a time of prayer—and a reminder to bring the wedding license to the rehearsal.

The rehearsal

Here's the typical agenda:

Greeting. I invite everyone to the front rows of the church. I introduce myself and briefly share my perspective that weddings are times of reverential worship and joy and that *both* are my goals for the ceremony. I also give a quick overview of the rehearsal agenda.

Prayer. I lead the wedding party in asking God's blessing on the service, reaffirming the purpose of the ceremony.

Introductions. I then introduce the wedding coordinator, expressing appreciation for her work and competence. She presides over the remaining introductions.

Instructions. The coordinator reviews several important items. She restates the *time* of the wedding and the time everyone must be there, and she asks the group to repeat it back to her. She offers reminders for *dressing,* telling the men, for instance, that when they pick up their tuxedos, they should try on the suit and the shirt to check the fit and should also make sure the tie, cuff links, suspenders, and shoes are included. Groomsmen and bridesmaids are shown their respective dressing rooms after the rehearsal. She gives advice about *posture,* including the warning about locking the legs and instructions to the men to keep their hands at their sides and smile.

Last, the coordinator displays her Emergency Kit (a carryall bag). It contains "everything experience has shown us people forget," she says with a smile. "What do you think is in here?"

With some good-natured joking, she describes the contents: thread (selection of colors), needles, pins, shirt buttons, thimble, pin cushion, scissors, nail file and emery board, nail polish, hair spray, bobby and hair pins, comb, mirror, talcum powder, tissues, breath mints, aspirin, antacid, small first-aid kit, capsules of ammonia, static cling spray, lint clothes brush, cleaning fluid, pen, pencil, plain envelopes, name tags ("in case you forget who you are!"), all-purpose glue, cellophane tape, masking tape, matches, and tape measure.

Perhaps the real purpose of the Emergency Kit, however, is to assure the nervous couple they are indeed in good hands, and they can relax and enjoy the occasion.

We then walk through the entire ceremony. Afterward, the bride and groom, the maid of honor, and the best man meet with me to sign most of the wedding certificate, leaving only a couple of signatures for the next day.

The ceremony

As pastor, I have always made it my business to be present during those forty-five minutes before the wedding to soothe frazzled nerves and complete the signing of the marriage documents. My role is to be calm and unflappable, to care for the couple, reassuring them everything will go well, and to remind them their role is to enjoy this moment.

But even more, I am there to pray separately with the groomsmen and bridesmaids, inviting God's blessing on the moments to follow, asking that he will preserve in their hearts and minds the sacred ambiance of the candlelit sanctuary, the radiant faces of well-wishing family and friends, and the joy of love exchanged in holy commitment.

During the ceremony, my role is to remind the people, by

word and bearing, that this is a worship service. I try to guard against talking too fast or saying the familiar words in a perfunctory manner. Wanting this to be a personal experience, I speak directly yet conversationally to the two people in front of me, not to the crowd behind them.

I also make creative use of silence, which we so rarely enjoy these days. For instance, I prefer no music at all when the bride ascends the platform, so everyone can hear the rustle of the dress.

Then the couple repeat solemn vows very similar to those said by their parents and ancestors, thus affirming their solidarity with the past and their fidelity to the high call of God.

I'm sometimes surprised but always delighted by how my attention to a few details during the preparation, rehearsal, and ceremony can release the couple from nervous tension. When I am able to move a couple's thinking from anxious performance to tender worship, I feel I've accomplished my pastoral role.

WEDDING CEREMONY PLANNING SHEET

PRELUDE
   Time prelude begins: Time candles lighted:
SOLO/SPECIAL MUSIC (optional)
SEAT MOTHERS
AISLE RUNNER (optional)
PROCESSIONAL
PRESENTATION OF BRIDE
WELCOME/CALL TO WORSHIP
   Example: *We are gathered here to worship God and to witness the marriage vows of _____ and _____ (full names). Let your light so shine before people that they may see your good works and give glory to your Father who is in heaven. Let us worship God.*
CHARGE
   Example: _____ *and* _____, *marriage is an honorable estate whose bond and covenant were instituted by God in creation. Our Lord Jesus Christ adorned and beautified this holy estate by his presence and first miracle at a wedding in Cana of Galilee. It signi-*

fies to us the mystery of the union between Christ and his Church. And the holy Scripture commends it to be honored among all people. Therefore, no one should enter this state of life unadvisedly, lightly, or wantonly; but reverently, discreetly, advisedly, soberly, and in the fear of God; duly considering the causes for which matrimony was ordained.

CONGREGATION SEATED

DECLARATION OF INTENT

    Example: "_____, *will you take* _____ *to be your wife, and will you be faithful to her, love her, honor her, live with her, and cherish her, according to the commandments of God in holy marriage?"*

    "_____, *will you take* _____ *to be your husband, and will you be faithful to him, love him, honor him, live with him, and cherish him, according to the commandments of God in holy marriage?"*

PRAYER

ASCEND PLATFORM

HYMN or SPECIAL MUSIC (may go *before* ascending platform)

SCRIPTURES

    Examples: Gen. 2:18–23; Eccles. 4:19–21; Matt. 5:13–16; John 2:1; Eph. 5:21–33; Col. 3:12–17; 1 John 4:7–12; Song of Songs 8:6–7.

HOMILY (7–10 minutes)

VOWS

    Example: "*I,* _____, *take you* _____, *to be my wedded wife, to have and to hold from this day forward, for better or for worse, for richer or for poorer, in sickness and in health, to love and to cherish, and according to God's holy plan, I give you my love."*

    "*I,* _____, *take you,* _____, *to be my wedded husband . . ."* (*as above*)

RING

    "_____/_____, *what token do you give of your love?"*

    "A ring."

    "_____, *with this ring I thee wed, and with all my worldly goods I thee endow; in the name of the Father, and of the Son, and of the Holy Spirit. Amen."*

PRAYER

Example: *Bless, O Lord, these rings to be a symbol of the solemn vows by which this man and this woman have bound themselves to each other in holy matrimony, through Jesus Christ our Lord. Amen.*
DECLARATION

Those whom God has joined together let no one put asunder.
PRONOUNCEMENT

Example: *Forasmuch as* _____ *and* _____ *have consented together in holy wedlock, and have witnessed the same before God and this congregation, and in so doing have given and pledged their vows to each other, and have declared the same by the giving and receiving of a ring, I pronounce them man and wife together, in the name of the Father, and of the Son, and of the Holy Spirit. Amen.*
LIGHTING OF CHRIST OR UNITY CANDLE (optional)
VOWS OF THE CHRISTIAN HOME (optional)

Depending upon God for strength and wisdom, we pledge ourselves to the establishment of a Christian home. Together we will constantly seek God's will and honor Christ in our marriage.
PRAYER (kneeling)
SOLO or SPECIAL MUSIC (optional)
KISS
RECESSIONAL

29

Life-Giving Funerals

How we bury the dead goes a long way in determining our acceptance in a community and the depth of our spiritual impact on a congregation.

—Calvin Ratz

I love funerals. Not that I enjoy death, it's just that I agree with Solomon, who said, "It is better to go to a house of mourning than to go to a house of feasting" (Eccles. 7:2 NIV). After talking and praying with the bereaved, I go home feeling I've made a difference; I've touched people at the point of their deepest need.

Burying the dead is part of pastoral turf. How we handle it goes a long way in determining our acceptance in a community and the depth of our spiritual impact on a congregation. Any strengths I muster can lose their power if I can't help people who are bereaved.

A well-handled funeral can be the best opportunity for genuine public relations a church and its pastor can have. It doesn't lead to instant church growth, but it breaks down barriers and builds an attitude of respect and appreciation. It's a positive point of contact with people who have drifted away from the church.

Whenever I've gone to a new congregation, I realize my first funeral is a chance to let the people see a side of me not obvious from the pulpit. Parishioners are initially skeptical about a new leader. They're wondering what the new pastor will be like and how much they can trust him or her. When they see me conduct a funeral service, people notice whether I care about them as individuals, even in their darkest moments.

The pastor's role

I was surprised to find that nowhere in the Bible does it tell pastors to bury the dead. Yet when I was ordained to the Christian ministry, part of the charge given was to "bury the dead." The church and its leaders have quite properly accepted this responsibility and privilege.

Why don't we let professional funeral directors care for the dead? Why do we not only get involved but take a leading part in the events surrounding death? When someone dies, what can we do that no one else can do?

As a pastor, I have a unique perspective. I'm a friend, but I'm also in a position of authority. I'm close enough to "weep with those who weep" but removed enough to bring objective truth.

Schooled in the details of death, a funeral director is helpful because he knows the right ways to embalm, arrange flowers, and approach the grave. A pastor's job goes beyond getting the dead body into the ground with decorum. I offer both faith and friendship to the living—those grieving people looking for help. They need someone calm to hold their hands; someone who can offer them hope, not sentiment; someone close enough to feel some of the pain. As a pastor, I have this role.

For this role, I need a realistic view of life and death. I've learned to accept the inevitability of death. I *am* going to die; it's only a question of when. Further, I accept the temporary nature of all present relationships. I can't try to hang on to what God says won't last.

In addition, because I am a Christian, death is not something to be feared but rather to be anticipated. Paul made this very clear. He told the Corinthians, "Therefore we are always confident and know that as long as we are at home in the body we are away from the Lord. . . . We are confident, I say, and would prefer to be away from the body and at home with the Lord" (2 Cor. 5:6–8 NIV). He also said, "For to me, to live is Christ and to die is gain" (Phil. 1:21 NIV).

Death is an opportunity to share the gospel with the living, teaching the brevity of life, the importance of preparing for our own inevitable deaths, and the good news that God will comfort those who sorrow.

What do I want to accomplish when there's a death? I approach funerals with three basic objectives. First, I want to get the surviving family through the days surrounding the funeral. Second, I want to get the dead person appropriately buried (or cremated). Third, I want to get the gathered family and friends to think about life, death, and meeting God.

Pulling the family through

My involvement usually starts with the phone call that brings the announcement of death. I visit the family as soon as I can. At death, more than a person dies; a network of relationships ceases. So there are shock, disbelief, guilt, resentment, and a whole range of other emotional responses of those close by. My first priority is to hold their hands, let them cry, and give them support in a variety of ways.

Seldom do I start any funeral arrangements during this initial visit. If the deceased has just passed away, there's too much shock. It's too harsh to talk of caskets and burial plots in those first few minutes. I let them know that tomorrow is soon enough for those decisions, and I'll be back to help them then.

On my second visit, I try to build a consensus of what should take place at the funeral service. I prefer to have as many of the family members present for this as possible. I determine who is in charge and who is going to make the major decisions. Sometimes that isn't clear. I want to establish not only who has the right, but who, emotionally or through force of personality, is going to make the arrangements. At times conflict or disagreement within the family places me in a crossfire.

On one occasion, the widow, who had the right to make the decisions, was out of town, and I had to finalize arrangements for the service. By telephone she specifically told me what she wanted, but the sister of the man who had died came into my office and told me the widow's arrangements were inappropriate.

I was caught between the strong feelings of the wife and those of the sister. It was impossible to come out a winner.

If there's a question about the decisions, I'll sometimes say to those gathered, "Now I know we are all involved and want to do what's right, but I understand Peter is in charge of making the arrangements. Peter, what do you think we should do?"

During this time, I observe how the family is coping with death. I try to distinguish between hysteria and grief, between legitimate sorrow and hopeless despair, trying to anticipate those who'll have emotional difficulty during the funeral. I watch nonverbal communication. Who's afraid to look at my face? Who walks out of the room when we talk about the service? This helps me avoid problems later on.

I pay particular attention to family photos and artifacts in the home. Asking questions about family photos is an indirect way of gathering useful information from families that aren't well known. These clues help me personalize the service and counsel the family afterward. I jot them on a card either in the home or as soon as I get to my car.

For the service, I try to honor personal requests—a favorite hymn or passage of Scripture. I gather the obituary information or have one of the family write it up for me. Prior to the service, I verify the accuracy of my information and the pronunciation of names with someone in the family.

Primarily, however, I want to explain to the family the sequence of events and how they will likely feel during the service. I talk about the value of tears. Walking the family through the service in advance sets them at ease and enables me to accomplish more when the service actually happens. I let the family know that I will meet them before the service for a final word of prayer prior to entering the sanctuary.

I realize that at this moment, I'm in a position of great power and tremendous trust. I carry a spiritual authority that normally I am not given. The family is looking for help. They hang on to my words. I also realize I'm told things in the time of bereavement that are strictly confidential. People say things out of guilt or grief that should never be repeated. I'm careful to observe confidentiality.

I conclude this second visit with a strong but brief statement about the biblical perspective of death. I'm careful not to minimize grief and may even point out how some Bible characters want to give a message of assurance and confidence. I sometimes read a portion of Scripture. I then pray with the family, thanking God for the memory of one who was loved, and asking God to sustain and comfort the family.

Burying the dead

The dominant theme of a funeral service has to be that Jesus Christ is alive. Christ's death and resurrection supply meaning to our deaths. His resurrection provides a stream of grace that enables us to cope with grief. This message must be heard above all the emotion and tradition surrounding a funeral service.

I want the funeral service to help people get their eyes off themselves and their circumstances and onto God, who in his great wisdom and love has everything under control. Due respect and tribute need to be given to the deceased, but I want the service to witness to God's provision of life through Jesus Christ, who brings a whole new dimension to living.

I want people to feel I've prepared this service just for them. I've attended some services where the name of the deceased was not even mentioned. It's obvious the words had all been said before for someone else. I definitely want those grieving to know I share their sorrow and genuinely want to help.

At some time during the service, I speak directly to the key members of the grieving family by name: "Mary, you've been through a lot. This has been a great shock. You had a wonderful husband. I want you to know God will help you in the days ahead. My prayers are with you." Of course, this is what we're trying to do with the whole service, but I find the person's name gives the message impact.

At times I ask someone capable of public speaking to make remarks about the life of the deceased. This is particularly helpful for those situations where I haven't known the person. When I know the person well, I try to go beyond giving the essential facts by recalling positive experiences. For example: "I remember visiting Dorothy both at her home and in the hospital. Though she knew she had cancer, she never seemed to doubt her faith or feel regret. She had strong courage even though she was aware of what was happening. She spoke only of her concern for her children."

There's even a place for humor, although not jokes. Death is serious, but brief, tasteful remembrances of humorous events can break the tension and bring a sense of release. At one service an eldest son brought tribute to his father. He mentioned several serious qualities and then concluded by relating how his father had always chided him for leaving the bathroom messy. This middle-aged son ended his remarks by looking up toward heaven and saying, "Dad, I just want you to know I cleaned up the bathroom before I came to your service." In some services, such a comment might have been out of place, but that day it fit. It helped the family get through the day.

Obviously, I'm as positive about the deceased as possible. There's something good to say about everyone. But several years ago, I learned I had to be honest. I was preparing for the funeral of a man I didn't know, gathering some biographical information from his grown daughter. She simply said, "Please don't say a lot of nice things about my father. I loved him, but he was not a good man. If you say he was good, people won't believe anything else you say."

The cause of death and the person's character or "credentials" determine the type and tone of the funeral service. Services for prominent church officials, well-known pastors, and former missionaries tend to involve more speeches of tribute and are more structured. During such services, I fight to control time by giving specific time limitations.

A service for a known unbeliever or someone who has lived an unwholesome life is much briefer. The emphasis of the service shifts from giving thanks for the deceased to providing comfort and encouragement to the bereaved. This is particularly the case in the death of a non-Christian spouse. I say little about the deceased. Rather I focus on how God will help the believing partner who remains.

In services for elderly, well-known church members, I'll often make the emphasis one of thanksgiving for a life well lived. For one man who had been active in the ministries of the church until the time of his death, I used Hebrews 11:13 as a text: "All these people were still living by faith when they died" (NIV). It was an opportunity to speak of his involvement, his acts of kindness, and his faith in God that remained strong for a lifetime.

I vary the sequence, but somewhere there's a hymn, usually a solo, and, depending on the circumstances, a few comments on the life of the deceased. I always include a message based on Scripture. I pray at least twice during the service, once asking for the Lord's presence and help during the service, and once asking for the Lord's counsel, comfort, and wisdom for the grieving family. I don't allow the prayers to become either minisermons or counseling sessions. I make them short and conversational; flowery language and theological jargon don't make sense to the sorrowing family.

I base my encouragement in Scripture. I shy away from sentimental poetry. I'm a preacher, not a poet. The underlying thought I want to leave is that the Bible provides solid answers about life and death, and Jesus Christ provides meaningful support to those who grieve.

The logistics of funerals and burials vary greatly. There's certainly no right or wrong way, only what's appropriate to the situation and community. My job is to provide the necessary outlet for legitimate grief.

The graveside service

The traditional burial following the funeral service can destroy the positive tone established during the service. Many people have told me the burial service was the hardest part of their grief experience. The big struggle was to walk away from the grave. So I suggest having the burial *before* the service to relieve the family of some of this pressure and to free them to hear the comforting words of the service.

If the burial service is for just the immediate family, the time at the graveside becomes more personal and family oriented. The service in the church or funeral chapel can then conclude on a positive note of hope and encouragement. In addition, relatives and friends are available immediately following the service to support the family; they don't have to wait till after the burial.

I tell the family the graveside part of the service is short, so they're not surprised by its brevity. Depending on the mix and number of people present at the graveside, I may have them sing a chorus or verse of a familiar hymn to involve them in the burial, helping them express their grief and affirm their faith. The overriding word at the graveside is *resurrection*. Since the grave is but a temporary resting place for the body, I don't dwell on the end of life but the hope of the resurrection.

Following my benediction, I greet each member of the immediate family individually by name. I don't say much; it's just a final personal touch. I then quickly withdraw and leave the family alone. They need private time to say things they might feel uncomfortable saying in my presence.

Speaking of life and death

The heart of the funeral has to be the sermon. A funeral message isn't lengthy, but it should be long enough to provide substance for faith to grasp. I aim for a ten- to twelve-minute message. I try to make my style conversational. There's no place for the bombastic, the flamboyant, or the spectacular.

Regardless of my text, I include a brief statement of what happens when a person dies, how God helps those who sorrow, and how we can prepare for our own eventual deaths. I have a congregation at a funeral that I don't have any other time. I don't abuse the privilege, but I've concluded that outsiders feel cheated if, as a man of God, I don't tell it like it is and say something of substance.

I recently went through an unusually hectic three weeks. In addition to a number of other pressing situations in the church, I had five funerals. Yet I preached a new and different sermon at each service.

How did I find time to prepare five new funeral messages? Several years ago I accepted the fact that death is going to happen, and I will be called upon to conduct the services. Further, I've learned that since funerals don't happen at convenient times, I have to be ready before I'm asked to perform them. So I keep a file of potential funeral texts. Perhaps calling it a file is a little strong. It's really just a folder with scraps of paper on which I've scribbled a potential text and a seed thought or two. When I'm called about a death, I go to my folder with possible texts, and usually there's an appropriate one to give me a place to start.

I tend to stay away from the most obvious texts. On the other hand, I try to stay away from obscure texts. A funeral message is too short to give background information and explanation. People want something familiar. They need to fasten their faith onto what they know.

The underlying message of every funeral service is hope. Believers can have assurance and confidence in facing the grave. As a pastor, I bring divine help to enable the family to cope with change, loss, and the process of rebuilding.

Following the service

After the service is when ministry is often most needed. Immediately following the service, the women of our church provide a luncheon. This relaxed time gives family and friends an opportunity to express their concern and love to each other. It's the start of the healing process.

Sometimes during these informal gatherings we've had a time when folk were encouraged to make some personal comments about the deceased or family members. This was particularly moving following the death of a young lady, Elfrieda, who died in her thirties. Many people told how she had blessed their lives. One girl spoke of how Elfrieda had brought her to the Lord. This was not only a fitting tribute to Elfrieda but brought healing and release to those who participated.

I let the family know I'm available to help. There's a follow-up visit to assess the situation and determine ongoing ministry. I make sure there is public prayer for the family during the first Sunday service bereaved family members are back in church.

In addition, I seek to connect each bereaved person with someone in the church who can befriend and encourage in an ongoing way. Pearl was widowed several years ago. Today she is reaching out to another widow who is struggling. Pearl phones her each morning, meets her often for coffee, and sees to it that she gets to church. This continuing ministry of comfort is too great for me to handle, and not my sole territory anyway. Godly women like Pearl minister in ways I can't.

Three women approached me recently following a funeral service for a friend. They paid me the compliment that I'm sure has been given to many other pastors: "Pastor, we hope you stay in this church a long time, because we don't plan to die for several years. But when we do, we want you to preach our funerals."

I had passed their test.

30

Mastering Ceremonies

*This is our real work: holding marriages and death,
growing lives and lasting achievements, before God in a
continuing community of prayer.*

—Eugene H. Peterson

Most pastoral work takes place in obscurity, deciphering grace in the shadows, blowing on the embers of a hard-used life.

Pastors stay with their people week in and week out, year after year, to proclaim and guide, encourage and instruct as God works his purposes (gloriously, it will eventually turn out) in the meandering and disturbingly inconstant lives that compose our congregations.

This necessarily means taking seriously, and in faith, the full routines of life. It means witnessing to the transcendent in the fog and rain. It means living hopefully among people who from time to time get flickering glimpses of the Glory but then live through long stretches of unaccountable grayness. This is hard work and not conspicuously glamorous.

But there are frequent interruptions in this work in which the significance blazes all of itself. The bush burns and is not quenched. Our work is done for us, or so it seems, by the event. We do nothing to get these occasions together: no prayer meeting, no strategic planning, no committee work, no altar call. They are given—redolent with meaning and almost always, even among unbelievers, a sense of reverence. These interruptions of the ordinary become occasions of ceremony and celebration: weddings, funerals, baptisms, dedications, anniversaries, graduations, events in which human achievements are honored.

Instead of deficiency of meaning, which characterizes so many lives and for which people compensate in frenzy or fantasy, there is an excess: the ecstasy of love, the dignity of death, the wonder of life, the nobility of achievement.

These occasions burst the containers of the everyday and demand amplitude and leisure in which to savor the fullness. No love was ever celebrated enough, no death ever mourned enough, no life adored enough, no achievement honored enough. People set aside time, clear space, call friends, gather families, assemble the community. Almost always, the pastor is invited to preside.

But when we arrive, we are, it seems, hardly needed and, in fact, barely noticed. One of the ironies of pastoral work is that on these occasions when we are placed at the very center of the action, we are perceived by virtually everyone there to be on the margins. No one would say that, of course, but the event that defines the occasion—love, death, birth, accomplishment—also holds everyone's attention. No one inquires of the pastor what meaning there is in this. Meaning is there, overwhelmingly obvious, in the bride and groom, in the casket, in the baby, in the honored guest.

The pastor is, in these settings, what the theater calls "fifth business"—required by the conventions but incidental to the action, yet, in its own way, important on the sidelines. This is odd, and we never quite get used to it, at least I never do. In the everyday obscurities in which we do most of our work, we often have the sense of being genuinely needed. Even when unnoticed, we are usually sure our presence makes a difference, sometimes a critical difference, for we have climbed to the abandoned places, the bereft lives, the "gaps" that Ezekiel wrote of (22:30) and have spoken Christ's word and witnessed Christ's mercy. But in these situations where we are given an honored place at the table, we are peripheral to everyone's attention.

Where is the spotlight?

At weddings, love is celebrated. The atmosphere is luminous with adoration. Here are two people at their best, in love, venturing a life of faithfulness with each other. Everyone senses both how difficult and how wonderful it is. Emotions swell into tears and laughter, spill over in giggles, congeal into pomposity. In the high drama that pulls families and friends together for a few moments on the same stage, the pastor is practically invisible, playing a bit part at best. We are geometrically at the center of the ceremony, but every eye is somewhere else.

At funerals, death is dignified. The not-being-there of the deceased is set in solemn ritual. Absence during this time is more powerful than presence. Grief, whether expressed torrentially or quietly, is directed into channels of acceptance and gratitude that save it from wasteful spillage into regret and bitterness. The tears that blur perception of the living, including the pastor, clarify appreciation of the dead.

At the baptisms and dedications of infants, the sheer wonder of infant life upstages the entire adult world. The glory that radiates from the newborn draws even bystanders into praise. In the very act of holding an infant in the sacrament of baptism or the service of dedication, the pastor, though many times larger, stronger, and wiser, is shadowed by the brightness of the babe.

At anniversaries and graduations, ground breakings and inaugurations—the various community occasions when achievements are recognized and ventures launched—the collective admiration or anticipation produces a groundswell of emotion that absorbs everything else. Every eye is focused on, and every ear is tuned to, the person honored, the project announced, the task accomplished, the victory won. The pastor, praying in the spotlight and with the amplification system working well, is not in the spotlight and barely heard.

And so it happens that on the occasions in our ministry when we are most visible, out in front giving invocations and benedictions, directing ceremonies and delivering addresses, we are scarcely noticed.

The one thing needful

If no one perceives our presence the way we ourselves perceive it—directing operations, running the show—what is going

on? We are at the margins during these occasions. No one came
to see us. No one came to hear us. We are not at all needed in
the way we are accustomed to being needed.

No one needs us to tell the assembled people that things of
great moment are taking place. No one needs us to proclaim that
this is a unique event, never to be repeated, in which we are all
privileged participants. All this is unmistakably obvious and not
to be missed by even the stiff-necked and uncircumcised of
heart.

So why are we there? We are there to say *God*. We are there for
one reason and one reason only: to pray. We are there to focus
the brimming, overflowing, cascading energies of joy, sorrow,
delight, or appreciation, if only for a moment but for as long as
we are able, in God. We are there to say *God* personally, to say
his name clearly, distinctly, unapologetically, in prayer. We are
there to say it without hemming and hawing, without throat
clearing and without shuffling, without propagandizing, prosely-
tizing, or manipulating. We have no other task on these occasions. We are not needed to add to what is there; there is already
more than anyone can take in. We are required only to say the
Name: Father, Son, Holy Ghost.

All men and women hunger for God. The hunger is masked
and misinterpreted in many ways, but it is always there. Everyone is on the verge of crying out "My Lord and my God!" if only
circumstances push them past their doubts or defiance, push
them out of the dull ache of their routines or their cozy accom-
modations with mediocrity. On the occasions of ceremony and
celebration, there are often many people present who never enter
our churches, who do their best to keep God at a distance and
never intend to confess Christ as Lord and Savior. These people
are not accustomed to being around pastors, and not a few of
them politely despise us. So it is just as well that we are perceived to be marginal to the occasion. The occasions themselves
provide the push toward an awareness of an incredible Grace, a
dazzling Design, a defiant Hope, a courageous Faithfulness.

But awareness, while necessary, is not enough. Consciousness
raising is only prolegomena. Awareness, as such, quickly trickles
into religious sentimentalism or romantic blubbering, or hardens

into patriotic hubris or pharisaic snobbery. Our task is to nudge the awareness past these subjectivities into the open and say *God.*

The less we say at these times the better, as long as we say *God.* We cultivate unobtrusiveness so that we do not detract from the sermon being preached by the event. We must do only what we are there to do: pronounce the name, name the hunger. But it is so easy to get distracted. There is so much going on, so much to see and hear and say. So much emotion. So much, we think, "opportunity." But our assignment is to the "one thing needful," the invisible and quiet center, God.

We do best on these occasions to follow the sermonic advice of the Rebbe Naphtali of Ropshitz: make the introduction concise and the conclusion abrupt—with nothing in between.

Such restraint is not easy. Without being aware of it, we are apt to resent our unaccustomed marginality and push ourselves to the fore, insisting we be noticed and acknowledged. We usually do this through mannerism or tone: stridency, sentimentality, cuteness. We do it, of course, in the name of God, supposing we are upholding the primacy of the one we represent. This is done with distressing regularity by pastors. But such posturing does not give glory to God; it only advertises clerical vanity. We are only hogging the show, and not very successfully, either. For no matter how resplendent we are in robes and "Reverends," we are no match for the persons or events that gave rise to the occasion to which we were asked to come and pray.

In golden-calf country

But there is another reason for keeping to our position on the margins of ceremony and celebrations. This is golden-calf country. Religious feeling runs high, but in ways far removed from what was said on Sinai and done on Calvary. While everyone has a hunger for God, deep and insatiable, none of us has any great desire for him. What we really want is to be our own gods and to have whatever other gods that are around help us in this work. This is as true for Christians as for non-Christians.

Our land lies east of Eden, and in this land Self is sovereign. The catechetical instruction we grow up with has most of the questions couched in the first person: How can I make it? How can I maximize my potential? How can I develop my gifts? How can I overcome my handicaps? How can I cut my losses? How can I live happily ever after, increase my longevity, preferably all the way into eternity? Most of the answers to these questions include the suggestion that a little religion along the way wouldn't be a bad idea.

Every event that pulls us out of the ordinariness of our lives puts a little extra spin on these questions. Pastors, since we are usually present at the events and have a reputation of being knowledgeable in matters of religion, are expected to legitimize and encourage the religious dimensions in the aspirations. In our eagerness to please, and forgetful of the penchant for idolatry in the human heart, we too readily leave the unpretentious place of prayer and, with the freely offered emotional and religious jewelry the people bring, fashion a golden calf-god— Romantic Love, Beloved Memory, Innocent Life, Admirable Achievement—and proclaim a "feast to the LORD" (Exod. 32:5 KJV). Hardly knowing what we do, we meld the religious aspirations of the people and the religious dynamics of the occasion to try to satisfy one and all.

Calvin saw the human heart as a relentlessly efficient factory for producing idols. People commonly see the pastor as the quality-control engineer in the factory. The moment we accept the position, we defect from our vocation. People want things to work better; they want a life that is more interesting; they want help through a difficult time; they want meaning and significance in their ventures. They want God, in a way, but certainly not a "jealous God," not the "God and Father of our Lord Jesus Christ." Mostly they want to be their own god and stay in control, but have ancillary divine assistance for the hard parts.

There are a thousand ways of being religious without submitting to Christ's lordship, and people are practiced in most of them. They are trained from an early age to be discriminating consumers on their way to higher standards of living. It should be no great surprise when they expect pastors to help them do it.

But it is a great apostasy when we go along. "Moses said to Aaron, 'What did this people do to you that you have brought so great a sin upon them?' " (Exod. 32:21 NRSV). Aaron's excuse is embarrassingly lame, but more than matched by the justifications we make for abandoning prayer in our enthusiasm to make the most of the occasion.

Our real work

Our churches and communities assign us ceremonial duties on these occasions, which we must be careful to do well. There are right and wrong ways to act and speak, better and worse ways to prepare for and conduct these ceremonies and celebrations. No detail is insignificant: gesture conveys grace, tone of voice inculcates awe, demeanor defines atmosphere, preparation deepens wonder. We must be diligently skillful in all of this.

But if there is no will to prayer in the pastor—a quietly stubborn and faithful centering in the action and presence of God— we will more than likely end up assisting, however inadvertently, in fashioning one more golden calf of which the world has more than enough. What is absolutely critical is that we attend God in these occasions: his Word, his presence. We are there to say the name, and by saying it guide lament into the depths where Christ descended into hell, not letting it digress into self-pity. We are there to say the name, and by saying it direct celebration into praise of God, not letting it wallow in gossipy chatter.

Our real work in every occasion that requires a priestly presence is prayer. Whether anyone there knows or expects it, we arrive as persons of prayer. The margins are the best location for maintaining that intention. Our vocation is to be responsive to what God is saying at these great moments, and simply be there in that way as salt, as leaven. Most of our prayer will be inaudible to those assembled. We are not praying to inspire them (they are inspired enough already) but to intercede for them. The action of God is intensified in these prayers and continued in the lives of the participants long after the occasion. The ceremonies are over in an hour or so; the prayers continue. This is our real work: holding marriages and death, growing lives and lasting achievements, before God in a continuing community of prayer.